MYTHS, RITES, SYMBOLS

MYTHS, RITES, SYMBOLS:

A Mircea Eliade Reader

Edited by

WENDELL C. BEANE

and

WILLIAM G. DOTY

Volume 1

❧

HARPER TORCHBOOKS
Harper & Row, Publishers
New York, Cambridge, Hagerstown, Philadelphia, San Francisco
London, Mexico City, São Paulo, Sydney

MYTHS, RITES, SYMBOLS: A MIRCEA ELIADE READER. Copyright © 1975 by Wendell
C. Beane and William G. Doty. All rights reserved. Printed in the United
States of America. No part of this book may be used or reproduced in any
manner without written permission except in the case of brief quotations embodied in critical articles and reviews. For information address Harper & Row,
Publishers, Inc., 10 East 53d Street, New York, N.Y. 10022. Published simultaneously in Canada by Fitzhenry & Whiteside Limited, Toronto.

First HARPER COLOPHON editions published 1976

LIBRARY OF CONGRESS CATALOG NUMBER: 75-7931

ISBN: 0-06-131955-4

Designed by Stephanie Krasnow

80 10 9 8 7 6 5 4

Contents

CHAPTER 2

VOLUME 2

Contents

Abbreviations and Acknowledgments

AR   *Australian Religions. An Introduction.* Ithaca, N.Y.: Cornell University Press, 1973. © 1973 by Cornell University Press. Originally: *History of Religions*, Vols. 6 (1966) and 7 (1967). Reprinted by permission of The University of Chicago Press, © 1966, 1967.

CH   *The Myth of the Eternal Return,* or *Cosmos and History.* Translated by Willard R. Trask. Bollingen Series 46. Princeton, N.J.: Princeton University Press, 1954. Copyright © 1954 by Bollingen Foundation. Reprinted by permission of Princeton University Press, a total of 8,130 words. Reprinted by permission of Routledge & Kegan Paul, Ltd., London.

FC   *The Forge and the Crucible (The Origins and Structures of Alchemy).* Translated by Stephen Corrin. New York: Harper & Row, 1971; © English translation by Rider & Company, 1962; © by Ernest Flammarion, 1956. Reprinted by permission of Hutchinson Publishing Group, Ltd., London.

FPZ   *From Primitives to Zen. A Thematic Sourcebook of the History of Religions.* New York: Harper & Row, 1967. © 1967 by Mircea Eliade. Reprinted by permission of Harper & Row, Publishers, Inc.

IS   *Images and Symbols. Studies in Religious Symbolism.* Translated by Philip Mariet. New York: 1969. © Librairie Gallimard, 1952. © in the English translation Harvill Press, 1961, published by Sheed and Ward, Inc., New York. Reprinted by permission of Harvill Press, Ltd., London, and Sheed and Ward, Inc., New York.

MDM   *Myths, Dreams, and Mysteries. The Encounter Between Contemporary Faiths and Archaic Realities.* Translated by Philip Mairet. New York: Harper & Row, 1967. © 1957 Libraire Gallimard; © 1960 in the English translation Harvill Press. Reprinted by permission of Harper & Row, Publishers, Inc. Reprinted by permission of Harvill Press, Ltd., London.

MR   *Myth and Reality.* Translated by Willard R. Trask. New York: Harper & Row, 1963. © 1963 by Harper & Row, Publishers, Inc. Reprinted by permission of Harper & Row, Publishers, Inc.

MRS   "Methodological Remarks on the Study of Religious Symbol-
         ism," in Mircea Eliade and J. M. Kitagawa, eds., *The History of
         Religions: Essays in Methodology*. Chicago: The University of
         Chicago Press, 1959, pp. 86–107. © 1959 by The University of
         Chicago. Reprinted by permission of The University of Chicago
         Press.

PCR   *Patterns in Comparative Religions* by Mircea Eliade. New
         York: 1958. © Sheed and Ward, Inc. 1958. Reprinted by per-
         mission of Sheed and Ward, Inc., New York.

Q   *The Quest. History and Meaning in Religion*. Chicago: The
         University of Chicago Press, 1969. © 1969 by The University
         of Chicago. Reprinted by permission of The University of
         Chicago Press.

RSI   *Rites and Symbols of Initiation. The Mysteries of Birth and
         Rebirth* (also as title: *Birth and Rebirth*). Translated by Wil-
         lard R. Trask. New York: Harper & Row, 1965. © 1958 by
         Mircea Eliade. Reprinted by permission of Harper & Row, Pub-
         lishers, Inc.

S   *Shamanism, Archaic Techniques of Ecstasy* by Mircea Eliade.
         Translated by Willard R. Trask. Bollingen Series 76. Princeton,
         N.J.: Princeton University Press, 1964. Copyright © 1964 by
         Bollingen Foundation. Reprinted by permission of Princeton
         University Press, a total of 10,670 words.

SMA   "The Sacred and the Modern Artist," *Criterion* 4, no. 2
         (Spring, 1965): 22–24. Reprinted by permission of *Criterion*,
         The University of Chicago, The Divinity School.

SP   *The Sacred and the Profane. The Nature of Religion*. Trans-
         lated by Willard R. Trask. New York: Harcourt Brace Jovano-
         vich, 1959. Copyright © 1959 by Harcourt Brace Jovanovich,
         Inc. Reprinted by permission of Harcourt Brace Jovanovich.
         Reprinted by permission of Rowohlt Taschenbuch Verlag
         G.m.b.H. from *The Sacred and the Profane* by Mircea Eliade.
         Copyright © 1957, Rowohlt Taschenbuch Verlag G.m.b.H.,
         Hamburg.

TO   *The Two and the One*. Translated by J. M. Cohen. New York:
         Harper & Row, 1965. © 1962 Editions Gallimard. © 1965 in the
         English translation by Harvill Press, London, Sheed and Ward,
         Inc., and Harper & Row, Publishers, Inc., New York. Reprinted
         by permission from Harvill Press, Ltd., London, and Sheed and
         Ward, Inc., New York.

Y   *Yoga: Immortality and Freedom*, by Mircea Eliade. Translated
         by Willard R. Trask, Bollingen Series 56. Princeton, N.J.:

Princeton University Press, 1970. Copyright © 1958 and © 1969 by Bollingen Foundation. Reprinted by permission of Princeton University Press, a total of 8,760 words.

Z   *Zalmoxis. The Vanishing God. Comparative Studies in the Religions and Folklore of Dacia and Eastern Europe.* Translated by Willard R. Trask. Chicago: The University of Chicago Press, 1972. © 1972 by The University of Chicago. © 1970, Payot, Paris. Reprinted by permission of The University of Chicago Press.

Preface

To begin, I should like to express my deep gratitude to the editors of this volume, Professors Wendell C. Beane and William G. Doty. They have gone to a great deal of trouble in excerpting selections from various publications that have spanned the last forty years, and I believe that they have been enormously successful in choosing passages that effectively and honestly present my essential ideas on the interpretation of religious ideology, behavior, and institutions. It is their hope and mine that such a compilation will prove useful to students and others interested in problems relating to the field of History of Religions.

Over the years, I have had occasion to publish numerous books and articles in which I sought to address myself to a variety of different audiences—usually scholars or specialists in studies of religion, Orientalists, anthropologists, and so on—but also readers interested in such broader fields as history of culture or ideas, literary criticism, psychology, and the arts. As a result, the structure and style of my writing has often shifted in accord with the intended audience, and I am afraid that this has made it more difficult than it might have been for Messrs. Beane and Doty to select out of my *oeuvre* materials for a unified reader such as this one. Yet, I feel that they have done a marvelous job in this respect. I am delighted with their choice of texts, and their careful editing has made them uniformly accessible for the use of the nonspecialist.

This is of great importance to me, for I have always been of the opinion that the results of the investigations made by those who practice History of Religions as their trade are of real interest to the modern reader, and transcend the boundaries of narrow scholasticism. For, at a certain level, the study of the History of Religions is a continuous encounter with things that are "wholly other" to us as modern Westerners: other cultures, other times, other systems of speculation and reflection. Such an encounter with the foreign or bewildering has great potential for catalyzing creative experiences of all types, as the discovery of African art forms by European artists at the turn of this century has so clearly demonstrated. But the delimitation of this experience within a limited preserve that is open only to scholars is no less stultifying than the dismissal of all that is foreign as "primitive" or "nonsense." It is my fondest hope that the encounter with archaic, Oriental, and exotic cultures can serve to provoke thought and understanding, deepening our appreciation of man and his imagination—religious and otherwise—while provoking our own. It is this which I meant in earlier works when I spoke of History of Religions opening doors toward a "new humanism."[1]

My own experience of the creative possibilities contained within the "other" began with India, and I have since had occasion to make studies touching on numerous other areas as well: Siberia, Australia, the Ancient Near East, South America, and others. As a result, my writings have not always borne the mark of a systematic scheme of organization on a grand scale. Rather, I have pursued various questions as they aroused my interest, turning to new problems on the basis of their intrinsic fascination and not because they fit neatly into a preconceived niche. This approach has served to keep my discipline always fresh and exciting for me, but I am afraid that it may have caused problems for my readers at times, and for this reason I am again most grateful to Professors Doty and Beane. The organization that they have set up for the selections included in this book is an extremely useful one, bringing together passages that are thematically very close, but often chronologically distant within the unfolding of my work. In this way, they may well have served to make my thinking more accessible to the reader, and for this I am extremely grateful.

University of Chicago   MIRCEA ELIADE
June 1975

1. See "History of Religions and a New Humanism," in *History of Religions* 1, no. 1 (Summer 1961), pp. 1–8, reprinted in *The Quest* (Chicago, 1969).

On Using These Volumes

WILLIAM G. DOTY

The origins of these volumes date back to several years ago when I told my new colleague, Wendell Beane, about my frustration in wanting to use more of Eliade's writings in my courses, but finding it almost impossible to select only one or two volumes from the sixteen or so Eliade had written. And when several volumes were used, students found themselves reading duplicate accounts of some materials—since Professor Eliade has often provided in a second book a résumé of an earlier work. Dr. Beane, even though he was a student of Mircea Eliade, could not be enticed into compiling the anthology I thought most helpful; eventually, however, we did agree to become collaborators, and have produced this book. We have jointly shared responsibility for making selections, writing continuity-material, and the completing of many hours of tedious checking, seeking permissions, and the like that are required by such a composite product.

We have not tried to replace the writings available (for the most part in inexpensive paperback translations), but rather to bring together in one volume many of the observations and insights Professor Eliade makes in the approximately 5,000 pages of his writings in English. For the beginning student, especially, we felt the need of a volume that would concentrate upon the "essential" Eliade, highlighting a wide range of his observations rather than arguing a particular method or series of results.

In each section we indicate in our footnotes further or parallel readings in the Eliade corpus, and of course the interested reader can find further elaboration by tracking down the context in the original volume from which a specific quotation is taken. The standard bibliography of books and essays by Professor Eliade (in Romanian, French, English, German, and nine other languages) is in J. M. Kitagawa and Charles H. Long, eds., *Myths and Symbols: Studies in*

Honor of Mircea Eliade.[1] At his suggestion, our selections are almost exclusively from his books, since his articles are usually reworked into volumes published sometime after the articles appear.

Before mentioning something about Eliade's context in the study of religions, there are conventions used in this book which the reader should have in mind:

1. Abbreviations follow the list of "Abbreviations and Acknowledgements" at the front of this volume. In footnotes, source notes, and text references abbreviations are separated from page numbers with a slash. For example, *SP*/15, refers to *The Sacred and the Profane: The Nature of Religion*, p. 15.

2. Footnotes in the text by the editors rather than by Professor Eliade are indicated by "Eds."

3. We have standardized spellings of technical terms in the history of religions, and have used this spelling throughout, rather than following the varying conventions in Eliade's many books; *The Two and the One* provided the model for most Sanskrit terms.

4. We have omitted most of the technical footnotes from the original publications, especially the extensive bibliographic materials given by Professor Eliade and cross-references to his own works, and we have reduced many footnotes in size, retaining only necessary references, as when a source or translation is cited in the text (interested readers will be able to pursue bibliographic references and comments in the original publications, but we did not have space for repeating this rich store of resources in this volume; see selection 145 for an example of the extent of cutting necessary).

5. The source of each selection is indicated at the bottom of the first page on which a selection begins.

6. Standard elipsis marks (. . .) or asterisks (***) indicate places where we have omitted materials from the original published versions; materials in brackets [ ] provide our own emendations; and the subtitles in this volume are a mixture of our own work and Eliade's original subtitles.

7. Throughout these two volumes, the design element of a solid black diamond is employed to introduce new sections prefaced by

1. (Chicago, 1969), pp. 415–33.

editorial commentary: two diamonds (◆ ◆) indicate the beginning of a main division; one diamond (◆) indicates a subdivision. Italic text that directly follows a selection title indicates editorial comment.

Professor Eliade met with the two editors in Chicago in October 1973, and has responded a number of times to queries about policies and details; before the work went to the publisher, he reviewed the entire manuscript and made critical suggestions. For his continued encouragement and assistance the editors are extremely grateful and sympathetic as well, for it must have been painful to see his writings cut up and pieced together into this totally new format.

We hope the book will provide a readable introduction for the individual reader as well as providing convenient access to Eliade's thought for classroom work. We know of interest in Eliade's studies that range from scholarly works in the history of religions, anthropology and literature departments, to communes that have sought guidance for their communal living in his analyses of earlier societies. Our hope, therefore, is that this volume will encourage further attention to this scholar's works, and that persons who disagree with something in a selection will frown at us and go to the original sources to see if the selection adequately represents Eliade's own work before frowning at him as well!

Thanks are due to our families, our students, and to the several persons who have assisted with the actual day-to-day mechanics of producing this volume: they have all shown marvelous patience, and have given us the needed encouragement and help to see it through.

Understanding Mircea Eliade
as Historian of Religions

WENDELL C. BEANE

It is not easy to introduce someone whose writings have concerned themselves with such a wide spectrum of human religiosity as Mircea Eliade. The threefold division of this book ("Myths," "Rites," and "Symbols") by no means reflects the complete picture;[1] thus we have thought to include some inferential remarks on his method of reflecting on the meaning of religious data. Nonetheless, the foregoing threefold division is chosen by us because these terms, simply, are the substance of any religious world view, whether it take the form of an intensely rationalized but unsystematic array of cultural traditions, or else a critically ratiocinated and systematized theology of culture. What we shall attempt to do here is merely to suggest some contours of contacts with other exemplary scholars of religion and culture whose thoughts may be taken as models of field perspectives and thereby to highlight some of the working principles of Eliade's own approach.

It should be recognized at once that it is hard to avoid a certain relativity of scholarly portraiture and inference regarding method, especially when it comes to intellectual giants. There is, then, some basis for saying that there is no universally recognized authority on the thought of Mircea Eliade. At any rate, for the student who wants to become more acquainted with Eliade's thought and works, it would be helpful to consider the following items.

First of all, Mircea Eliade, though aware of the fact that humankind has "evolved" in one way or another as cultural beings, is not

---

1. See, for example, discussions on Eliade, the novelist, in J. M. Kitagawa and Charles H. Long, eds., *Myths and Symbols: Studies in Honor of Mircea Eliade* (Chicago, 1969), pp. 327–414.

himself an "evolutionist" scholar in the sense of J. G. Frazer (*The Golden Bough*, 1890), E. B. Tylor (*Primitive Culture*, 1871), or R. Marett (*The Threshold of Religion*, 1909); nor is he a "degeneration-ist" (= supporting an original monotheism that later becomes poly-theism, ancestor worship, spiritism, etc.) in the sense of Andrew Lang (*The Making of Religion*, 1898), or Pater Wilhelm Schmidt (*Der Ursprung der Gottesidee*, 1912–15).[2] Rather, an idea which underlies the superabundance of sacred phenomena Eliade includes in his works is that the ancient world is characterized by a "multiplicity of hiero-phanies"; that is to say, many of the religious ideas and forms which have tended to become the subjects of scholarly debate in the quest to achieve the final generalization in the study of religion's origins, Eliade believes, *coexisted* (though not in every time and place) as parts of the primitive ethos or world-orientation. Hence (types of) monotheism: male- or female-symbol dominated; polytheism, ances-tor worship, animism, etc., might all be symbolizations of the amaz-ing varieties of religious experience characterizing humankind's sa-cred past. The significance of this guideline should be an important consideration to both the introductory and the advanced reader, in light of the comments by Eliade's critics that his works ignore the factor of sociocultural stratification; that is, the questionableness of placing (so-called) "primitive" and "high culture" religious phe-nomena in juxtaposition, or raising particular elements out of their peculiar context to the level of becoming mere "snippets of ethnog-raphy."[3] As our Reader will show, however, Eliade's own conten-tion is that "nothing can take the place of the example, the concrete fact" (*SP/15*); therefore, the student will find much to ponder as he or she finds among the reading selections an emphasis upon symbols that Eliade believes can allow persons of different cultural back-ground "to intercommunicate."

Second, Eliade's use of the phrase "the Sacred and the Profane" requires an important announcement concerning their *relation*: that they are not rigidly antithetical descriptions of the primitive and

2. For Schmidt, students might better profit from a reading of Wilhelm Schmidt, *The Origin and Growth of Religion: Facts and Theories*, trans. H. J. Rose (New York, 1931).

3. See, e.g., Thomas J. J. Altizer, *The Sacred and the Profane: Mircea Eliade and the Dialectic of the Sacred* (Philadelphia, 1963), p. 42 and *passim*. Also see Edmund Leach, "Man on a Ladder," *The New York Review of Books*, October 20, 1966, pp. 28–31.

modern worlds as religious environments. While it may be accurate to say that of the two worlds the "primitive" lends himself more appropriately to the occasion of being a model of the pan-sacralized mentality, this does not mean that the modern world knows nothing of sacred things. In fact, our author would have us know that both primitive *and* modern religious beings know the Sacred but the Profane as well. Hence the title: "The Sacred *and* the Profane," not "the Sacred *versus* the Profane." However, it is the "modern" human being that presents himself as more appropriately the model of the desacralized mentality. In between these two extremes, therefore, there is Eliade's discernment of the essential relation between a primitive rite of annual community- or world-renewal rooted in Primordial Time and a modern liturgical rehearsal of a redemptive revelation rooted in Historical Time. What these two *sacred worlds* have in common, then, despite their limitations as cultural situations in the profane sense, is that the participants in these sacred worlds both insist upon understanding their frames of reference and their centers of gravity as rooted in a transcendental reality: the Sacred, the Holy, the Religious. In a word, it is this Reality which enables them to live *in* history and time with a genuine sense of being *beyond* time and history.

Finally, there is Eliade's attitude toward the problem of the *interpretation* of religion in the face of what seems to be an utterly unmanageable maze of data in the form of myths, rites, and symbols. Here are three specific and useful directives that we can detect in Eliade's works as his way of interpreting a vast array of sacred phenomena:

1. The need to recognize, on the basis of cumulative investigations by scholars from various disciplines, that sacred words and things always point beyond themselves to what Eliade calls "a meta-empirical reality and purpose" (i.e., they are material means to *spiritual* ends).

2. The need to adopt an attitude of radical displacement of one's personal biases concerning what "ought" to be thought, said, and done by other religious peoples, in order to begin not only to understand *how* religious symbols relate to their historical environment, but also *what* such symbols *intend* as sacred realities worth discovering again and again.

3. The need to compare and integrate the elements of religious traditions as a means of arriving at even tentative generalizations about humankind's religious ways of being in the world, which may lead us to understand anew the essential relation between the *human* and the religious.

As an historian of religions Eliade, to be sure, does not stand in complete opposition to all that has gone before him, either in the area of comparative religion or, for that matter, other fields of inquiry such as anthropology. In a broad sense, it were better to say that his way of doing things is distinctively a matter of *emphasis* rather than discontinuity with other students of religion and culture.

For example, Bronislaw Malinowski (d. 1942) is still recalled today as the chief pioneer and advocate of a *pragmatic* approach to the intentionality of myth as a religious form. His definition of myth, again, is classical in religious field studies and defies improvement by any scholar. Indeed, Eliade himself shows admiration for that scholar's remarkable achievement in this regard by citing Malinowski's definition. (*MR*/19 f.). Malinowski himself, of course, was an advocate of firm ethnographic principles, such as being scientific-minded and knowing field values, showing fellow-feeling and a willingness to "live in" among the subjects (= beings) of one's interest, and knowing how to gather, control, and classify one's overall data.

Malinowski, however, had a vital interest in the economic dynamics of the primitive social world, and this influenced him decisively when it came to his comprehension of the relation, for instance, between primitive magic, science, and religion.[4] Following and, in a real sense, succeeding his original inspiration (i.e., Frazer's *The Golden Bough*), he saw primitive man as a practical being who resorted to magical rites only when his everyday "scientific" know-how proved to be an ineffective mode of activity. The primary value in Malinowski's work, nonetheless, was a "functional" one, which placed more emphasis on the role of myth as a socioeconomic reality than *a religious reality in itself*.

Claude Lévi-Strauss, on the other hand, having also lent himself to solid traditional ethnographic principles, has recently appeared to have by-passed the foregoing functionalist vogue and has developed

4. See Bronislaw Malinowski, *Magic, Science and Religion, and Other Essays* (New York, 1948).

what Edmund Leach refers to as "a revised form of 'symbolist' analysis that he calls structural." Lévi-Strauss's distinctive lesson for us as an attitude toward the study of myth, however, comes in the form of his understanding of myth not as a "disease of language" but as a religious-cultural art form. It is this nature of myth as such which permits us to uncover its own inherent genius and to understand it as a well thought out structural reality; although this perspective demands a detailed study of the words, images, and symbols of myth. When this is done, even apart from their distinct historical or social setting, the discovery can be made that these myths are ardent and deliberate attempts to overcome the contradictions that human beings find both in nature and society—indeed in themselves. Through a series of symbols which form complex interrelations in the mythic structure the aim is at bottom the resolution of life's anomalies and the transformation of natural disorder into culturally understandable values. Here we include but move ultimately beyond Malinowski's sheer pragmatic approach to an emphasis upon the rational, humanistic, and, even, existentialist concerns of "les sauvages"; but, moreover, we have an understanding that, despite the *recurrent usefulness of myth-telling*, the key to the meaning of myth as a religious form lies in its *linguistic* structure.[5]

Mircea Eliade, as historian of religions, brings us a view of myth which engulfs the pragmatism of Malinowski and the symbolic linguistics of Lévi-Strauss, though we must be careful not to infer that they have had any direct influence upon him as an historian of religions. On the one hand, Eliade entertains the notion of the "ambivalence of the sacred," which is an ongoing recognition of the practical reality (= concreteness) of an object that has become a sacred symbol (e.g., a stone or tree *remains* what it is even while becoming something "*wholly other*"). On the other hand, Eliade understands the existentialist function of myth as an art form, which is both an act of creative thought and an effort to make a "world" out of often chaotic natural reality. Yet Eliade's distinctive approach as historian of religions is best understood when we notice the pervasive attention that he gives to the element of religious experience in both myth and ritual as symbolic realities. He thus calls our attention to some-

---

5. See Claude Lévi-Strauss, *Structural Anthropology*, trans. C. Jacobsen and B. G. Schoepp (New York, 1963), Ch. XI, "The Structural Study of Myth."

thing in the life of primitive peoples that is critically important beyond the anthropological confirmation that they are indeed human
beings with the art of common sense and a remarkable inclination
toward myth-making. Eliade, in sum, insists that behind and beyond
the linguistic structure and pragmatic function of myth lies the
conception, gestation, and birth of myth *out of the depths of a
genuine religious experience*. It is ultimately this element of religious
experience of the Sacred which is the true source of its structure,
practicality, and repeatability. In the final analysis myth is a "living"
testimony not only to its capacity to be ritually reenacted as a presen-
tation of sacred human convictions; but, also, in terms of method, it
points to the necessity of leaving room for the interpretation of the
transcendental milieu of myth as uniquely the essence of religion.

1

Myths—Sacred History, Time, and Intercommunication

Introduction

The materials in chapter one are quite varied. We have tried to provide a balance of theory and illustration that will demonstrate Professor Eliade's approach to mythology. The first subsections deal with structures of myths and the ways they function in mythic societies, then with the rationalization of the mythic mentality in modern societies. The founding myth—especially the cosmogonic myth, which relates how reality came to exist—is shown as the essential element in creating a sacred history and a sacred time; and all profane time is dependent upon this primal time.

Various understandings of the primal time are discussed, including the understandings of the West and the East, and extending into the present, as in the section on psychoanalytic concepts of time. The section concludes with the ways myths are passed around and on, the corruption and infantilization of symbolic meaning in cultures where the primary mythic orientation falls prey to demystification.

◆ ◆

The Structure of Myths

Eliade's *Myths and Reality* contains some of his most pointed statements about the nature of myths and the ways they are related to the communities that revere them. The first readings here present major parts of the argument of that book, concentrating on definition and the distinction between types of mythic narrative, and then moving in the next subsection to the ways myths came to be regarded in modern societies.

1. THE DEFINITION OF MYTH

For the past fifty years at least, Western scholars have approached the study of myth from a viewpoint markedly different from, let us say, that of the nineteenth century. Unlike their predecessors, who treated myth in the usual meaning of the word, that is, as "fable," "invention," "fiction," they have accepted it as it was understood in the archaic societies, where, on the contrary, "myth" means a "true story" and, beyond that, a story that is a most precious possession

Source: *MR*/1–6.

because it is sacred, exemplary, significant. This new semantic value given the term "myth" makes its use in contemporary parlance somewhat equivocal. Today, that is, the word is employed both in the sense of "fiction" or "illusion" and in that familiar especially to ethnologists, sociologists, and historians of religions, the sense of "sacred tradition, primordial revelation, exemplary model." ...

It is not in this sense—the most usual one in contemporary parlance—that we understand "myth." More precisely, it is not the intellectual stage or the historical moment when myth became a "fiction" that interests us. Our study will deal primarily with those societies in which myth is—or was until very recently—"living," in the sense that it supplies models for human behavior and, by that very fact, gives meaning and value to life. To understand the structure and function of myths in these traditional societies not only serves to clarify a stage in the history of human thought but also helps us to understand a category of our contemporaries. ...

It would be hard to find a definition of myth that would be acceptable to all scholars and at the same time intelligible to nonspecialists. Then, too, is it even possible to find *one* definition that will cover all the types and functions of myths in all traditional and archaic societies? Myth is an extremely complex cultural reality, which can be approached and interpreted from various and complementary viewpoints.

Speaking for myself, the definition that seems least inadequate because most embracing is this: Myth narrates a sacred history; it relates an event that took place in primordial Time, the fabled time of the "beginnings." In other words, myth tells how, through the deeds of Supernatural Beings, a reality came into existence, be it the whole of reality, the Cosmos, or only a fragment of reality—an island, a species of plant, a particular kind of human behavior, an institution. Myth, then, is always an account of a "creation"; it relates how something was produced, began to *be*. Myth tells only of that which *really* happened, which manifested itself completely. The actors in myths are Supernatural Beings. They are known primarily by what they did in the transcendent times of the "beginnings." Hence myths disclose their creative activity and reveal the sacredness (or simply the "supernaturalness") of their works. In short, myths describe the various and sometimes dramatic breakthroughs of the sacred (or the "supernatural") into the World. It is this sudden breakthrough of the sacred that really *establishes* the World and makes it what it is today. Furthermore, it is as a result of the intervention of Supernatural Beings that man himself is what he is today, a mortal, sexed, and cultural being.

... At this point it is necessary to emphasize a fact that we consider essential: the myth is regarded as a sacred story, and hence a "true history," because it always deals with *realities*. The cosmogonic myth is "true" because the existence of the World is there to prove it; the myth of the origin of death is equally true because man's mortality proves it, and so on.

Because myth relates the *gesta*[1] of Supernatural Beings and the manifestation of their sacred powers, it becomes the exemplary model for all significant human activities. ...

2. "TRUE STORIES" AND "FALSE STORIES"

... In societies where myth is still alive the natives carefully distinguish myths—"true stories"—from fables or tales, which they call "false stories." ...

This is why myths cannot be related without regard to circumstances. Among many tribes they are not recited before women or children, that is, before the uninitiated. Usually the old teachers communicate the myths to the neophytes during their period of isolation in the bush, and this forms part of their initiation. ...

This distinction made by natives between "true stories" and "false stories" is significant. Both categories of narratives present "histories," that is, relate a series of events that took place in a distant and fabulous past. Although the actors in myths are usually Gods and Supernatural Beings, while those in tales are heroes or miraculous animals, all the actors share the common trait that they do not belong to the everyday world. Nevertheless, the natives have felt that the two kinds of "stories" are basically different. For everything that the myths relate *concerns them directly*, while the tales and fables refer to events that, even when they have caused changes in the World (cf. the anatomical or physiological peculiarities of certain animals), have not altered the human condition as such.

Source: *MR*/8–11, 13, 15, 17–18; cf. *CH*/44–46 on myth *vs*. facts.
1. *Gesta:* primal sacred acts. Eds.

Myths, that is, narrate not only the origin of the World, of animals, of plants, and of man, but also all the primordial events in consequence of which man became what he is today—mortal, sexed, organized in a society, obliged to work in order to live, and working in accordance with certain rules. If the World *exists*, if man *exists*, it is because Supernatural Beings exercised creative powers in the "beginning." But after the cosmogony and the creation of man other events occurred, and man *as he is today* is the direct result of those mythical events, *he is constituted by those events*. He is mortal because something happened *in illo tempore*.[1] If that thing had not happened, man would not be mortal—he would have gone on existing indefinitely, like rocks; or he might have changed his skin periodically like snakes, and hence would have been able to renew his life, that is, begin it over again indefinitely. But the myth of the origin of death narrates what happened *in illo tempore*, and, in telling the incident, explains *why* man is mortal. . . .

. . . A "primitive" could say: I am what I am today because a series of events occurred before I existed. But he would at once have to add: events that took place *in mythical times* and therefore make up a *sacred history* because the actors in the drama are not men but Supernatural Beings. In addition, while a modern man, though regarding himself as the result of the course of Universal History, does not feel obliged to know the whole of it, the man of the archaic societies is not only obliged to remember mythical history but also to *re-enact* a large part of it periodically. It is here that we find the greatest difference between the man of the archaic societies and modern man: the irreversibility of events, which is the characteristic trait of History for the latter, is not a fact to the former. . . .

For [the man of the archaic societies], then, the essential thing is to know the myths. It is essential not only because the myths provide him with an explanation of the World and his own mode of being in the World, but above all because, by recollecting the myths, by re-enacting them, he is able to repeat what the Gods, the Heroes, or the Ancestors did *ab origine*. . . . For knowing the origin of an object, an animal, a plant, and so on is equivalent to acquiring a magical power over them by which they can be controlled, multiplied, or reproduced at will. . . . In most cases it is not enough to *know* the

---

1. *In illo tempore:* in the primal time. Eds.

origin myth, one must *recite* it; this, in a sense, is a proclamation of one's knowledge, *displays* it. But this is not all. He who recites or performs the origin myth is thereby steeped in the sacred atmosphere in which these miraculous events took place. The mythical time of origins is a "strong" time because it was transfigured by the active, creative presence of the Supernatural Beings. By reciting the myths one reconstitutes that fabulous time and hence in some sort becomes "contemporary" with the events described, one is in the presence of the Gods or Heroes. As a summary formula we might say that by "living" the myths one emerges from profane, chronological time and enters a time that is of a different quality, a "sacred" Time at once primordial and indefinitely recoverable. . . .

3. THE STRUCTURE AND FUNCTION OF MYTHS

. . . In general it can be said that myth, as experienced by archaic societies (1) constitutes the History of the Acts of the Supernaturals; (2) that this History is considered to be absolutely *true* (because it is concerned with realities) and *sacred* (because it is the work of the Supernaturals); (3) that myth is always related to a "creation," it tells how something came into existence, or how a pattern of behavior, an institution, a manner of working were established; this is why myths constitute the paradigms for all significant human acts; (4) that by knowing the myth one knows the "origin" of things and hence can control and manipulate them at will; this is not an "external," "abstract" knowledge but a knowledge that one "experiences" ritually, either by ceremonially recounting the myth or by performing the ritual for which it is the justification; (5) that in one way or another one "lives" the myth, in the sense that one is seized by the sacred, exalting power of the events recollected or re-enacted.

"Living" a myth, then, implies a genuinely "religious" experience, since it differs from the ordinary experience of everyday life. The "religiousness" of this experience is due to the fact that one re-enacts fabulous, exalting, significant events, one again witnesses the creative deeds of the Supernaturals; one ceases to exist in the everyday world and enters a transfigured, auroral world impregnated with the Super-

SOURCE: *MR*/18–19; cf. *SP*/95–99 on myths as paradigmatic models.

naturals' presence. What is involved is not a commemoration of mythical events but a reiteration of them. The protagonists of the myth are made present, one becomes their contemporary. This also implies that one is no longer living in chronological time, but in the primordial Time, the Time when the event *first took place*. This is why we can use the term the "strong time" of myth; it is the prodigious, "sacred" time when something *new*, *strong*, and *significant* was manifested. To reexperience that time, to re-enact it is often as possible, to witness again the spectacle of the divine works, to meet with the Supernaturals and relearn their creative lesson is the desire that runs like a pattern through all the ritual reiterations of myths. In short, myths reveal that the World, man, and life have a supernatural origin and history, and that this history is significant, precious, and exemplary....

◆ ◆

The Greatness and Decadence of Myths

4. KEEPING THE WORLD OPEN

On the archaic levels of culture religion maintains the "opening" toward a superhuman world, the world of axiological values. These values are "transcendent," in the sense that they are held to be revealed by Divine Beings or mythical Ancestors. Hence they constitute absolute values, paradigms for all human activities. . . . These models are conveyed by myths. Myths are the most general and effective means of awakening and maintaining consciousness of another world, a beyond, whether it be the divine world or the world of the Ancestors. This "other world" represents a superhuman, "transcendent" plane, the plane of *absolute realities*. It is the experience of the sacred—that is, an encounter with a transhuman reality—which gives birth to the idea that something *really exists*, that hence there are absolute values capable of guiding man and giving a meaning to human existence. It is, then, through the experience of the sacred that the ideas of *reality*, *truth*, and *significance* first dawn, to be later elaborated and systematized by metaphysical speculations.

The apodictic value of myth is periodically reconfirmed by the rituals. Recollection and re-enactment of the primordial event help

SOURCE: *MR*/139–42, 144–47; cf. *SP*/99–104 on reactualizing myths.

"primitive" man to distinguish and hold to the *real*. By virtue of the continual repetition of a paradigmatic act, something shows itself to be *fixed* and *enduring* in the universal flux. This periodic reiteration of what was done *in illo tempore* makes it inescapably certain that something *exists absolutely*. This "something" is "sacred," that is, transhuman and transmundane, but it is accessible to human experience. "Reality" unveils itself and admits of being constructed from a "transcendent" level, but this "transcendence" can be ritually experienced and finally becomes an integral part of human life. . . .

Myth assures man that what he is about to do *has already been done*, in other words, it helps him to overcome doubts as to the result of his undertaking. There is no reason to hesitate before setting out on a sea voyage, because the mythical Hero has already made it in a fabulous Time. All that is needed is to follow his example. Similarly, there is no reason to fear settling in an unknown, wild territory, because one knows what one has to do. One has merely to repeat the cosmogonic ritual, whereupon the unknown territory (= "Chaos") is transformed into "Cosmos," becomes an *imago mundi*[1] and hence a ritually legitimized "habitation." The existence of an exemplary model does not fetter creative innovation. The possibilities for applying the mythical model are endless.

The man of the societies in which myth is a living thing lives in a World that, though "in cipher" and mysterious, is "open." The World "speaks" to man, and to understand its language he needs only to know the myths and decipher the symbols. Through the myths and symbols of the Moon man grasps the mysterious solidarity among temporality, birth, death and resurrection, sexuality, fertility, rain, vegetation, and so on. The World is no longer an opaque mass of objects arbitrarily thrown together, it is a living Cosmos, articulated and meaningful. In the last analysis, *the World reveals itself as language*. It speaks to man through its own mode of being, through its structures and its rhythms.

That the World exists is due to a divine act of creation, its structures and its rhythms are the product of events that took place at the beginning of Time. The Moon has its mythical history, but so have the Sun and the Waters, plants and animals. Every significant cosmic object has a "history." This is as much as to say that it can "speak"

---

1. *Imago mundi:* image of the universe. Eds.

to man. Because it "speaks" of itself—above all of its "origin," the primordial event in consequence of which it came into being—the object becomes *real* and *significant*. It is no longer something "unknown," that is, an opaque object, inapprehensible, meaningless, and in the last analysis "unreal." It shares in the same "World" as man.

This co-participation not only makes the World "familiar" and intelligible, it makes it transparent. Through the objects of this present World one perceives traces of the Beings and powers of another world. . . .

Myth, in itself, is not a guarantee of "goodness" or morality. Its function is to reveal models and, in so doing, to give a meaning to the World and to human life. This is why its role in the constitution of man is immense. It is through myth, as we said before, that the ideas of *reality, value, transcendence* slowly dawn. Through myth, the World can be apprehended as a perfectly articulated, intelligible, and significant Cosmos. In telling how things were made, myth reveals by whom and why they were made and under what circumstances. All these "revelations" involve man more or less directly, for they make up a Sacred History.

In short, myths are a constant reminder that grandiose events took place on Earth and that this "glorious past" is partly recoverable. The imitation of paradigmatic acts also has a positive aspect: the rite forces man to transcend his limitations, obliges him to take his place with the Gods and the mythical Heroes so that he can perform their deeds. Directly or indirectly, myth "elevates" man. This becomes even clearer if we bear in mind that in archaic societies recitation of the mythological traditions remains the prerogative of a few individuals. In some societies the reciters are recruited among the shamans and medicine men or among members of the secret societies. In any case, he who recites the myths has had to prove his vocation and receive instruction from the old masters. . . .

. . . It is the specialists in ecstasy, the familiars of fantastic universes, who nourish, increase, and elaborate the traditional mythological motifs.

. . . In the last analysis, in the archaic societies as everywhere else, culture arises and is renewed through the creative experiences of a few individuals. But since archaic culture gravitates around myths, and these are constantly being studied and given new, more profound interpretations by the specialists in the sacred, it follows that the society as a whole is led toward the values and meanings discovered and conveyed by these few individuals. It is in this way that myth helps man to transcend his own limitations and conditions and stimulates him to rise to "where the greatest are."

5. HOMER

An entire study could well be devoted to the relations between the great religious personalities, especially the reformers and prophets, and the traditional mythological schemas. The messianic and millennialist movements among the peoples of the former colonies represent a practically unlimited field for research. It would be possible to reconstruct, at least in part, the impact of Zarathustra on Iranian mythology or that of the Buddha on the traditional mythologies of India. As for Judaism, the great "demythicization" performed by the prophets has long been known....

The problem of Greek myth is one to give the investigator pause. Only in Greece did myth inspire and guide not only epic poetry, tragedy, and comedy but also the plastic arts; on the other hand, only in the culture of Greece was myth submitted to a long and penetrating analysis, from which it emerged radically "demystified." The rise of Ionian rationalism coincides with a more and more damaging criticism of the "classic" mythology as it found expression in the works of Homer and Hesiod. If in every European language the word "myth" denotes a "fiction," it is because the Greeks proclaimed it to be such twenty-five centuries ago.

Willy-nilly, every attempt to interpret Greek myth, at least within a culture of the Western type, is in some sort conditioned by the critique of the Greek rationalists. As we shall see in a moment, this critique was seldom directed against what we have called "mythical thought" or the resultant type of behavior. The criticisms were aimed primarily at the doings of the Gods as narrated by Homer and Hesiod. We may well wonder what a Xenophanes would have thought of the Polynesian cosmogonic myth or of a speculative Vedic myth such as that in *Rig Veda* X, 129. Obviously, we cannot know. But it is important to emphasize the fact that the target of the rationalists' attacks was primarily the adventures and arbitrary decisions of the Gods, their capricious and unjust behavior, their "immorality." And the main critique was made in the name of an increasingly higher idea of God: a true God could not be unjust, immoral, jealous, vindictive, ignorant, and the like. The same critique was later renewed and exacerbated by the Christian apologists. This thesis—more particularly the objection that the divine myths as presented by the poets cannot be true—triumphed, at first among the Greek intellectual elites and finally, after the victory of Christianity, everywhere in the Greco-Roman world.

But it is only justice to remember that Homer was neither a theologian nor a mythographer. In other words, he laid no claim to presenting the whole body of Greek religion and mythology systematically and exhaustively. Though, as Plato put it, Homer had educated all Greece, he had composed his poems for a specific audience: the members of a military and feudal aristocracy. His literary genius had exercised a fascination never equaled by any other author; hence his works greatly contributed toward unifying and articulating Greek culture. But since he was not writing a treatise on mythology, he did not record all the mythological themes that were in circulation in the Greek world. Then too, he avoided evoking religious or mythological conceptions that were either foreign to his essentially patriarchal and military auditors or in which they took little interest. Concerning all that could be called the nocturnal, chthonian, funereal side of Greek religion and mythology, Homer says next to nothing. . . .

6. THEOGONY AND GENEALOGY

Hesiod addressed a different audience. That is why he narrates myths that are passed over in silence or barely alluded to in the Homeric poems. For example, he is the first to tell of Prometheus. But he could not know that the central myth of Prometheus was based on a misapprehension, or, more precisely, on its primordial religious meaning having been "forgotten." The fact is that Zeus takes vengeance on Prometheus because the latter, summoned to preside over the sharing out of the first sacrificial victim, had covered the bones

SOURCE: *MR*/150–51.

with a layer of fat, and the flesh and entrails with the stomach. Attracted by the fat, Zeus had chosen the poorer share for the Gods, leaving the flesh and entrails to men (*Theogony*, 534 ff.). Now, Karl Meuli[1] has compared this Olympian sacrifice with the rituals of the archaic North Asian hunters; the latter venerate their celestial Supreme Beings by offering them the animal's bones and head. The same ritual custom has survived among the pastoral peoples of Central Asia. What, during an archaic stage of culture, had been considered the most perfect homage to a celestial God had in Greece become the consummate example of cheating, the crime of lèse-majesté against Zeus, the supreme God. We do not know when this shift of the original ritual meaning occurred, nor how Prometheus came to be accused of the crime. We have given the example only to show that Hesiod cites extremely archaic myths, rooted deep in pre-History; but these myths had undergone a long process of transformation and modification before the poet recorded them. . . .

7. THE RATIONALISTS AND MYTH

We cannot here even summarize the long process of erosion by which the Homeric myths and Gods were finally emptied of their original meanings. If we are to believe Herodotus (I, 32), Solon already said that "the deity is full of envy and instability." In any case, the earliest Milesian philosophers refused to see the Figure of the true divinity in Homer's descriptions. When Thales affirmed that "every thing is full of gods" (A 22), he was revolting against the Homeric idea that the Gods inhabited only certain regions of the Cosmos. Anaximander attempts to present a total conception of the Universe, without gods and without myths. As for Xenophanes (born *ca. 565*), he does not hesitate to attack the Homeric pantheon openly. He refuses to believe that God moves about from place to place, as Homer tells (B 26). He rejects the immortality of the Gods as described by Homer and Hesiod: ". . . Homer and Hesiod say that the gods do all manner of things which men would consider disgraceful:

SOURCE: *MR*/152–54.

1. Karl Meuli, "Griechische Opfergebräuche," *Phyllobolia für Peter Von der Mühl* (Basel, 1946), pp. 185–288.

adultery, stealing, deceiving each other" (B 11, B 12).[1] Nor will he accept the idea of divine procreation: ". . . But mortals consider that the gods are born, and that they have clothes and speech and bodies like their own" (B 14).[2] He especially criticizes the anthropomorphism of the Gods: "But if cattle and horses or lions had hands, or were able to draw with their hands and do the works that men can do, horses would draw the forms of gods like horses, and cattle like cattle, and they would make their bodies such as they each had themselves" (B 15).[3] For Xenophanes, "One god is the highest among gods and men; in neither his form nor his thought is he like unto mortals" (B 23, trans. W. Jaeger).

In these critiques of "classical" mythology we can see an effort to free the concept of divinity from the anthropomorphic expressions of the poets. Even a profoundly religious author like Pindar rejects the "incredible" myths (*I Olympic*, 28 ff.). Euripides' conception of God had been wholly influenced by Xenophanes' critique. In Thucydides' day the adjective *mythodes* meant "fabulous and unauthenticated," in contrast to every kind of truth or reality.[4] When Plato (*Republic*, 378 ff.) blamed the poets for the way in which they had presented the Gods, he was probably addressing an audience that was already convinced.

The criticism of mythological traditions was almost pedantically elaborated by the Alexandrian rhetoricians. As we shall see, the Christian apologists patterned themselves on these authors when they in turn were called on to deal with the problem of distinguishing the historical elements in the Gospels. The Alexandrian Aelius Theon (*ca.* second century A.D.) discourses at length on the arguments by which it is possible to demonstrate the "incredibility" of a myth or a historical narrative, and he illustrates his methods by a critical analysis of the myth of Medea. Theon considers that a mother could not kill her own children. In addition, the act is "incredible" because Medea could not have slaughtered her children in the very city (Corinth) in which their father Jason was living. Then again, the

---

1. Trans. W. Jaeger, *The Theology of the Early Greek Philosophers* (Oxford, 1947), p. 47.
2. Trans. G. S. Kirk and J. E. Raven, *The Presocratic Philosophers* (Cambridge, Mass., 1957), p. 168.
3. *Ibid.*, p. 169.
4. Cf. Thucydides, *History*, i. 21.

way in which the crime was committed is improbable: Medea would have tried to hide her guilt and, being a witch, she would have used poison instead of the sword. Finally the alleged reason for her act is highly improbable: anger against her husband could not have driven her to cut the throats of their children, which were at the same time her own; in doing so, the person she hurt most was herself, since women are more prone to emotions than men.[5]

8. ALLEGORIZATION AND EUHEMERISM

This is more than a devastating critique of the myth; it is a critique of any imaginary world, leveled in the name of a simplistic psychology and an elementary rationalism. Nevertheless, the mythology of Homer and Hesiod continued to interest the elites in all parts of the Hellenistic world. But the myths were no longer taken literally: what was now sought was their "hidden meanings" (*hyponoiai*; the term *"allegoria"* was used later). Theagenes of Rhegium (fl. *ca.* 525) had already suggested that the names of the Gods in Homer represented either the human faculties or the natural elements. But it was especially the Stoics who developed the allegorical interpretation of Homeric mythology and, in general, of all religious traditions. Chrysippus reduced the Greek Gods to physical or ethical principles. In the *Quaestiones Homericae* of Heraclitus (first century A.D.) there is a whole series of allegorical interpretations: for example, when the myth tells that Zeus bound Hera, the episode really signifies that the ether is the limit of the air, and so on. The allegorical method was applied by Philo to decipher and illustrate the "enigmas" of the Old Testament. As we shall see later, allegorical interpretation of a sort, particularly typology (that is, the correspondence between the two Testaments), was freely used by the Fathers, especially Origen.

Some scholars hold that allegory was never very popular in Greece and had more success in Alexandria and Rome. It is none the less true that various allegorical interpretations "saved" Homer and Hesiod

Source: *MR*/154–57.
5. Aelius Theon, *Progymnasmata* (94, 12–32), summarized by Robert M. Grant, *The Earliest Lives of Jesus* (New York, 1961), pp. 41–42; cf. also *ibid.*, pp. 120 ff.

in the eyes of the Greek elites and made it possible for the Homeric Gods to retain a high cultural value. The rescue of the Homeric pantheon and mythology is not the work of the allegorical method alone. At the beginning of the third century B.C. Euhemerus published a romance in the form of a philosophical voyage, *Sacred Writing* (*Hyera anagraphe*), the success of which was great and immediate. Ennius translated it into Latin; indeed, it was the first Greek text to be translated. Euhemerus believed that he had discovered the origin of the Gods: they were ancient kings deified. Here was another "rational" way to preserve the Gods of Homer. They now had a "reality": it was historical (or, more precisely, prehistorical); their myths represented the confused memory or an imaginative transfiguration of the exploits of the primitive kings.

This allegorizing in reverse had wide repercussions, undreamed of by Euhemerus and Ennius, and even by Lactantius and other Christian apologists when the latter took their stand on Euhemerus to demonstrate the humanity, and hence the unreality, of the Greek Gods. By force of allegorical interpretation and euhemerism, and more especially of the fact that all literature and all plastic art had developed around the divine and heroic myths, the Greek Gods and Heroes did not sink into oblivion after the long process of "demythicization" or even after the triumph of Christianity.

On the contrary, as Jean Seznec has shown in his excellent book, *The Survival of the Pagan Gods*, the euhemerized Greek Gods survived all through the Middle Ages, though they had shed their classic forms and were camouflaged under the most unexpected disguises. The "rediscovery" of the Renaissance consists primarily in the restoration of the pure, "classic" forms.[1] And in fact it was toward the end of the Renaissance that the Western world realized there was no longer any possibility of combining Greco-Latin "paganism" with Christianity; whereas in the Middle Ages antiquity was not regarded as a "distinct historical milieu, as a period that had run its course."[2]

So it is that a secularized mythology and a euhemerized pantheon managed to survive and, from the time of the Renaissance, to become a subject of scientific investigation—precisely because dying antiq-

1. Jean Seznec, *The Survival of the Pagan Gods. The Mythological Tradition and its Place in Renaissance Humanism and Art* (New York, 1953), pp. 320 ff.

2. *Ibid.*, p. 322.

uity no longer believed in Homer's Gods or in the original meaning of their myths. All this mythological heritage could be accepted and assimilated by Christianity because it no longer carried living religious values. It had become a "cultural treasure." In the last analysis, the classical heritage was "saved" by the poets, the artists, and the philosophers. From the end of antiquity—when no cultivated person any longer took them literally—the Gods and their myths were conveyed to the Renaissance and the seventeenth century by *works*, by creations of literature and art.

9. WRITTEN DOCUMENTS AND ORAL TRADITIONS

Through *culture*, a desacralized religious universe and a demythicized mythology formed and nourished Western civilization—that is, the only civilization that has succeeded in becoming exemplary. There is more here than a triumph of *logos* over *mythos*. The victory is that of *the book* over oral tradition, of the document—especially of the written document—over a living experience whose only means of expression were preliterary. A great many antique written texts and works of art have perished. Yet enough remain to enable the admirable Mediterranean civilization to be reconstructed in outline. This is not the case with the preliterary forms of culture, in Greece as well as in ancient Europe. We know very little about the popular religions and mythologies of the Mediterranean, and that little we owe to the monuments and a few written documents. In some cases—the Eleusinian mysteries, for example—the scantness of our information is explained by the fact that initiatory secrecy was well kept. In other cases what we know of one or another popular belief or cult is due to some lucky chance. To give only one example, if Pausanias had not recorded his personal experience at the oracle of Trophonius in Lebadeia (IX, 39), we should have had to make do with the few vague allusions in Hesiod, Euripides, and Aristophanes. In other words, we should not have suspected the significance and importance of that religious center.

The "classic" Greek myths already represent the triumph of the literary *work* over religious *belief*. Not a single Greek myth has

Source: *MR*/157–58, 160–61.

come down to us in its cult context. We know the myths as literary and artistic "documents," not as the sources, or expressions, of a religious experience bound up with a rite. The whole *living* and popular side of Greek religion escapes us, precisely because it was not systematically expressed in writing.

We must not judge the vitality of Greek religious feeling and practice solely by the degree to which the Olympian myths and cults found adherents. Criticism of the Homeric myths did not necessarily imply rationalism or atheism. The fact that the *classic forms* of mythical thought had been "compromised" by the rationalists' criticism does not mean that all mythical thought was discarded. The intellectual elites had discovered other mythologies able to justify and articulate new religious concepts. On the one hand, there were the Mystery religions, from Eleusis and the Orphico-Pythagorean brotherhoods to the Greco-Oriental mysteries that were so popular in Imperial Rome and the provinces. In addition, there were what could be called the mythologies of the soul, the soteriologies elaborated by the Neo-Pythagoreans, the Neo-Platonists, and the Gnostics. To all this we must add the spread of solar mythologies and cults, the astral and funerary mythologies, as well as all kinds of popular "superstitions" and "minor mythologies." . . .

* * *

. . . We may conclude that Greek religion and mythology, radically secularized and demythicized, survived in European *culture*, for the very reason that they had been expressed by literary and artistic masterpieces. Whereas the popular religions and mythologies, the only *living* pagan forms when Christianity triumphed (but about which we know almost nothing, since they were not expressed in writing), survived in Christianized form in the traditions of the various rural populations. Since this rural religion was essentially agricultural in structure, with roots going back to the Neolithic Age, in all probability European religious folklore still preserves a prehistoric heritage.

But these survivals of archaic myths and religious attitudes and practices, although representing an important spiritual phenomenon, had very little effect on the cultural plane. The revolution brought about by writing was irreversible. Henceforth the history of culture will consider only archaeological documents and written texts. A people without *this* kind of documents is considered a people without history. Popular creations and oral traditions will be granted value only very late, in the period of German Romanticism; the interest in them is already antiquarian. The popular creations in which mythical behavior and the mythical universe still survive have sometimes served as the source of inspiration for a few great European artists. But such popular creations have never played an important role in culture. They have ended by being regarded as "documents," and as such have tempted the curiosity of certain specialists. To interest a modern man, this *oral* traditional heritage has to be presented in the form of a *book*. . . .

◆ ◆

Cosmogonic Myth and Sacred History

In the following excerpts Eliade introduces an approach to the religious interpretation of myth based on seeing myths as "living things," not as "fictions" in the Greek tradition, and then he exemplifies the approach by specific applications. Two societies are discussed, the Ngadju Dayak, of Borneo, a region in Southeast Asia about 400 miles east of Singapore, and the Aranda tribes of Central Australia. It is important in these excerpts to notice that the Ngadju and Aranda mythical traditions establish *sacred worlds*, not just optional religious beliefs that can be held alongside others. The cosmogonic myth is thus seen as encompassing decisive valuations of existence, humankind, and society.

10. THE LIVING MYTH AND THE HISTORIAN OF RELIGIONS

It is not without fear and trembling that a historian of religion approaches the problem of myth. This is not only because of that preliminary embarrassing question: what is intended by myth? It is also because the answers given depend for the most part on the documents selected by the scholar. From Plato and Fontenelle to Schelling and Bultmann, philosophers and theologians have proposed innumerable definitions of myth. But all of these have one thing in common: they are based on the analysis of Greek mythology. Now, for a his-

SOURCE: Q/72–76; cf. AR/44–50.

torian of religions this choice is not a very happy one. It is true that only in Greece did myth inspire and guide epic poetry, tragedy, and comedy, as well as the plastic arts; but it is no less true that it is especially in Greek culture that myth was submitted to a long and penetrating analysis, from which it emerged radically "demythicized." . . . What is even more serious for an historian of religion: we do not know a single Greek myth within its ritual context. Of course this is not the case with the paleo-oriental and Asiatic religions; it is especially not the case with the so-called primitive religions. As is well known, a *living myth* is always connected with a cult, inspiring and justifying a religious behavior. None of this of course means that Greek myth should not figure in an investigation of the mythical phenomenon. But it would seem unwise to begin our kind of inquiry by the study of Greek documents, and even more so to restrict it to such documents. The mythology which informs Homer, Hesiod, and the tragic poets represents already a selection and an interpretation of archaic materials, some of which had become almost unintelligible. In short, our best chance of understanding the structure of mythical thought is to study cultures where myth is a "living thing," where it constitutes the very ground of the religious life; in other words, where myth, far from indicating a *fiction*, is considered to reveal the *truth par excellence*.

This is what anthropologists have done, for more than half a century, concentrating on "primitive" societies. . . . Reacting against an excessive concern with comparison, most of the authors have neglected to supplement their anthropological research with a rigorous study of other mythologies, for example those of the ancient Near East, in the first place of Mesopotamia and Egypt, those of the Indo-Europeans—especially the grandiose, exuberant mythologies of ancient and medieval India—and those, finally, of the Turco-Mongols, the Tibetans, and the peoples of Southeast Asia. A restriction of the inquiry to "primitive" mythologies risks giving the impression that there is no continuity between archaic thought and the thought of the peoples who played an important role in ancient history. Now, such a solution of continuity does not exist. Moreover, by limiting the research to primitive societies, we are left with no measure of the role of myths in complex and highly developed religions, like those of the ancient Near East and India. To give only one example, it is impossible to understand the religion and, in general, the style of

Mesopotamian culture if we ignore the cosmogonic myth and the origin myths preserved in *Enuma elish* and in the Gilgamesh Epic. At every New Year the fabulous events related in *Enuma elish* were ritually reenacted; every New Year the world needed to be re-created —and this necessity reveals a profound dimension of Mesopotamian thought.[1] Moreover, the myth of the origin of man illuminates, at least in part, the tragic world-view and pessimism characteristic of Mesopotamian culture: for man has been molded by Marduk from clay, that is, from the very body of the primordial monster Tiamat, and from the blood of the arch-demon Kingu. And the myth clearly indicates that man has been created by Marduk in order that the gods may be nourished by human labor. Finally, the Gilgamesh Epic presents an equally pessimistic vision by explaining why man did not, and could not, obtain immortality.

This is the reason why the historians of religions prefer the approach of their colleagues—a Raffaelle Pettazzoni or a Gerardus van der Leeuw—or even the approach of certain scholars in the field of comparative anthropology, like Adolf Jensen or H. Baumann, who deal with all categories of mythological creativity, those of the "primitives" as well as of the peoples of high cultures. While one may not always agree with the results of their researches, one is at least certain that their documentation is sufficiently broad to permit valid generalizations.

But the divergences resulting from an incomplete documentation do not constitute the only difficulty in the dialogue between the historian of religions and his colleagues from other disciplines. It is his very approach which separates him, for instance, from the anthropologist or the psychologist. The historian of religions is too conscious of the axiological difference of his documents to marshal them on the same level. Aware of nuances and distinctions, he cannot ignore the fact that there exist great myths and myths of less importance; myths which dominate and characterize a religion, and secondary myths, repetitious and parasitical. *Enuma elish*, for example, cannot figure on the same plane with the mythology of the female demon Lamashtu; the Polynesian cosmogonic myth has not the same weight as the myth of the origin of a plant, for it precedes it and serves as a model for it. Such differences may not be important for an anthropologist

---

1. Cf. selection 18 below, "Annual Repetition of the Creation." Eds.

or a psychologist. For instance, a sociologist concerned to study the French novel in the nineteenth century or a psychologist interested in literary imagination might discuss Balzac and Eugène Sue, Stendhal or Jules Sandeau indifferently, irrespective of the quality of their art. But for a literary critic such conflation is simply unthinkable, for it annihilates his own hermeneutical principles.

When, in one or two generations, perhaps even earlier, we have historians of religions who are descended from Australian, African, or Melanesian tribal societies, I do not doubt that, among other things, they will reproach Western scholars for their indifference to the scale of values *indigenous* to these societies. Let us imagine a history of Greek culture in which Homer, the tragic poets, and Plato are passed by silently while the *Book of Dreams* of Artemidorus and the novel of Heliodorus from Emessa are laboriously commented on, under the pretext that such works better illuminate the specific traits of the Greek genius and help us to understand its destiny. To come back to our theme, I do not think that we can grasp the structure and function of mythical thought in a society which has myth as its foundation if we do not take into account the *mythology in its totality* and, at the same time, the *scales of values* which such mythology implicitly or explicitly proclaims.

Now in every case where we have access to a still living tradition, and not to an acculturated one, one thing strikes us from the very beginning: the mythology not only constitutes, as it were, the "sacred history" of the tribe, not only does it explain the total reality and justify its contradictions, but it equally reveals a hierarchy in the series of fabulous events that it reports. In general, one can say that any myth tells how something came into being, the world, or man, or an animal species, or a social institution, and so on. But by the very fact that the creation of the world precedes everything else, the cosmogony enjoys a special prestige. In fact, . . . the cosmogonic myth furnishes the model for all myths of origin. The creation of animals, plants, or man presupposes the existence of a world.

Certainly, the myth of the creation of the world does not always look like a cosmogonic myth *stricto sensu*, like the Indian or Polynesian myth, or the one narrated in *Enuma elish*. In a great part of Australia, for example, such cosmogonic myths are unknown. But there is always a central myth which describes the beginnings of the world, that is, what happened before the world became as it is today.

Thus, there is always a *primordial history* and this history has a *beginning*: a cosmogonic myth proper, or a myth that describes the first, germinal stage of the world. This beginning is always implied in the sequence of myths which recounts the fabulous events that took place after the creation or the coming into being of the universe, namely, the myths of the origin of plants, animals, and man, or of the origin of marriage, family, and death, etc. Taken all together, these myths of origin constitute a fairly coherent history. They reveal how the cosmos was shaped and changed, how man became mortal, sexually diversified, and compelled to work in order to live; they equally reveal what the supernatural beings and the mythical ancestors did, and how and why they abandoned the earth and disappeared. We can also say that any mythology that is still accessible in an appropriate form contains not only a beginning but also an end, determined by the last manifestation of the supernatural beings, the cultural heroes, or the ancestors.

Now this primordial, sacred history, brought together by the totality of significant myths, is fundamental because it explains, and by the same token justifies, the existence of the world, of man and of society....

11. MEANING AND FUNCTION OF A COSMOGONIC MYTH

My first example is the mythology of the Ngadju Dayak of Borneo. I have chosen it because there is available a work about it which deserves to become a classic: *Die Gottesidee der Ngadju Dajak in Süd-Borneo* (Leiden, 1946) by Hans Schärer.[1] The author, who unfortunately died prematurely, studied these people for many years. The mythological documents which he collected, if ever printed, would cover 12,000 pages. Hans Schärer not only mastered the language of these people and thoroughly knew their customs, but he also understood the structure of mythology and its role in the life of

Source: Q/77–80.
1. The book has recently been translated into English by Rodney Needham, *Ngaju Religion. The Conception of God among a South Borneo People* (The Hague, 1963).

the Dayak. As for many other archaic peoples, for the Dayak the cosmogonic myth discloses the eventful creation of the world and of man and, at the same time, the principles which govern the cosmic process and human existence. One must read this book to realize how much everything attains consistency in the life of an archaic people, how the myths succeed each other and articulate themselves into a sacred history which is continuously recovered in the life of the community as well as in the existence of each individual. Through the cosmogonic myth and its sequel, the Dayak progressively unveils the structures of reality and of his own proper mode of being. What happened in the beginning describes at once both the original perfection and the destiny of each individual.

At the beginning, so the myth goes, the cosmic totality was still undivided in the mouth of the coiled watersnake. Eventually two mountains arise and from their repeated clashes the cosmic reality comes progressively into existence: the clouds, the hills, the sun and the moon, and so on. The mountains are the seats of the two supreme deities, and they are also these deities themselves. They reveal their human forms, however, only at the end of the first part of the creation. In their anthropomorphic form, the two supreme deities, Mahatala and his wife Putir, pursue the cosmogonic work and create the upperworld and the underworld. But there is still lacking an intermediary world, and mankind to inhabit it. The third phase of the creation is carried out by two hornbills, male and female, who are actually identical with the two supreme deities. Mahatala raises the tree of life in the "Center," the two hornbills fly over toward it, and eventually meet each other in its branches. A furious fight breaks out between the two birds, and as a result the tree of life is extensively damaged. From the knotty excrescences of the tree and from the moss falling out from the throat of the female hornbill, a maiden and a young man come forth, the ancestors of the Dayak. The tree of life is finally destroyed and the two birds end by killing each other.

In sum, during the work of creation the deities reveal themselves under three different forms: cosmic (the two mountains), anthropomorphic (Mahatala and Putir), theriomorphic (the two hornbills).[2] But these polar manifestations represent only one aspect of

2. Anthropomorphic: deities in human forms; theriomorphic: deities in animal forms. Eds.

the divinity. Not less important are the godhead's manifestations as a *totality*: the primordial watersnake, for instance, or the tree of life. This totality—which Schärer calls divine/ambivalent totality—constitutes the fundamental principle of the religious life of the Dayak, and it is proclaimed again and again in different contexts. One can say that, for the Dayaks, every divine form contains its opposite in the same measure as itself: Mahatala is also his own wife and *vice versa*, and the watersnake is also the hornbill and *vice versa*.

The cosmogonic myth enables us to understand the religious life of the Dayaks as well as their culture and their social organization. The world is the result of a combat between two polar principles, during which the tree of life—i.e., their own embodiment—is annihilated. "But from destruction and death spring the cosmos and a new life. The new creation originates in the death of the total godhead."[3] In the most important religious ceremonies—birth, initiation, marriage, death—this creative clash is tirelessly reiterated. As a matter of fact, everything which is significant in the eyes of a Dayak is an imitation of exemplary models and a repetition of the events narrated in the cosmogonic myth. The village as well as the house represent the universe and are supposed to be situated at the Center of the World. The exemplary house is an *imago mundi*: it is erected on the back of the watersnake, its steep roof symbolizes the primeval mountain on which Mahatala is enthroned, and an umbrella represents the tree of life on whose branches one can see the two birds.

During the ceremonies of marriage, the couple return to the mythical primeval time. Such a return is indicated by a replica of the tree of life that is clasped by the bridal pair. Schärer was told that clasping the tree of life means to form a unity with it. "The wedding is the reenactment of the creation, and the reenactment of the creation is the creation of the first human couple from the Tree of Life."[4] Birth also is related to the original time. The room in which the child is born is symbolically situated in the primeval waters. Likewise, the room where the young girls are enclosed during initiation ceremonies is imagined to be located in the primordial ocean. The young girl descends to the underworld and after some time assumes the form of

3. Schärer, *Ngaju Religion*, p. 34.
4. *Ibid.*, p. 85.

a watersnake. She comes back to earth as a new person and begins a new life, both socially and religiously.[5] Death is equally conceived as a passage to a new and richer life. The deceased person returns to the primeval era, his mystical voyage indicated by the form and decorations of his coffin. In fact, the coffin has the shape of a boat, and on its sides are painted the watersnake, the tree of life, the primordial mountains, that is to say the cosmic/divine totality. In other words, the dead man returns to the divine totality which existed at the beginning.

On the occasion of each decisive crisis and each *rite de passage*, man takes up again *ab initio* the world's drama. The operation is carried out in two times: (1) the return to the primordial totality, and (2) the repetition of the cosmogony, that is to say, the breaking up of the primitive unity. The same operation takes place again during the collective annual ceremonies. Schärer points out that the end of the year signifies the end of an era and also of a world;[6] the ceremonies clearly indicate that there is a return to the precosmic time, the time of the sacred totality embodied in the watersnake and in the tree of life. In fact, during this period, sacred *par excellence*, which is called *helat nyelo*, "the time between the years," a replica of the tree of life is erected in the village and all the population returns to the primeval (i.e., precosmogonic) age. Rules and interdictions are suspended since the world has ceased to exist. While waiting for a new creation the community lives near the godhead, more exactly lives *in* the total primeval godhead. The orgiastic character of the interval between the years ought not to obscure its sacrality. As Schärer puts it, "there is no question of disorder (even if it may appear so to us) but of another order."[7] The orgy takes place in accordance with the divine commandments, and those who participate in it recover in themselves the total godhead. As is well known, in many other religions, primitive as well as historical, the periodical orgy is considered to be the instrument *par excellence* to achieve the perfect totality. It is from such a totality that a new creation will take place—for the Dayaks as well as for the Mesopotamians.

5. *Ibid.*, p. 87.
6. *Ibid.*, pp. 94 ff.
7. *Ibid.*, p. 97.

12. PRIMORDIALITY AND TOTALITY

Even this imperfect résumé of an immense amount of material has enabled us to grasp the considerable role that the cosmogonic myth plays in an archaic society. The myth unveils the religious thought of the Dayaks in all its depth and complexity. As we have just seen it, the individual and collective life has a cosmological structure: every life constitutes a cycle, whose model is the sempiternal creation, destruction, and re-creation of the world. Such a conception is not restricted to the Dayak, or even to peoples having their type of culture. In other words, the Dayak myth reveals to us a meaning which transcends its ethnographic frontiers. Now, what is striking in this mythology is the great importance bestowed upon the *primordial totality*. One may almost say that the Dayaks are obsessed by two aspects of the sacred: the *primordiality* and the *totality*. This does not mean that they belittle the work of creation. There is nothing of the Indian or gnostic pessimism in the Dayak conception of the cosmos and of life. The world is good and significant because it is sacred, since it came out from the tree of life, that is to say from the total godhead. But only the primordial total godhead is perfect. If the cosmos must be periodically abolished and re-created, it is not because the first creation did not succeed, but because it is only that stage which precedes the creation which represents a plenitude and a beatitude otherwise inaccessible in the created world. On the other hand, the myth points out the necessity of creation, that is, of the breaking up of the primeval unity. The original perfection is periodically reintegrated, but such perfection is always transitory. The Dayak myth proclaims that the creation—with all that it made possible: human existence, society, culture—cannot be definitively abolished. In other words, a "sacred history" has taken place, and this history must be perpetuated by periodical reiteration. It is impossible to freeze the reality in its germinal modality, such as it was in the beginning, immersed as it were in the primordial divine totality.

Now, it is this exceptional value conferred upon the "sacred history," ground and model of all human history, that is significant. Such attribution of value is recognizable in many other primitive mythologies, but it becomes particularly important in the mythologies of the ancient Near East and of Asia. If we examine a mythology in

SOURCE: *Q*/80–82.

its totality we learn the judgment of the particular people upon its own sacred history. Every mythology presents a successive and coherent series of primordial events, but different peoples judge these fabulous acts in different ways, underlining the importance of some of them, casting aside, or even completely neglecting, others. If we analyze the context of what may be called the myth of the estrangement of the creator god and his progressive transformation into a *deus otiosus*,[1] we notice a similar process, involving an analogous choice and judgment: out of a series of primordial creative events, only some of them are exalted, those in particular which are of consequence for human life. In other words, the coherent series of events which constitute the *sacred history* is incessantly remembered and extolled, while the previous stage, everything which existed *before* that sacred history—first and above all, the majestic and solitary presence of the creator God—fades away. If the High God is still remembered, he is known to have created the world and man, but this is almost all. Such a Supreme God seems to have ended his role by achieving the work of creation. He plays almost no role in the cult, his myths are few and rather banal, and, when he is not completely forgotten, he is invoked only in cases of extreme distress, when all other divine beings have proved utterly ineffectual.

13. THE "GREAT FATHER" AND THE MYTHICAL ANCESTORS

This lesson of the primitive myths is particularly revealing. It not only shows us that man, turning toward the divinities of life and fecundity, became as it were more and more incarnated. It also shows that early man assumes already, in his way, a history of which he is at once both the center and the victim. What happened to his mythical ancestors became, for him, more important than what happened *before* their appearance. One can illustrate this process with innumerable examples. . . . But I would like to examine now the mythical traditions of a people who for more than half a century have enjoyed a considerable vogue among anthropologists, sociologists, and psychologists, namely the Aranda tribes of Central Australia. I will draw

Source: *Q*/82–86.
1. See selection 13, n. 2. Eds.

exclusively from the materials collected by T. G. H. Strehlow,[1] the son of the famous missionary Carl Strehlow, whose writings gave rise to heated controversies in Durkheim's time. I think I choose the best living authority, for Aranda was the first language spoken by T. G. H. Strehlow, and he studied these tribes intensely for more than thirty years.

According to the Aranda, the sky and the earth have always existed and have always been inhabited by supernatural beings. In the sky there is an emu-footed personage, having emu-footed wives and children: it is the Great Father (*knaritja*), called also the Eternal Youth (*altjira nditja*). All these supernatural beings live in a perpetually green land, rich in flowers and fruits, traversed by the Milky Way. All of them are eternally young, the Great Father being in appearance as young as his children. And all of them are as immortal as the stars themselves, for death cannot enter their home.

Strehlow thinks that it would be impossible to regard this emu-footed Great Father as a supernatural being analogous to certain celestial gods of Southeast Australia. Indeed, he did not create or shape the earth, nor did he bring into existence either plants, animals, man, or the totemic ancestors, nor did he inspire or control the ancestors' activities. The Great Father and the other inhabitants of heaven were never interested in what happened on the earth. Evil-doers had to fear not the celestial Great Father but the wrath of the totemic ancestors and the punishment of the tribal authorities. For, as we shall see in a moment, all the creative and meaningful acts were effected by the earth-born totemic ancestors. In sum, one can see here, a drastic transformation of a celestial being into a *deus otiosus*.[2] The next step could only be his falling into total oblivion. This probably did happen outside of the western Aranda territory, where Strehlow could not find any comparable beliefs in sky beings.

Nevertheless, there are some characteristic traits which allow this otiose and transcendent Great Father and Eternal Youth a place in

1. Especially his *Aranda Traditions* (Melbourne, 1947) and his recent article "Personal Monototemism in a Polytotemic Community" in *Festschrift für Ad. E. Jensen* (Munich, 1964), pp. 723–54; cf. also "La gémellité de l'âme humaine" in *La Tour Saint-Jacques* (Paris, 1957), nos. 11–12, pp. 14–23.

2. *Deus otiosus* (plural: *dii otiosi*): a withdrawn, inactive, or hidden god. Eds.

the category of supreme beings. There is, first, his immortality, his youth, and his beatific existence; there is then his ontological anteriority with regard to the totemic heroes; indeed, he had been up there, in the sky, for a long time before the emergence of the totemic ancestors from under the earth. Finally, the religious importance of the sky is repeatedly proclaimed: for example, in the myths of certain heroes who conquered immortality by ascending to heaven, in the mythical traditions of trees or ladders connecting heaven and earth, and especially in the widespread Aranda beliefs that death came into being because the communications with heaven had been violently interrupted. Strehlow recalls the traditions concerning a ladder joining the earth to heaven, and describes the sites where, according to the legend, there grew gigantic trees which certain mythical ancestors were able to climb to heaven. Similar beliefs are to be found in many other archaic traditions, particularly in myths relating that after the interruption of the communications between heaven and earth, the gods retired to the highest sky and became more or less *dii otiosi*. From that moment on, only a few privileged personages—heroes, shamans, medicine men—have been able to ascend to heaven.[3] We do not know how much of this mythical theme was familiar to the Aranda. But the fact is that, despite the reciprocal indifference between the Aranda and the celestial beings, the religious prestige of heaven continues to survive along with the haunting memory of a conquest of immortality by an ascension to heaven. One is tempted to read in these mythical fragments a certain nostalgia for a primordial situation irretrievably lost.

In any case the *primordium* represented by the celestial Great Father does not have any immediate significance for the Aranda. On the contrary, the Aranda seem to be interested exclusively in what happened at a certain moment *on the earth*. Such happenings are supremely significant; that is to say, in our terminology, they have a religious value. Indeed, the events that took place in the mythical times, in the "Dream Time," are religious in the sense that they constitute a paradigmatic history which man has to follow and repeat in order to assure the continuity of the world, of life and society.

While the Great Father and his family lived a sort of paradisiacal

3. On this theme, cf. selections 51–53 below. Eds.

existence in the sky, without any responsibility, on the surface of earth there existed even from time immemorial amorphous, semi-embryonic masses of half-developed infants. They could not develop into individual men and women, but neither could they grow old or die. Indeed, neither life nor death was known on earth. Life existed fully *below* the surface of the earth, in the form of thousands of slumbering supernatural beings. They also were uncreated (as a matter of fact they are called "born out of their own eternity," *altijirana nambakala*). Finally they awoke from their sleep and broke through the surface of the earth. Their birthplaces are impregnated with their life and power. One of these supernatural beings is the sun, and when he emerged out of the ground the earth was flooded with light.

The forms of these chthonian beings[4] were varied; some emerged in animal forms, others as men and women. But all of them had something in common: the theriomorphic ones acted and thought like humans, and those in human forms could change at will into a particular species of animal. These chthonian beings, commonly designated totemic ancestors, began to wander on the surface of the earth and to modify the land, giving the Central Australian landscape its actual physical features. Such works constitute properly speaking a cosmogony; the ancestors did not create the earth, but they gave form to a pre-existent *materia prima*. And the anthropogony repeats the cosmogony. Some of the totemic ancestors took on the roles of culture heroes, slicing apart the semi-embryonic aggregate, then shaping each individual infant by slitting the webs between his fingers and toes and cutting open his ears, eyes, and mouth. Other culture heroes taught men how to make tools and fire and to cook food, and they also revealed social and religious institutions to them.

As a result of all these labors, an extreme fatigue overpowered the ancestors, and they sank into the ground or turned into rocks, trees, or ritual objects (*tjurunga*). The sites which marked their final resting places are, like their birth places, regarded as important sacred centers, and are called by the same name, *pmara kutata*. But the disappearance of the ancestors, which put an end to the primordial age, is not final. Though reimmersed in their initial slumber under the surface of the earth, they watch over the behavior of men. Moreover, the ancestors reincarnate themselves perpetually; as Strehlow has

4. Chthonian beings: of the earth or underworld. Eds.

shown,[5] the immortal soul of each individual represents a particle of an ancestor's life.

This fabulous epoch when the ancestors were roaming about the land is for the Aranda tantamount to a paradisiacal age. Not only do they imagine the freshly formed earth as a paradise, where the different animals allowed themselves to be easily captured and water and fruits were in abundance, but the ancestors were free from the multitude of inhibitions and frustrations that inevitably obstruct all human beings who are living together in organized communities.[6] This primordial paradise still haunts the Aranda. In a certain sense, one can interpret the brief intervals of ritual orgy, when all the interdictions are suspended, as ephemeral returns to the freedom and beatitude of the ancestors.

Such a terrestrial and paradisiacal primordiality—which constitutes both a history and a propaedeutic—is the one that interests the Aranda. In this mythical time man became what he is today, not only because he was then shaped and instructed by the ancestors, but also because he has to repeat continuously everything that the ancestors did *in illo tempore*. The myths disclose this sacred and creative history. Moreover, through initiation, every young Aranda not only learns what happened *in principio*, but ultimately discovers *that he was already there*, that somehow he participated in those glorious events. The initiation brings about an *anamnesis*.[7] At the end of the ceremony, the novice finds out that the hero of the myths just communicated to him is himself. He is shown a sacred and well-guarded ritual object, a *tjurunga*, and one old man tells him: This is your own body!—for that *tjurunga* represents the body of one of the ancestors. This dramatic revelation of the identity between the eternal ancestor and the individual in which he is reincarnated can be compared with *tat tvam asi* of the Upanishads. These beliefs are not exclusively Aranda. In Northeast Australia, for instance, when an Unambal proceeds to repaint the image of a Wondjina on the rock wall (the Wondjina are the equivalent of the Central Australian totemic ancestors), he says: "I am going now to refresh and invigorate myself; I paint myself anew, so that the rain can come."

5. Cf. "Personal Monototemism in a Polytotemic Community," p. 730.
6. *Ibid.*, p. 729. Cf. also *Aranda Traditions*, pp. 36 ff., on the "Golden Age" of the totemic ancestors.
7. *Anamnesis:* a recollection, remembering; see selections 23, 31, 32. Eds.

To the irrevocability of death, as a result of the brutal interruption of the communications between earth and heaven, the Aranda replied with a theory of transmigration thanks to which the ancestors —that is to say, they themselves—are supposed to return perpetually to life. One can distinguish, then, two sorts of *primordiality*, to which two types of nostalgia correspond: (1) the *primordium* represented by the celestial Great Father and by the celestial immortality that is inaccessible to ordinary human beings; (2) the fabulous epoch of the ancestors, when life in general and human life in particular was brought about. The Aranda yearn above all for the terrestrial paradise represented by this second *primordium*.[8]

◆ ◆

Sacred Time and Myths

Time is a motif of primary importance in Eliade's work. To be sure, there is a sense in which Time is the very stuff of "sacred history." For it appears that a history only becomes sacred as it is either contemplated as having an *absolute beginning* (e.g., the Dream Time) or as it is construed as *another Time* (e.g., the Great Time) outside of ordinary time either because of its infinite duration or its distinctive quality and power. The element of quality and power is, nonetheless, shared by both views.

Eliade recognizes that ". . . the archaic ideology of ritual repetition [of the primal time] . . . does not always imply the 'myth of the eternal return' [of the primal time]."[1] Moreover, the oft-made generalization by critics, that Eliade holds that primitive peoples live in an omnisacral world is not accurate. The following excerpts from *The Sacred and the Profane* and other sources will show that: (1) both the Sacred *and* the Profane are found in both the world of the primitive and that of the ancients; (2) that the archaic religious man would *prefer* to live in an omnisacral world; and (3) that there is Time, and there are "times," and these "times" offer us varying perspectives on the valuation of Time in relation to the desire for ultimate salvation.

8. The Aranda myth of origins is discussed in *AR*/44–50. Eds.
1. *CH*/vii; this point is sometimes overlooked or ignored by secondary studies of Eliade. See also *PCR*/Ch. XI, "Sacred Time and the Myth of the Eternal Renewal," a comprehensive discussion.

14. PROFANE DURATION AND SACRED TIME

For religious man time too, like space, is neither homogeneous nor continuous. On the one hand there are the intervals of a sacred time, the time of festivals (by far the greater part of which are periodical); on the other there is profane time, ordinary temporal duration, in which acts without religious meaning have their setting. Between these two kinds of time there is, of course, solution of continuity; but by means of rites religious man can pass without danger from ordinary temporal duration to sacred time.

One essential difference between these two qualities of time strikes us immediately: *by its very nature sacred time is reversible* in the sense that, properly speaking, it is *a primordial mythical time made present*. Every religious festival, any liturgical time, represents the reactualization of a sacred event that took place in a mythical past, "in the beginning." Religious participation in a festival implies emerging from ordinary temporal duration and reintegration of the mythical time reactualized by the festival itself. Hence sacred time is indefinitely recoverable, indefinitely repeatable. From one point of view it could be said that it does not "pass," that it does not constitute an irreversible duration. It is an ontological, Parmenidean time; it always remains equal to itself, it neither changes nor is exhausted. With each periodical festival, the participants find the same sacred time—the same that had been manifested in the festival of the previous year or in the festival of a century earlier; it is the time that was created and sanctified by the gods at the period of their *gesta*,[1] of which the festival is precisely a reactualization. In other words the participants in the festival meet in it *the first appearance of sacred time*, as it appeared *ab origine, in illo tempore*. For the sacred time in which the festival runs its course did not exist before the divine *gesta* that the festival commemorates. By creating the various realities that today constitute the world, the gods *also founded sacred time*, for the time contemporary with a creation was necessarily sanctified by the presence and activity of the gods.

Hence religious man lives in two kinds of time, of which the more important, sacred time, appears under the paradoxical aspect of a

SOURCE: *SP*/68–72, 107.
1. *Gesta:* primal sacred acts. Eds.

circular time, reversible and recoverable, a sort of eternal mythical present that is periodically reintegrated by means of rites. This attitude in regard to time suffices to distinguish religious from nonreligious man; the former refuses to live solely in what, in modern terms, is called the historical present; he attempts to regain a sacred time that, from one point of view, can be homologized to eternity.

What time is for the nonreligious man of modern societies would be more difficult to put into a few words. We do not intend to discuss the modern philosophies of time nor the concepts that modern science uses in its own investigations. Our aim is to compare not systems or philosophies but existential attitudes and behaviors. Now, what it is possible to observe in respect to a nonreligious man is that he too experiences a certain discontinuity and heterogeneity of time. For him too there is the comparatively monotonous time of his work, and the time of celebrations and spectacles—in short, "festal time." He too lives in varying temporal rhythms and is aware of times of different intensities; when he is listening to the kind of music that he likes or, being in love, waits for or meets his sweetheart, he obviously experiences a different temporal rhythm from that which he experiences when he is working or bored.

But, in comparison with religious man, there is an essential difference. The latter experiences intervals of time that are "sacred," that have no part in the temporal duration that precedes and follows them, that have a wholly different structure and origin, for they are of a primordial time, sanctified by the gods and capable of being made present by the festival. This transhuman quality of liturgical time is inaccessible to a nonreligious man. This is as much as to say that, for him, time can present neither break nor mystery; for him, time constitutes man's deepest existential dimension; it is linked to his own life, hence it has a beginning and an end, which is death, the annihilation of his life. However many the temporal rhythms that he experiences, however great their differences in intensity, nonreligious man knows that they always represent a human experience, in which there is no room for any divine presence.

For religious man, on the contrary, profane temporal duration can be periodically arrested; for certain rituals have the power to interrupt it by periods of a sacred time that is nonhistorical (in the sense that it does not belong to the historical present). Just as a church constitutes a break in plane in the profane space of a modern city, the service celebrated inside it marks a break in profane temporal duration. It is no longer today's historical time that is present—the time that is experienced, for example, in the adjacent streets—but the time in which the historical existence of Jesus Christ occurred, the time sanctified by his preaching, by his passion, death, and resurrection. But we must add that this example does not reveal all the difference between sacred and profane time; Christianity radically changed the experience and the concept of liturgical time, and this is due to the fact that Christianity affirms the historicity of the person of Christ. The Christian liturgy unfolds in *a historical time sanctified by the incarnation of the Son of God*. The sacred time periodically reactualized in pre-Christian religions (especially in the archaic religions) is a *mythical time*, that is, a primordial time, not to be found in the historical past, an *original time*, in the sense that it came into existence all at once, that it was not preceded by another time, because no time could exist *before the appearance of the reality narrated in the myth.* . . .

* * *

The perspective changes completely when the sense of *the religiousness of the cosmos becomes lost.* This is what occurs when, in certain more highly evolved societies, the intellectual élites progressively detach themselves from the patterns of the traditional religion. The periodical sanctification of cosmic time then proves useless and without meaning. The gods are no longer accessible through the cosmic rhythms. The religious meaning of the repetition of paradigmatic gestures is forgotten. But *repetition emptied of its religious content necessarily leads to a pessimistic vision of existence.* When it is no longer a vehicle for reintegrating a primordial situation, and hence for recovering the mysterious presence of the gods, that is, *when it is desacralized*, cyclic time becomes terrifying; it is seen as a circle forever turning on itself, repeating itself to infinity. . . .

15. THE STRUCTURAL MORPHOLOGY OF THE SACRED

. . . One of the major differences separating the people of the early cultures from people today is precisely the utter incapacity of the

SOURCE: *PCR*/31–33.

latter to live their organic life (particularly as regards sex and nutrition) as a sacrament. Psychoanalysis and historical materialism have taken as surest confirmation of their theses the important part played by sexuality and nutrition among peoples still at the ethnological stage. What they have missed, however, is how utterly different from their modern meaning are the value and even the function of eroticism and of nutrition among those peoples. For the modern they are simply physiological acts, whereas for primitive man they were sacraments, ceremonies by means of which he communicated with the *force* which stood for Life itself. . . . This force and this life are simply expressions of ultimate reality, and such elementary actions for the primitive become a rite which will assist man to approach reality, to, as it were, wedge himself into Being, by setting himself free from merely automatic actions (without sense or meaning), from change, from the profane, from nothingness.

We shall see that, as the rite always consists in the repetition of an archetypal action performed *in illo tempore* (before "history" began) by ancestors or by gods, man is trying, by means of the hierophany, to give "being" to even his most ordinary and insignificant acts. By its repetition, the act coincides with its archetype, and time is abolished. We are witnessing, so to speak, the same act that was performed *in illo tempore*, at the dawn of the universe. Thus, by transforming all his physiological acts into ceremonies, primitive man strove to "pass beyond," to thrust himself out of time (and change) into eternity. I do not want to stress here the function fulfilled by ritual, but we must note at once that it is the normal tendency of the primitive to transform his physiological acts into rites, thus investing them with spiritual value. When he is eating or making love, he is putting himself on a plane which is not simply that of eating or sexuality. This is true both of initiatory experiences (first-fruits, first sexual act), and also of the whole of erotic or nutritional activity. One might say that here you have an indistinct religious experience, different in form from the distinct experiences represented by the hierophanies of the unusual, the extraordinary, *mana*, etc. But the part this experience plays in the life of primitive man is none the less for that, though it is, by its very nature, liable to escape the eye of the observer. This explains my earlier statement that the religious life of primitive peoples goes beyond the categories of *mana*, hierophanies and startling kratophanies.[1] A real religious experience, indistinct in form, results from this effort man makes to enter the real, the sacred, by way of the most fundamental physiological acts transformed into ceremonies.

Then, too, the religious life of any human group at the ethnological stage will always include certain elements of theory (symbols, ideograms, nature- and genealogy-myths, and so on). As we shall see later, such "truths" are held to be hierophanies by primitive peoples —not only because they reveal modalities of the sacred, but because these "truths" help man to protect himself against the meaningless, nothingness; to escape, in fact, from the profane sphere. Much has been said of the backwardness of primitives in regard to theory. Even if this were the case (and a great many observers think otherwise), it is too often forgotten that the workings of primitive thought were not expressed only in concepts or conceptual elements, but also, and primarily, in symbols. We shall see later on how the "handling" of symbols works according to its own symbolic logic. It follows from this that the apparent conceptual poverty of the primitive cultures does not imply an inability to construct theory, but implies rather that they belong to a style of thinking totally different from our modern style, with its roots in the speculation of the Greeks. Indeed we can identify, even among the groups least developed ethnologically, a collection of truths fitting coherently into a system or theory (among, for instance, the Australians, Pygmies, and Fuegians). That collection of truths does not simply constitute a *Weltanschauung*, but a pragmatic ontology (I would even say soteriology) in the sense that with the help of these "truths" man is trying to gain salvation by uniting himself with reality.[2]

To quote only one example, we shall see that the greater part of primitive man's actions were, so he thought, simply the repetition of a primeval action accomplished at the beginning of time by a divine being, or mythical figure. An act only had meaning in so far as it repeated a transcendent model, an archetype. The object of that repetition was also to ensure the *normality* of the act, to legalize it

1. Hierophany: a manifestation of the sacred; kratophany: a manifestation of a supernal power. Eds.

2. *Weltanschauung*: world-view; ontology: theory of being; soteriology: theory of salvation. Eds.

by giving it an ontological status; it only became real in so far as it repeated an archetype. Now, every action performed by the primitive supposes a transcendent model—his actions are effective only in so far as they are real, as they follow the pattern. The action is both a ceremony (in that it makes man part of a sacred zone) and a thrusting into reality. . . .

16. TWO KINDS OF "PRIMORDIALITY"

. . . Apparently the irrelevance, the vagueness, or the absence of a celestial High Being does not modify the pan-Australian pattern of the religious life. As Elkin puts it: to say that a custom is *altjira*, "dreaming," is the same as to say of a custom: "Baiame say so." . . . What is important in this process is that the religious function of the *primordial* and *primordiality* remains the same. Whatever the context may be—supernatural Sky Gods, Culture Heroes, Wondjina or Ungud . . . the primordial mythical time has an overwhelming significance. Only that which was effected *in illo tempore* is real, meaningful, exemplary, and of inexhaustible creativity. Among the western Aranda we noted a passage from what might be called a "speculative" primordial time—the epoch of the celestial, eternal Great Father—to a primordial time rich in existential values, the fabulous epoch of the "dreaming" when the totemic Ancestors (or Culture Heroes) shaped the world, created the animals, and completed and civilized man. The "primordiality" of the Great Father was not of immediate relevance to the Aranda's existence; once the communication with heaven had been interrupted and death had come into the world, it was not very helpful to know about the immortality of Altjira's family or of those who had ascended to heaven. The only "immortality" accessible to the Aranda and to other Australian tribes was the reincarnation, the perennial return to life of the primordial Ancestors. . . .

Thus it seems as if the pattern of Australian religions implies the substitution of a "primordial" directly related to the human condition for the "primordial" preceding this condition. Such a process is

SOURCE: *AR*/39–41.

known in other religions too; we might refer, for example, to the "primordiality" of Tiamat and the passage to the creative primordial epoch represented by the victory of Marduk, the cosmogony, anthropogony, and the founding of a new divine hierarchy. Or we might compare the primordiality of Ouranos with the establishment of Zeus' supremacy—or point to the passage from the almost forgotten Dyaus to Varuna and later still to the consecutive supremacies of Indra, Shiva, and Vishnu.

What is significant in this substitution of an "existential" primordiality for a "speculative" one is that this process represents a more radical incarnation of the *sacred* in *life* and *human existence*. . . . The abundance of embryological imagery is not without a profound religious meaning. It is as if the entire grandiose cosmogonic drama were being interpreted in terms of procreation, pregnancy, embryonic existence, and obstetric operations. But none of these fabulous events is either "human" or "profane" in nature. They are primordial, creative, exemplary, and thus religious acts. Ultimately they represent mysteries which only the fully initiated men will be able to grasp. . . .

◆ ◆

Varieties of Sacred Time

That there is thought to exist an intimate relationship between the cosmos and time is a widespread feature of mythic thought. But there are various ways of relating time and the cosmos, and we look here at some of these. The primal time can be renewed, brought forward to the present, transcended, prolonged, annulled, redeemed, and so forth; and we begin to see that a religion's evaluation of the nature of time is an important factor in understanding it.

Perhaps this subsection discloses something of the strength of Eliade's cross-cultural and comparative approach to religions: under the theme of "time," we have a basis for comparing Chinese alchemy, the Australian Dream Time, Christian eschatologies, and Freudian psychoanalysis! This comparative method does not assume that these phenomena are all at the same level of sophistication or religious development at all—it merely isolates one theme and asks how it can provide a key to comparative study.

17. *TEMPLUM—TEMPUS*

We shall begin our investigation by presenting certain facts that have the advantage of immediately revealing religious man's behavior in respect to time. First of all, an observation that is not without importance: in a number of North American Indian languages the term world (= Cosmos) is also used in the sense of year. The Yokuts say "the world has passed," meaning "a year has gone by." For the Yuki, the year is expressed by the words for earth or world. Like the Yokuts, they say "the world has passed" when a year has passed. This vocabulary reveals the intimate religious connection between the world and cosmic time. The cosmos is conceived as a living unity that is born, develops, and dies on the last day of the year, to be reborn on New Year's Day. We shall see that this *rebirth* is a *birth*, that the cosmos is reborn each year because, at every New Year, time begins *ab initio*.

The intimate connection between the cosmos and time is religious in nature: the cosmos is homologizable[1] to cosmic time (= the Year) because they are both sacred realities, divine creations. Among some North American peoples this cosmic-temporal connection is revealed even in the structure of sacred buildings. Since the temple represents the image of the world, it can also comprise a temporal symbolism. We find this, for example, among the Algonquins and the Sioux. . . . Their sacred lodge represents the universe; but at the same time it symbolizes the year. For the year is conceived as a journey through the four cardinal directions, signified by the four doors and four windows of the lodge. The Dakotas say: "The Year is a circle around the world"—that is, around their sacred lodge, which is an *imago mundi*.[2]

A still clearer example is found in India. We saw that the erection of an altar is equivalent to a repetition of the cosmogony. The texts add that "the fire altar is the year" and explain its temporal system as follows: the 360 bricks of the enclosure correspond to the 360 nights of the year, and the 360 *yajusmati* bricks to the 360 days

---

Source: *SP*/73–76.

1. Homologous: matching in structure or function. Eliade uses this word frequently to compare religious phenomena that look different but function similarly in distinct cultures. Eds.

2. Werner Müller, *Die blaue Hütte* (Wiesbaden, 1954), p. 133.

(*Shatapatha Brahmana*, X, 5, 4, 10; etc.). This is as much as to say that, with the building of each fire altar, not only is the world remade but the year is built too; in other words, *time is regenerated by being created anew*. But then, too, the year is assimilated to Prajapati, the cosmic god; consequently, with each new altar Prajapati is reanimated—that is, the sanctity of the world is strengthened. It is not a matter of profane time, of mere temporal duration, but of the sanctification of cosmic time. What is sought by the erection of the fire altar is to sanctify the world, hence to place it in a sacred time.

We find a similar temporal symbolism as part of the cosmological symbolism of the Temple at Jerusalem. According to Flavius Josephus (*Ant. Jud.*, III, 7, 7), the twelve loaves of bread on the table signified the twelve months of the year and the candelabrum with seventy branches represented the decans (the zodiacal division of the seven planets into tens). The Temple was an *imago mundi*; being at the Center of the World, at Jerusalem, it sanctified not only the entire cosmos but also cosmic life—that is, time.

Hermann Usener has the distinction of having been the first to explain the etymological kinship between *templum* and *tempus* by interpreting the two terms through the concept of "intersection," (*Schneidung, Kreuzung*).[3] Later studies have refined the discovery: "*templum* designates the spatial, *tempus* the temporal aspect of the motion of the horizon in space and time."[4]

The underlying meaning of all these facts seems to be the following: for religious man of the archaic cultures, *the world is renewed annually*; in other words, *with each new year it recovers* its original sanctity, the sanctity that it possessed when it came from the Creator's hands. This symbolism is clearly indicated in the architectonic structure of sanctuaries. Since the temple is at once the holy place par excellence and the image of the world, it sanctifies the entire cosmos and also sanctifies cosmic life. This cosmic life was imagined in the form of a circular course; it was identified with the year. The year was a closed circle; it had a beginning and an end, but it also had the peculiarity that it could be reborn in the form of a *new* year. With each New Year, a time that was "new," "pure," "holy"—because not yet worn—came into existence.

3. H. Usener, *Götternamen*, 2d. ed. (Bonn, 1920), pp. 191 ff.
4. Werner Müller, *Kreis und Kreuz* (Berlin, 1938), p. 39; cf. also pp. 33 ff.

But time was reborn, began again, because with each New Year the world was created anew. In the preceding chapter we noted the considerable importance of the cosmogonic myth as paradigmatic model for every kind of creation and construction. We will now add that the cosmogony equally implies the creation of time. Nor is this all. For just as the cosmogony is the archetype of all creation, cosmic time, which the cosmogony brings forth, is the paradigmatic model for all other times—that is, for the times specifically belonging to the various categories of existing things. To explain this further: for religious man of the archaic cultures, every creation, every existence begins in time; *before a thing exists, its particular time could not exist.* Before the cosmos came into existence, there was no cosmic time. Before a particular vegetable species was created, the time that now causes it to grow, bear fruit, and die did not exist. It is for this reason that every creation is imagined as having taken place *at the beginning of time, in principio.* Time gushes forth with the first appearance of a new category of existents. This is why myth plays such an important role; as we shall show later, the way in which a reality came into existence is revealed by its myth.

18. ANNUAL REPETITION OF THE CREATION

It is the cosmogonic myth that tells how the cosmos came into existence. At Babylon during the course of the *akitu* ceremony, which was performed during the last days of the year that was ending and the first days of the New Year, the *Poem of Creation*, the *Enuma elish*, was solemnly recited. This ritual recitation reactualized the combat between Marduk and the marine monster Tiamat, a combat that took place *ab origine* and put an end to chaos by the final victory of the god. Marduk created the cosmos from Tiamat's dismembered body and created man from the blood of the demon Kingu, Tiamat's chief ally. That this commemoration of the Creation was in fact a *reactualization* of the cosmogonic act is shown both by the rituals and in the formulas recited during the ceremony.

The combat between Tiamat and Marduk, that is, was mimed by a battle between two groups of actors, a ceremonial that we find again

Source: *SP*/77–80; cf. *CH*/112–37.

among the Hittites (again in the frame of the dramatic scenario of the New Year), among the Egyptians, and at Ras Shamra. The battle between two groups of actors *repeated the passage from chaos to cosmos*, actualized the cosmogony. The mythical event became *present* once again. "May he continue to conquer Tiamat and shorten his days!" the priest cried. The combat, the victory, and the Creation took place *at that instant, hic et nunc*.

Since the New Year is a reactualization of the cosmogony, it implies *starting time over again at its beginning*, that is, restoration of the primordial time, the "pure" time, that existed at the moment of Creation. This is why the New Year is the occasion for "purifications," for the expulsion of sins, of demons, or merely of a scapegoat. For it is not a matter merely of a certain temporal interval coming to its end and the beginning of another (as a modern man, for example, thinks); it is also a matter of abolishing the past year and past time. Indeed, this is the meaning of ritual purifications; there is more than a mere "purification"; the sins and faults of the individual and of the community as a whole are annulled, *consumed as by fire*.

The Nawroz—the Persian New Year—commemorates the day that witnessed the creation of the world and man. It was on the day of Nawroz that the "renewal of the Creation" was accomplished, as the Arabic historian al-Biruni expressed it. The king proclaimed: "Here is a new day of a new month of a new year; what time has worn must be renewed." Time had worn the human being, society, the cosmos—and this destructive time was profane time, duration strictly speaking; it had to be abolished in order to reintegrate the mythical moment in which the world had come into existence, bathed in a "pure," "strong," and sacred time. The abolition of profane past time was accomplished by rituals that signified a sort of "end of the world." The extinction of fires, the return of the souls of the dead, social confusion of the type exemplified by the Saturnalia, erotic license, orgies, and so on, symbolized the retrogression of the cosmos into chaos. On the last day of the year the universe was dissolved in the primordial waters. The marine monster Tiamat—symbol of darkness, of the formless, the nonmanifested—revived and once again threatened. The world that had existed for a whole year *really* disappeared. Since Tiamat was again present, the cosmos was annulled; and Marduk was obliged to create it once again, after having once again conquered Tiamat.

The meaning of this periodical retrogression of the world into a chaotic modality was this: all the "sins" of the year, everything that time had soiled and worn, was annihilated in the physical sense of the word. By symbolically participating in the annihilation and re-creation of the world, man too was created anew; he was reborn, for he began a new life. With each New Year, man felt freer and purer, for he was delivered from the burden of his sins and failings. He had reintegrated the fabulous time of Creation, hence a sacred and strong time—sacred because transfigured by the presence of the gods, strong because it was the time that belonged, and belonged only, to the most gigantic creation ever accomplished, that of the universe. Symbolically, man became contemporary with the cosmogony, he was present at the creation of the world. In the ancient Near East, he even participated actively in its creation (cf. the two opposed groups, representing the god and the marine monster).

It is easy to understand why the memory of that marvelous time haunted religious man, why he periodically sought to return to it. *In illo tempore* the gods had displayed their greatest powers. *The cosmogony is the supreme divine manifestation*, the paradigmatic act of strength, superabundance, and creativity. Religious man thirsts for the real. By every means at his disposal, he seeks to reside at the very source of primordial reality, when the world was *in statu nascendi*.[1]

19. REGENERATION THROUGH RETURN TO THE TIME OF ORIGINS

All this would warrant detailed study, but for the moment only two features will occupy our attention: (1) through annual repetition of the cosmogony, time was regenerated, that is, it began again as sacred time, for it coincided with the *illud tempus* in which the world had first come into existence; (2) by participating ritually in the end of the world and in its re-creation, any man became contemporary with the *illud tempus*; hence he was born anew, he began life over again with his reserve of vital forces *intact*, as it was at the moment of his birth.

Source: *SP*/80–85.
1. *In statu nascendi*: in a state of being born. Eds.

These facts are important; they reveal the secret of religious man's attitude and behavior in respect to time. Since the sacred and strong time is the *time of origins*, the stupendous instant in which a reality was created, was for the first time fully manifested, man will seek periodically to return to that original time. This ritual reactualizing of the *illud tempus* in which the first epiphany of a reality occurred is the basis for all sacred calendars; the festival is not merely the commemoration of a mythical (and hence religious) event; it *reactualizes* the event.

The paramount *time of origins* is the time of the cosmogony, the instant that saw the appearance of the most immense of realities, the world. This, as we saw in the preceding [section], is the reason the cosmogony serves as the paradigmatic model for every creation, for every kind of doing. It is for this same reason that *cosmogonic time* serves as the model for all *sacred times*; for if sacred time is that in which the gods manifested themselves and created, obviously the most complete divine manifestation and the most gigantic creation is the creation of the world.

Consequently, religious man reactualizes the cosmogony not only each time he creates something (his "own world"—the inhabited territory—or a city, a house, etc.), but also when he wants to ensure a fortunate reign for a new sovereign, or to save threatened crops, or in the case of a war, a sea voyage, and so on. But, above all, the ritual recitation of the cosmogonic myth plays an important role in healing, when what is sought is the *regeneration* of the human being. In Fiji, the ceremony for installing a new ruler is called creation of the world, and the same ceremony is repeated to save threatened crops. But it is perhaps Polynesia that exhibits the widest application of the cosmogonic myth. The words that Io spoke *in illo tempore* to create the world have become ritual formulas. Men repeat them on many occasions—to fecundate a sterile womb, to heal (mental as well as physical ailments), to prepare for war, but also on the occasion of a death or to stimulate poetic inspiration.

Thus the cosmogonic myth serves the Polynesians as the archetypal model for all creations, on whatever plane—biological, psychological, spiritual. But since ritual recitation of the cosmogonic myth implies reactualization of that primordial event, it follows that he for whom it is recited is magically projected *in illo tempore*, into the "beginning of the World"; he becomes contemporary with the cosmogony.

What is involved is, in short, a return to the original time, the therapeutic purpose of which is to begin life once again, a symbolic rebirth. The conception underlying these curative rituals seems to be
the following: life cannot be repaired, it can only be recreated
through symbolic repetition of the cosmogony, for, as we have said,
the cosmogony is the paradigmatic model for all creation.

The regenerative function of the return to the time of origins becomes still more clear if we make a detailed examination of an archaic
therapy, such, for example, as that of the Na-khi, a Tibeto-Bur-
mese people living in Southwest China (Yün-nan Province). The
therapeutic ritual proper consists in the solemn recitation of the myth
of the creation of the world, followed by myths of the origin of
maladies from the wrath of the snakes and the appearance of the first
Shaman-Healer who brought humanity the necessary medicines. Almost all the rituals invoke the mythical *beginning*, the mythical *illud
tempus*, when the world was not yet made: "In the beginning, at the
time when the heavens, sun, moon, stars, planets and the land had not
yet appeared, when nothing had yet come forth," etc. Then comes
the cosmogony and the appearance of the snakes: "At the time when
heaven came forth, the sun, moon, stars and planets, and the earth
was spread out; when the mountains, valleys, trees and rocks came
forth . . . at that time there came forth the Nāgas and dragons," etc.
The birth of the First Healer and the appearance of medicines is
then narrated. After this it is said: "Unless its origin is related one
should not speak about it."[1]

The important fact to be noted in connection with these magical
healing chants is that *the myth of the origin of the medicines employed* is always incorporated into the *cosmogonic myth*. It is well
known that in all primitive and traditional therapies a remedy becomes efficacious only if its origin is ritually rehearsed in the sick
person's presence. A large number of Near Eastern and European
incantations contain the history of the sickness or of the demon who
has provoked it, at the same time that they evoke the mythical moment in which a divinity or a saint succeeded in conquering the mal-
ady. But we consider it certain that the origin myth was copied after
the cosmogonic myth, for the latter is the paradigmatic model for

---

1. J. F. Rock, *The Na-khi Nāga Cult and Related Ceremonies* (Rome, 1952),
2: 279 ff.

all origins. This, moreover, is why, in therapeutic incantations, the origin myth is often preceded by the cosmogonic myth and even incorporated into it. An Assyrian incantation against toothache rehearses that "after Anu made the heavens, the heavens made the earth, the earth made the rivers, the rivers made the canals, the canals made the pools, the pools made the worm." And the worm goes "weeping" to Shamash and Ea and asks them what will be given it to eat, to destroy. The gods offer it fruits, but the worm asks them for human teeth. "Since thou hast spoken thus, O Worm, may Ea break thee with his powerful hand!"[2] Here are presented: (1) the creation of the world; (2) the birth of the worm and of the sickness; (3) the primordial and paradigmatic gesture of healing (Ea's destruction of the worm). The therapeutic efficacy of the incantation lies in the fact that, ritually uttered, it reactualizes the mythical time of origins, both the origin of the world and the origin of toothaches and their treatment.

20. CONTINUOUS REGENERATION OF TIME

. . . That within each group of analogous beliefs there are variations, differences, incompatibilities, that the origin and dissemination of these ceremonials raise a host of problems requiring further study, we are the first to admit. . . . Our ambition is to understand their meaning, to endeavor to see what they show us—leaving to possible future studies the detailed examination (genetic or historical) of each separate mythico-ritual complex.

It goes without saying that there are—we should almost feel justified in writing that there *must* be—very considerable differences between the various groups of periodic ceremonies, if only for the simple reason that we are dealing with both historical and "anhistorical" peoples or strata, with what are generally called "civilized man" and "primitive man." It is further of interest to note that the New Year scenarios in which the Creation is repeated are particularly explicit among the historical peoples, those with whom history, properly speaking, begins—that is, the Babylonians, Egyptians, Hebrews,

Source: *CH*/73–77.
2. Campbell Thompson, *Assyrian Medical Texts* (London, 1932), p. 59.

Iranians. It almost seems that these peoples, conscious that they were the first to build "history," recorded their own acts for the use of their successors (not, however, without inevitable transfigurations in the matter of categories and archetypes . . .). These same peoples also appear to have felt a deeper need to regenerate themselves periodically by abolishing past time and reactualizing the cosmogony.

As for the primitive societies that still live in the paradise of archetypes and for whom time is recorded only biologically without being allowed to become "history"—that is, without its corrosive action being able to exert itself upon consciousness by revealing the irreversibility of events—these primitive societies regenerate themselves periodically through expulsion of "evils" and confession of sins. The need these societies also feel for a periodic regeneration is a proof that they too cannot perpetually maintain their position in what we have just called the paradise of archetypes, and that their memory is capable (though doubtless far less intensely than that of a modern man) of revealing the irreversibility of events, that is, of recording history. Thus, among these primitive peoples too, the existence of man in the cosmos is regarded as a fall. The vast and monotonous morphology of the confession of sins, authoritatively studied by R. Pettazzoni in *La confessione dei peccati*, shows us that, even in the simplest human societies, "historical" memory, that is, the recollection of events that derive from no archetype, the recollection of personal events ("sins" in the majority of cases), is intolerable. We know that the beginning of the avowal of sins was a magical conception of eliminating a fault through some physical means (blood, speech, and so forth). But again it is not the confessional procedure in itself that interests us—it is magical in structure—but primitive man's need to free himself from the recollection of sin, i.e., of a succession of personal events that, taken together, constitute history.

Thus we observe the immense importance that collective regeneration through repetition of the cosmogonic act acquired among the peoples who created history. We might point out here that, for reasons which, of course, are various, but also because of the metaphysical and anhistorical structure of Indian spirituality, the Indians never elaborated a cosmological New Year scenario as extensive as those found in the ancient Near East. We might also point out that an outstandingly historical people, the Romans, were continuously obsessed by the "end of Rome" and sought innumerable systems of *renovatio*. But for the moment we do not wish to set the reader on this path. Hence we shall limit ourselves to pointing out that, aside from these periodic ceremonies of abolishing history, the traditional societies (that is, all societies down to those which make up the modern world) knew and applied still other methods intended to bring about the regeneration of time.

. . . Construction rituals likewise presuppose the more or less explicit imitation of the cosmogonic act.[1] For traditional man, the imitation of an archetypal model is a reactualization of the mythical moment when the archetype was revealed for the first time. Consequently, these ceremonies too, which are neither periodic nor collective, suspend the flow of profane time, of duration, and project the celebrant into a mythical time, *in illo tempore*. . . . All rituals imitate a divine archetype and . . . their continual reactualization takes place in one and the same atemporal mythical instant. However, the construction rites show us something beyond this: imitation, hence reactualization, of the cosmogony. A "new era" opens with the building of every house. Every construction is an absolute beginning; that is, tends to restore the initial instant, the plenitude of a present that contains no trace of history. Of course, the construction rituals found in our day are in great part survivals, and it is difficult to determine to what extent they are accompanied by an experience in the consciousness of the persons who observe them. But this rationalistic objection is negligible. What is important is that man has felt the need to reproduce the cosmogony in his constructions, whatever be their nature; that this reproduction made him contemporary with the mythical moment of the beginning of the world and that he felt the need of returning to that moment, as often as possible, in order to regenerate himself. It would require a most uncommon degree of perspicacity for anyone to be able to say to what extent those who, in the modern world, continue to repeat construction rituals still share in their meaning and their mystery. Doubtless their experiences are, on the whole, profane: the New Year signalized by a construction is translated into a new stage in the life of those who are to live in the house. But the structure of the myth and the rite remains unaltered by any of this, even if the experiences aroused by their actualization are no longer anything but profane: a construction is a new organi-

1. On construction rituals, see selection 91 below. Eds.

zation of the world and life. All that is needed is a modern man with a sensibility less closed to the miracle of life; and the experience of renewal would revive for him when he built a house or entered it for the first time (just as, even in the modern world, the New Year still preserves the prestige of the end of a past and the fresh beginning of a new life)....

21. THE AUSTRALIAN DREAM TIME

For the Australians, as well as for other primitive societies, the world is always "their own world," that is to say, the world in which they live and whose mythical history they know. Outside this familiar cosmos lie amorphous, unknown, dangerous lands, peopled by mysterious and inimical ghosts and magicians. The aborigines dread an adventure, even in numbers, into unknown territories. These strange lands do not belong to their "world" and consequently still partake of the uncreated mode of being.

Yet even the most arid and monotonous landscape can become a "home" for the tribe when it is believed to have been "created" or more exactly, transformed by Supernatural Beings. Giving shape to the land, the Supernatural Beings at the same time made it "sacred." The present countryside is the result of their work, and they themselves belong to a realm of being different from that of men. These Primordial Beings, moreover, not only molded the landscape; they also inserted in some places "spirit children" and "spirits" of various animals, brought forth from their own bodies.

The epoch when the Supernatural Beings appeared and began to transform the world, wandering across immense territories, producing plants and animals, making man as he is today, giving him his present institutions and ceremonies—this epoch was the "Dream Time" or, as some authors call it, the "Eternal Dream Time" or just "Dreaming." This mythical time is "sacred" because it was sanctified by the real presence and the activity of the Supernatural Beings. . . .

Ultimately, all Australian religious activities can be considered as so many different but homologous means of reestablishing contact

Source: *AR*/42–43, 84; cf. *Q*/84; *RSI*/19, 48–49.

with the Supernatural Beings and of immersing oneself in the sacred time of the "Dreaming." Every religious act—a ritual, the recital of a myth, a secret chant, the making of a sacred instrument, and so on—is only the *repetition* of an event that took place in the beginning of time, in short, an imitation of models revealed to the tribe by Supernatural Beings. On the other hand, every individual is fundamentally a "spiritual" being. His most secret self is a part of that sacred world he is periodically trying to recontact. But he does not know his own real identity: this must be revealed to him through the initiation rites. Thus, one may say that the initiation reinstates the young Australian in his original, spiritual mode of being. As W. Lloyd Warner says with regard to each Murngin male, "the personality before birth is purely spiritual; it becomes completely profane or unspiritual in the earlier period of its life when it is classed socially with the females, gradually becomes more and more ritualized and sacred as the individual grows older and approaches death, and at death once more becomes completely spiritual and sacred."[1]

22. THE MYTH OF BAGADJIMBIRI

The creative deeds of . . . mythological heroes are equivalent to a cosmogony. The world came into being as a result of their work. In some cases, the cosmogonic character of the Dream Time activity is quite evident. This is true, for example, of the mythology of the Karadjeri tribe, which centers around the two brothers Bagadjimbiri. Before their appearance there was nothing at all—neither trees, nor animals, nor human beings. The brothers arose from the ground in the form of dingos, but they later became two "human" giants, their heads touching the sky. They emerged from the earth just before twilight on the first day. When they heard the cry of a little bird (*duru*) that always sang at that time, they knew it was twilight. Previously they had known nothing at all. The two brothers subsequently saw all kinds of animals and plants and gave them names. That is to say, from that moment, because they had names, the ani-

Source: *AR*/53–55.
1. W. Lloyd Warner, *A Black Civilization: A Study of an Australian Tribe* (1937; New York, 1964), pp. 5–6.

mals and plants began to *really* exist. Next the brothers saw a star
and the moon and named them also. . . .

Then the Bagadjimbiri went toward the north. On their journey
they encountered men and women without genital organs, and the
brothers provided them with organs made from a species of mush-
room. They threw a *pirmal* (a long stick) at an animal and killed it;
the Karadjeri found the stick and have performed the same act ever
since. The two brothers founded the initiation ceremonies and utilized
for the first time the ritual instruments: a stone circumcision knife,
the bull-roarer, and the long *pirmal*. They saw a snake and sang the
song for the production of snakes. Then they differentiated the
dialects.

The two Bagadjimbiri had a great deal of hair, some of which they
pulled out and gave to every tribe. (Thus every tribe now possesses
a corporeal particle of the Heroes.) But a certain man killed the
brothers with a spear. Their mother, Dilga, who was far away, de-
tected the odor of corpses upon the wind. Milk streamed forth from
her breasts and flowed underground to the place where the brothers
lay dead. There it gushed like a torrent, drowning the murderer and
reviving the two brothers. The two Bagadjimbiri later transformed
themselves into water snakes, while their spirits became the Magel-
lanic Clouds.

This myth constitutes the foundation of all Karadjeri life. During
initiation the ceremonies instituted by the two Bagadjimbiri are re-
enacted, although the meaning of some of the rituals is no longer
clear to the aborigines. This mythical pattern is well known in different parts of Australia: the epiphany of the Culture Heroes, their
wanderings and their civilizing activities, their final disappearance. As
we shall see, every act of the Heroes (Ancestors) is duly repeated by
the members of the tribe. As Strehlow put it: "All occupations originated with the totemic ancestors; and here, too, the native follows
tradition blindly: he clings to the primitive weapons used by his forefathers, and no thought of improving them ever enters his mind."[1]
But of course this is true only up to a certain point: the Australians,
like other primitives, have changed their lives in the course of history;
but all such changes are considered to be new "revelations" of Supernatural Beings.

1. T. G. H. Strehlow, *Aranda Traditions* (Melbourne, 1947), p. 35.

23. A MYTHICAL GEOGRAPHY

Through the initiation rites the neophyte is gradually introduced to the tribal traditions; he discovers all that happened *ab origine*. This "knowledge" is total—that is to say, mythical, ritual, and geographic. In learning what took place in the Dream Time, the initiate also learns what must be done in order to maintain the living and productive world. Moreover, a mythical—or mystical—geography is revealed to him: he is introduced to the innumerable sites where the Supernatural Beings performed rituals or did significant things. The world in which the initiate henceforth moves is a meaningful and "sacred" world, because Supernatural Beings have inhabited and transformed it. Thus it is always possible to be "oriented" in a world that has a sacred history, a world in which every prominent feature is associated with a mythical event. W. E. H. Stanner writes, with regard to the Murinbata mythical geography: "The Murinbata considered the countryside filled with plain evidence that the dramas had occurred. The places of climax were known and named, and each one contained proof—a shape, or form, or pattern of a great event."[1] Likewise Spencer and Gillen, relating their journey to an important totemic center in the company of a small group of natives, disclose for us the mythical geography of the Warramunga tribe. A range of hills marked the path traversed by the mythical Ancestor of the bat totem. A column of rock represented another Ancestor, the opossum man; a low range of white quartzite hills indicated the white ant eggs thrown there in the Dream Time by some mythical women. "All the time, as we travelled along, the old men were talking amongst themselves about the natural features associated in tradition with these and other totemic ancestors of the tribe, and pointing them out to us."[2] And thus, during the three days of the journey, they passed near innumerable tangible traces of the Primordial totemic (cultural) Heroes. Finally they approached the famous water hole where the mythical snake Wollunka lived. Near the sacred pool the natives "became very quiet and solemn," and "the chief men of

SOURCE: *AR*/55–59; cf. selections 90–92. Eds.

1. W. E. H. Stanner, *On Aboriginal Religion* ("Oceania Monographs," No. 11 [Sydney, 1963]), p. 254.

2. B. Spencer and F. J. Gillen, *The Northern Tribes of Central Australia* (London: Macmillan & Co., 1904), p. 249.

the totemic group went down to the edge of the water and, with bowed heads, addressed the Wollunka in whispers, asking him to remain quiet and do them no harm, for they were mates of his. . . . We could plainly see that it was all very real to them, and that they implicitly believed that the Wollunka was indeed alive beneath the water, watching them, though they could not see him."[3]

One must read the descriptions of Spencer and Gillen *in extenso* to understand why even the most dreary landscape is, for the aborigines, charged with awe: every rock, spring, and water hole represents a concrete trace of a sacred drama carried out in the mythical times. For the Western reader, these endless wanderings and fortuitous meetings of the Dream Time Heroes seem excessively monotonous. (But then the wanderings of Leopold Bloom in *Ulysses* also seem monotonous for the admirer of Balzac or Tolstoi.) For the aborigines, the vestiges of the mythical drama are more than a cipher or stencil enabling him to read the sacred stories imprinted in the landscape. They reveal to him a history in which he is existentially involved. Not only is he the result of those endless wanderings and performances of the mythical Ancestors; in many cases he is the reincaration of one of those Ancestors. As T. G. H. Strehlow puts it: "The whole countryside is his living, age-old family tree. The story of his own totemic ancestor is to the native *the account of his own doings at the beginning of time*, at the dim dawn of life, when the world as he knows it now was being shaped and moulded by all-powerful hands. *He himself has played a part in that first glorious adventure*, a part smaller or greater according to the original rank of the ancestor of whom he is the present reincarnated form."[4]

Learning the mythical history of the familiar countryside, the initiate experiences a sort of *anamnesis*: he remembers his coming into being in the primordial time and his most remote deeds: "At the time of birth the totemic ancestor who has undergone reincarnation is totally unaware of his former glorious existence. For him the preceding months have been a 'sleep and a forgetting.' If he is born as a boy, the old men will later on initiate him and reintroduce him into the ancient ceremonies which he himself had instituted in his

3. *Ibid.*, pp. 252–53.
4. T. G. H. Strehlow, *Aranda Traditions* (Melbourne, 1947), pp. 30–31 [italics are Eliade's].

previous existence."[5] Through his initiation, the novice discovers that he *has already been here*, in the beginning; he was here under the appearance of the mythical Ancestor. In learning the deeds of his mythical Ancestor, he learns about his own glorious pre-existence. Ultimately, he is taught to repeat himself such as he was *ab origine*; that is to say, he is to imitate his own exemplary model.

. . . For the moment, it seems relevant for us to point out the Platonic structure of the Australian doctrine of *anamnesis*. As is well known, for Plato learning is recollecting; to *know* is to *remember* (cf. *Meno* 81). Between two existences on earth, the soul contemplates the Ideas: it shares in pure and perfect knowledge. But when the soul is reincarnated, it drinks of the spring of Lethe and forgets the knowledge it had obtained from its direct contemplation of the Ideas. Yet this knowledge is latent in the man in whom the soul is reincarnated, and it can be made patent by philosophical effort. Physical objects help the soul to withdraw into itself and, through a sort of "going back," to rediscover and repossess the original knowledge that it had possessed in its extra-terrestrial condition. Hence death is the return to a primordial and perfect state, which is periodically lost through the soul's reincarnation.

Of course, there can be no question of assimilating the Australian conception to Plato's doctrine of *anamnesis*. But it is significant that the belief in the perpetual reincarnation of the Ancestors has forced the Aranda to elaborate a theory of *anamnesis* fairly close to that of Plato. For Plato as well as for the Aranda, physical objects help the soul to *remember his real identity*. With this difference: for Plato, the soul through death is able to contemplate the Ideas, and thus to partake in Knowledge. For the Aranda, the knowledge in question is not philosophical but mythical and "historical": that which the novice discovers through initiation is what he did *in illo tempore*; he learns not ideas but his own primordial deeds and their meaning. He discovers in the mythology of a certain Hero his own fabulous biography. Certain physical objects (rocks, *tjurungas*, etc.) reveal themselves as proofs of his first and glorious existence on earth. For Plato, the physical objects help the soul to recover the knowledge of his extra-terrestrial condition. But for both Plato and the Aranda, the true *anamnesis* is the effect of a spiritual activity: philosophy for the Greek philosopher, initiation for the Australians.

5. *Ibid.*, p. 93.

24. CHINESE ALCHEMICAL TIME

The "return to the origin" is . . . highly esteemed as therapy in China. Taoism lays considerable stress on "embryonic breathing," *t'ai-si*. It consists in a closed-circuit respiration like that of a fetus; the adept tries to imitate the circulation of blood and breath between mother and child and vice versa. The preface to the *T'ai-si k'eou kiue* ("Oral formulas for embryonic breathing") expressly states: "By going back to the base, by returning to the origin, one drives away old age, one returns to the state of a fetus."[1] A text from modern syncretistic Taoism runs: "That is why the (Buddha) Ju-lai (= Tathagata), in his great mercy, revealed the method for the (alchemical) work by Fire and taught man to *re-enter the womb* in order to reconstitute his (true) nature and (the fullness of) his portion of life."[2]

Here, then, we have two different but related mystical techniques, both seeking to obtain the "return to the origin": "embryonic breathing" and the alchemical process. These two techniques are, of course, among the numerous methods employed by the Taoist to acquire youth and extreme longevity ("immortality"). Alchemical experimentation must be accompanied by an appropriate mystical meditation. During the fusion of metals the Taoist alchemist tries to bring about in his own body the union of the two cosmological principles, Heaven and Earth, in order to reproduce the primordial chaotic situation that existed before the Creation. This primordial situation (which, moreover, is called precisely the "chaotic" [*houen*] situation) corresponds both to the egg or the embryo and to the paradisal and innocent state of the uncreated World. The Taoist endeavors to obtain this primordial state either by the meditation that accompanies alchemical experiment or by "embryonic breathing." But in the last analysis "embryonic breathing" amounts to what the texts call "unification of the breaths," a quite complex technique, which we cannot examine here. Suffice it to say that "unification of the breaths," has a cosmological model. For according to Taoist traditions, in the

SOURCE: *MR*/83–84; *FC*/109–20, 172–78.

1. H. Maspéro, "Les procédés de 'Nourrir le Principe Vital' dans la religion taoïste ancienne," *Journal Asiatique* (April-June, 1937): 198.

2. *Houei-ming-king* by Lieou Houayang, cited by Rolf Stein, "Jardins en miniature d'Extrême Orient," *Bulletin de l'Ecole Française d'Extrême Orient* 42 (Hanoi, 1943): 97.

beginning the "breaths" were mingled and formed an egg, the Great-One, from which came Heaven and Earth.

The ideal of the Taoists—that is, obtaining the bliss of youth and longevity ("immortality")—had, then, a cosmological model: the state of primordial unity. Here we no longer have a re-enactment of the cosmological myth, as in the healing rituals cited earlier. The aim is no longer to reiterate the *cosmic creation*; it is to recover the state that *preceded the cosmogony*, the state of "chaos." But the line of thought is the same: health and youth are obtained by a "return to the origin," be it "return to the womb" or return to the cosmic Great-One. So we may note the important fact that, in China too, sickness and old age are believed to be cured by "return to the origin," the only method that archaic thought considered able to annul the work of Time. For, in the end, it is always a matter of abolishing past Time, of "going back" and beginning life over again with all its virtualities intact. . . .

* * *

To a certain extent it would be true to say that in China there was no break between mystical metallurgy and alchemy. . . . It was in Taoist and Neo-Taoist circles that alchemical techniques were propagated. . . .

. . . The alchemist, especially in the Neo-Taoist period, strove to recover an "ancient wisdom," adulterated or mutilated by the very transformation of Chinese society. The alchemist was a cultured man: his predecessors—hunters, potters, smiths, dancers, agriculturists, ecstatics—lived in the very heart of traditions orally transmitted by initiations and "trade-secrets." From the very first Taoism had turned with sympathy, even with fervor, to the representatives of these traditions. This has been described as the Taoists' infatuation for "popular superstitions," which included techniques of various kinds—dietetic, gymnastic, choreographic, respiratory, magic, shamanist, ecstatic and spiritualist, etc. Everything points to the notion that on the "popular" level on which they were sought, some of the traditional practices had already undergone numerous changes; we have only to recall the aberrant varieties of certain shamanist techniques of ecstasy. The Taoists somehow could sense beneath the crust of such superstitions authentic fragments of an ancient wisdom which they strove to recapture and make their own.

It was in this rather vague area, in which primitive intuitions and traditions of great antiquity lingered on, unaffected by the vicissitudes of cultural history, that Taoism collected its crop of precepts, secrets and recipes. (These traditions derived from spiritual situations long past, situations connected with the magic of the hunt, the discovery of pottery, agriculture and metallurgy, and the experiences and ecstasies that went with them.) One may say, therefore, that the Taoist alchemists, despite inevitable innovations, continued and prolonged an ageless tradition. Their ideas of longevity and immortality belong to the sphere of mythologies and folklore which is virtually universal. The notions of the "herb of immortality," of animal or vegetable substances charged with "vitality" and containing the elixir of eternal youth, as well as the myths concerning inaccessible regions inhabited by immortals, are part of a primitive ideology going far beyond the confines of China. . . . Let us simply point out in what sense those rudimentary intuitions in the myths and rites of smelters and smiths were taken up and interpreted by the alchemists. It will be especially edifying to highlight the subsequent development of a few fundamental ideas concerning the growth of ores, the natural transformation of metals into gold and the mystic value of gold. As for the ritual complex, comprising brotherhoods of smiths and initiatory trade-secrets, something of its structure was transmitted to the Chinese alchemist, and not *only* to him. Initiation by a master, and the initiatory communication of secrets, for long continued to be the norm in alchemical teaching.

Specialists are not all agreed about the origins of Chinese alchemy; the *dates of the earliest texts* which mention alchemical operations are still under discussion. . . . It is important to distinguish the *historical beginning* and development of a *pre-chemistry* from alchemy as a soteriological technique. As we have already said, this latter was identifiable with the methods and mythologies, mainly Taoist, whose aim was quite other than that of "making gold" (it remained so up to the end of the eighteenth century).

Indeed, Chinese alchemy was built up, in so far as it is an autonomous discipline, by utilizing (1) traditional cosmological principles; (2) myths connected with the elixir of immortality and the immortal saints; (3) techniques pursuing the prolongation of life, beatitude and spiritual spontaneity.

These three elements—principles, myths, and techniques—belonged to the cultural heritage of protohistory. It would be an error to believe that the date of the first documents which gives evidence of them also establishes their age. There is a very obvious and close connection between the "preparation of gold," the "drug of immortality" and the "evocation" of the Immortals. Luan Tai presents himself to the Emperor Wu and assures him that he can perform these three miracles but he only succeeds in "materializing" the Immortals.

The magician Li Chao Kuin advises the Emperor Wu Ti of the Han dynasty as follows: "Sacrifice to the furnace (*tsao*) and you will be able to summon (supernatural) beings; when you have called forth these beings, the powder of cinnabar can be transformed into yellow gold; when the yellow gold is produced you will be able to make of it utensils for drinking and eating and in so doing you will have a prolonged longevity. When your longevity is prolonged you will be able to see the blessed (*hsien*) of the island of P'eng Lai which is in the midst of the seas. When you have seen them and have made the *feng* and *chan* sacrifices, then you will not die" (Ssu-ma Chien, vol. III, p. 465). Another celebrated personage, Liu Hsiang (79–8 B.C.), claimed to be able "to make gold" but failed.[1] A few centuries later, the most celebrated Chinese alchemist, Pao Pu'tzu (pseudonym of Ko Hung, 254–334), attempts to explain Liu Hsiang's failure, by telling us that he was not in possession of "true medicine" (the philosopher's stone) and that he was not spiritually prepared (for the alchemist must fast a hundred days and purify himself with perfumes, etc.). This transmutation cannot be brought about in a palace, adds Pao Pu'tzu: one must live in solitude apart from ordinary people. Books are not enough; what one finds in books is only for beginners, the rest is secret and communicable only by oral teaching, etc.

The quest for the elixir was thus bound up with the search for distant mysterious islands where the "Immortals" lived: to encounter these Immortals was to transcend the human condition and share in an existence of timeless bliss. This search for the Immortals in distant islands exercised the minds of the early emperors of the Tsin dynasty (219 B.C.; Ssu-ma Chien, *Memoirs*, II, 143, 152; III, 437) and the Emperor Wu of the Han dynasty (110 B.C.; *ibid.*, III, 499; Dubs, p. 66).

1. Texts in H. H. Dubs, "The Beginnings of Alchemy," *Isis* 38 (1947): 62–86, 74.

The search for gold was also a spiritual quest. Gold was imperial; it was to be found in the "Center" of the earth and was mystically connected with the *chue* (realgar or sulphur), yellow mercury and life in the hereafter (the "yellow sources"). This is how it was presented in a text dated 122 B.C., *Huai Nan Tzu*, where we likewise find evidence for the belief in an *accelerated metamorphosis of metals* (fragment translated by Dubs, pp. 71–3). It is possible that this text may derive from the school of Tsou Yen, if not from the Master himself (*ibid.*, p. 74). . . . Belief in the natural metamorphosis of metals was common in China. The alchemist only accelerates the growth of metals. Like his Western colleague, the Chinese alchemist contributes to Nature's work by precipitating the tempo. But we should not forget that the transmutation of metals into gold also has a spiritual aspect; gold being the imperial metal, "perfect," freed from impurities, the alchemical operation must seek to imitate the perfection of nature which is, in the final instance, its absolution and its liberty. The gestation of metals in the bowels of the earth obeys the same temporal rhythms as those which bind man to his carnal and fallen condition; to hasten the growth of metals by the operation of alchemy is tantamount to absolving them from the laws of Time.

Gold and jade, since they take part in the *yang* cosmological principle, preserve bodies from corruption. "If there is gold and jade in the nine apertures of the corpse, it will preserve the body from putrefaction," writes the alchemist Ko Hung. And T'ao Hung Ching (fifth century) gives the following details: "When on opening an ancient grave, the corpse seems alive, then there is inside and outside the body a large quantity of gold and jade. According to the regulations of the Han dynasty, princes and lords were buried in clothes adorned with pearls and boxes of jade for the purpose of preserving the body from decay."[2] For the same reason, vases of alchemical gold have a specific virtue; they prolong life indefinitely. Ko Hung writes: "If with this alchemical gold you make dishes and bowls and if you eat and drink out of them you shall live long."[3] The same author on another occasion says: "As to the true man, he makes gold because he wishes, by the medicinal use of it (that is, by assimilating it as a

2. B. Laufer, *Jade, a study in Chinese Archaeology and Religion* (Chicago, 1912), p. 299.

3. Trans. A. Waley, *Notes on Chinese Alchemy, Bull. School of Oriental Studies* 6 (1930): 1–24, 4.

food), to become an immortal."[4] But to be effective, gold had to be "prepared," "fabricated." Gold produced by the processes of alchemical sublimation and transmutation possessed a higher vitality by means of which one could achieve immortality.

The alchemist accepts the traditional identity of microcosm and macrocosm, so familiar to Chinese thought. The universal quintet, *wu-hsing* (water, fire, wood, gold, earth), is regarded as intimately allied with the organs of the human body: the heart with the essence of fire, the liver with the essence of wood, the lungs with the essence of metal, the kidneys with the essence of water, the stomach with the essence of earth (texts in Johnson, p. 102). The microcosm which the human body is, is likewise interpreted in alchemical terms. "The fire of the heart is red like cinnabar and the water of the kidneys is dark, as lead," writes a biographer of the famous alchemist Lü Tsu (eighth century A.D.).[5] Closely allied with the macrocosm, man possesses all the elements which constitute the cosmos and all the vital energies which secure his periodic renovation. All that is necessary is to reinforce certain essences. Hence the importance of cinnabar is due not so much to its red color (the color of blood, the vital principle) as to the fact that when put into fire cinnabar produces mercury. It therefore conceals the mysteries of regeneration by death (for combustion symbolizes death). It follows from this that it can ensure the perpetual regeneration of the human body and ultimately achieve immortality. Pao Pu'tzu writes that if one mixes three pounds of cinnabar with one pound of honey and if one dries the whole in the sun in order to obtain pills of the size of a grain of hemp, ten of such pills taken in the course of one year will restore the blackness to white hair and make decayed teeth grow again. And if one continues beyond one year, one becomes immortal (text in Johnson, p. 63). . . .

But cinnabar can also be made inside the human body, mainly by means of the distillation of sperm. "The Taoist, imitating animals and vegetables, hangs himself upside down, causing the essence of his sperm to flow up to his brain."[6] The *tan-t'ien*, the "famous fields of cinnabar," are to be found in the most secret recesses of the brain and belly: there it is that the embryo of immortality is alchemically prepared. Another name for these "cinnabar fields" is *K'un Lun*, mean-

4. Trans. O. Johnson, *A Study of Chinese Alchemy* (Shanghai, 1928), p. 71.
5. Quoted by W. A. Martin, *The Lore of Cathay* (New York, 1901), p. 60.
6. Rolf Stein, *Jardins en miniature d'Extrême-Orient* (Hanoi, 1943), p. 86.

ing both "mountain of the western sea"—a sojourn of the immortals —and a secret region of the brain, comprising the "chamber similar to a cave" (*tong-fang*, which also signifies "nuptial chamber") and the "nirvana" (*ni-wan*). "In order to enter therein by mystic medita- tion, one falls into a 'chaotic' state (*houen*) resembling the primordial, paradisal, 'unconscious' condition of the uncreated world" (R. Stein, *Jardins*, p. 54).

Two elements especially call for attention: (1) the parallelism of the mythical mountain, K'un Lun, with the secret regions of the brain and belly; (2) the role given to the "chaotic state" which, once at- tained by means of meditation, allows one to penetrate to those secret recesses of the "cinnabar fields," thus making possible the alchemical preparation of the embryo of immortality.

The identification of the *K'un Lun* in the human body confirms what we have several times emphasized: that the Taoist alchemist takes up and carries on a time-old tradition, embracing recipes for longevity and techniques of mystic physiology. Indeed the Mountain of the Western Sea, sojourn of the Immortals, is a traditional and very ancient image of the "world in little," of a universe in miniature. The Mountain of *K'un Lun* has two tiers: an upright circular cone sur- mounted by an inverted one, similar to the alchemist's furnace. But the calabash too consists of two superposed spheres. The calabash, of course, plays a considerable part in Taoist ideology and folklore and is regarded as representing the cosmos in miniature. In this gourd-shaped microcosm resides the source of Life and Youth. This theme—the universe having the shape of a calabash—is of undeniable antiquity. It is therefore significant that an alchemical text should declare: "He who cultivates cinnabar (that is, the pill of immortal- ity) takes Heaven as his model and fashions Earth. He seeks them by turning in on himself and then finds that a Heaven shaped like a gourd has come into spontaneous existence in his body."[7] Indeed, when the alchemist achieves the "chaotic" state of unconsciousness, he pene- trates "to the innermost recesses of the being, the space of the size of a thumb, round and square" (R. Stein, *Jardins* p. 59). This inner space is in the form of a gourd.

As for this "chaotic" state, attained through meditation and indis- pensable to the operations of alchemy, it is, for several reasons, of

---

7. Commentary quoted by the *P'ei-wen yun fou*, trans. R. Stein, p. 59.

interest to our investigation. And this is primarily because of the resemblance between this "unconscious" state (comparable to that of the embryo or the egg) and the *materia prima*, the *massa confusa* of Western alchemy. . . . The *materia prima* should not be understood merely as a primordial condition of the substance but also as an inner experience of the alchemist. The reduction of matter to its original condition of absolute indifferentiation, corresponds, on the plane of inner experience, to the regression to the pre-natal, embryonic state. The theme of rejuvenation and longevity by means of the *regressus ad uterum* is a leitmotif of Taoism. The most usual method is "embryonic respiration" (*t'ai-si*). But the alchemist also achieves this state by the smelting of various ingredients in his furnace. A text of modern syncretist Taoism expresses itself thus: "that is why the (Buddha) Jou-lai (= Tathagata), in his great mercy, has revealed to man the (alchemical) method of work with fire and has taught him to *penetrate anew to the matrix* in order to refashion its (true) nature and (the plenitude of) his lot in life" (quoted by R. Stein, p. 97).

We may add that this "return to the matrix," exalted both by Taoist writers and Western alchemists (R. Stein, pp. 154 sq.) is simply the development of a more ancient, more widespread conception already attested at primitive levels of culture: recovery from disease by a symbolic return to the origins of the world, that is, by a re-enactment of the cosmogony. Many primitive therapies include a ritual reiteration of the creation of the world, permitting the sick man to be born anew and thus to recommence existence with an intact reserve of the vital forces. The Taoist and Chinese alchemists have taken up and perfected this traditional method. Instead of reserving it for the healing of particular maladies, they have applied it, above all, to cure man of the illness resulting from the ravages of time, that is from old age and death.

* * *

The survival of the alchemist's ideology does not become immediately evident just when alchemy disappears from the pages of history and all its empirically valid chemical knowledge is being integrated into chemistry. The new science of chemistry makes use only of those empirical discoveries which do not represent—however numerous and important one may suppose them to be—the true spirit of alchemy. We must not believe that the triumph of experimental science reduced to nought the dreams and ideals of the alchemist. On the contrary, the ideology of the new epoch, crystallized around the myth of infinite progress and boosted by the experimental sciences and the progress of industrialization which dominated and inspired the whole of the nineteenth century, takes up and carries forward—despite its radical secularization—the millennary dream of the alchemist. It is in the specific dogma of the nineteenth century, according to which man's true mission is to transform and improve upon Nature and become her master, that we must look for the authentic continuation of the alchemist's dream. The visionary's myth of the perfection, or more accurately, of the redemption of Nature, survives, in camouflaged form, in the pathetic program of the industrial societies whose aim is the total transmutation of Nature, its transformation into "energy." It is in this nineteenth century, dominated by the physico-chemical sciences and the upsurge of industry, that man succeeds in supplanting Time. His desire to accelerate the natural tempo of things by an ever more rapid and efficient exploitation of mines, coal-fields and petrol deposits, begins to come true. Organic chemistry, fully mobilized to wrest the secrets of the mineral basis of life, now opens the way to innumerable "synthetic" products. And one cannot help noticing that these synthetic products demonstrate for the first time the possibility of eliminating Time and preparing, in factory and laboratory, substances which it would have taken Nature thousands and thousands of years to produce. And we know full well to what extent the "synthetic preparation of life," even in the modest form of a few cells of protoplasm, was the supreme dream of science throughout the whole second half of the nineteenth century and the beginning of the twentieth. This was the alchemist's dream too—the dream of creating the homunculus.[8]

On the plane of cultural history, it is therefore permissible to say that the alchemists, in their desire to supersede Time, anticipated what is in fact the essence of the ideology of the modern world. Chemistry has received only insignificant fragments of the alchemical heritage. The bulk of this heritage is to be found elsewhere—in the literary ideologies of Balzac and Victor Hugo, in the work of the naturalists, in the systems of political economy, whether capitalist, liberal or Marxist, in the secularized theologies of materialism, positiv-

8. Homunculus: a miniature human being. Eds.

ism and infinite progress—everywhere, in short, where there is faith in the limitless possibilities of *homo faber*; everywhere where the eschatological significance of labour, technology and the scientific exploitation of Nature reveals itself. The more one reflects, the more one discovers that this frantic enthusiasm feeds on a certitude: by conquering Nature through the physico-chemical sciences, man can become Nature's rival without being the slave of Time. Henceforth science and labour are to do the work of Time. With what he recognizes to be most essential in himself—his applied intelligence and his capacity for work—modern man takes upon himself the function of temporal duration; in other words he takes on the role of Time.

It is not our purpose to develop these few observations concerning the ideology and situation of *homo faber* in the nineteenth and twentieth centuries. It was simply our intention to point out that it is in this faith in experimental science and grandiose industrial projects that we must look for the alchemist's dreams. Alchemy has bequeathed much more to the modern world than a rudimentary chemistry; it has left us its faith in the transmutation of Nature and its ambition to control Time. It is true that this heritage has been interpreted and realized by modern man in a totally different way from that of the alchemist. The alchemist was still continuing the behaviour of primitive man, for whom Nature was the source of sacred revelations and work a ritual. But modern science could only come into its own by divesting Nature of these sacred attributes. Scientific phenomena are only revealed at the cost of the disappearance of the hierophanies. Industrial societies have nothing to do with the liturgical activity identifiable with craft-rites. That kind of work was useless in a factory, even if only for lack of any industrial initiation or "tradition."

It is worth recalling another fact. Although he put himself in the place of Time, the alchemist took good care not to assume its role. His dream was to accelerate the tempo of things, to create gold more quickly than Nature; but like the good "philosopher" or mystic that he was, he was afraid of Time. He did not admit himself to be an essentially temporal being, he longed for the beatitude of paradise, aspired to eternity and pursued immortality, the *elixir vitae*. In this respect, too, the alchemist was behaving like premodern man. By all sorts of means he tried to conceal from himself his awareness of the irreversibility of Time, either by regenerating it periodically by a re-enactment of the cosmogony, or by sanctifying it in the liturgy, or even by "forgetting" it, that is, by refusing to acknowledge the secular intervals between two significant (and hence sacred) acts. Above all we must bear in mind that the alchemist became master of Time when, with his various apparatus, he symbolically reiterated the primordial chaos and the cosmogony or when he underwent initiatory "death and resurrection." Every initiation was a victory over death, i.e., temporality; the initiate proclaimed himself "immortal"; he had forged for himself a post-mortem existence which he claimed to be indestructible.

But the moment the individual dream of the alchemist might have been realized by a whole society, and on the plane on which it was collectively realizable (the sphere of the physico-chemical sciences and industry), the defence against Time ceased to be possible. The tragic grandeur of modern man is bound up with the fact that he was the first to take on the work of Time in relation to Nature. We have seen how his spectacular conquests fulfil, on a different plane, the longings of the alchemists. But there is more yet: man in modern society has finally assumed the garb of Time not only in his relations with Nature but also in respect to himself. On the philosophical plane he has recognized himself to be essentially, and sometimes even uniquely, a temporal being, taking his existence from Time and bound by actuality. And the modern world, to the extent to which it asserts its own greatness and fully accepts its dramatic role, feels at one with Time in the way that nineteenth-century science and industry urged it to be. For they proclaimed that man can achieve things better and faster than Nature if he, by means of his intelligence, succeeds in penetrating to her secrets and supplementing, by his own operations, the multiple temporal durations (the geological, botanical, animal rhythms) required by Nature in order to bring her work to fruition. The temptation was too great to resist. Through innumerable millennia man has dreamed of improving upon Nature. It was inconceivable that he should hesitate when confronted by the fabulous perspectives opened out to him by his own discoveries. But the price had to be paid. Man could not stand in the place of Time without condemning himself implicitly to be identified with it, to do its work even when he would no longer wish to.

The work of Time could be replaced only by intellectual and manual (especially manual) work. Of course, Man has from time immemorial been condemned to work. But there is a difference, and it is a fundamental one. To supply the necessary energy to the dreams and ambitions of the nineteenth century, work had to be secularized. For the first time in his history, man assumed this very harsh task of "doing better and quicker than Nature," without now having at his disposal the liturgical dimension which in other societies made work bearable. And it is in work finally secularized, in work in its pure state, numbered in hours and units of energy consumed, that man feels the implacable nature of temporal duration, its full weight and slowness. All in all, one may say that man in modern society has taken on, in the literal sense of the word, the role of Time, exhausting himself by so doing and becoming a uniquely temporal being. And since the irreversibility and vacuity of Time has become a dogma for the modern world (or more exactly, for those who do not recognize themselves as being at one with the Judaeo-Christian ideology), the temporality assumed and experienced by man is translated, on the philosophical plane, into the tragic awareness of the vanity of all human existence. Happily, passions, images, myths, games, distractions, dreams—not to mention religion, which does not belong to the proper spiritual horizon of modern man—are there to prevent this tragic consciousness from imposing itself on planes other than the philosophic.

These considerations are no more a criticism of the modern world than they are a eulogy of other, primitive or exotic societies. One may criticize many aspects of modern society as one can those of other societies, but this is not our concern. It has been our desire simply to show in what direction the guiding ideas of alchemy, rooted in protohistory, have continued into the ideology of the nineteenth century, and with what results. As for the crises of the modern world, we must bear in mind that this world inaugurates a completely new type of civilization. It is not possible to foresee its future developments. But it is useful to remember that the only revolution comparable to it in the past history of humanity, that is, the discovery of agriculture, provoked upheavals and spiritual breakdowns whose magnitude the modern mind finds it well-nigh impossible to conceive. An ancient world, the world of nomadic hunters, with its religions, its myths, its moral conceptions, was ebbing away. Thousands and thousands of years were to elapse before the final lamentations of the old world died away, forever doomed by the advent of agriculture. One must also suppose that the profound spiritual crisis aroused by man's decision *to call a halt and bind himself to the soil*, must have taken many hundreds of years to become completely integrated. It is impossible to imagine the upheaval of all values caused by the change-over from the nomadic to the sedentary life and to appreciate its psychological and spiritual repercussions. The technical discoveries of the modern world, its conquest of Time and Space, represent a revolution of similar proportions, the consequences of which are still very far from having become part of us. The secularization of work is like an open wound in the body of modern society. There is, however, nothing to indicate that a resanctification may not take place in the future. As for the temporality of the human condition, it presents an even more serious discovery. But a reconciliation with temporality remains a possibility, given a more correct conception of Time. But this is not the place to deal with these problems. Our aim was simply to show that the spiritual crisis of the modern world includes among its remote origins the demiurgic dreams of the metallurgists, smiths and alchemists. It is right that the historiographic consciousness of Western man should be at one with the deeds and ideals of his very remote ancestors—even though modern man, heir to all these myths and dreams, has succeeded in realizing them only by breaking loose from their original significance.

25. INDIAN SYMBOLISM OF TIME AND ETERNITY

India has elaborated a doctrine of cosmic cycles by amplifying the number of periodic creations and destructions of the Universe to ever more terrifying proportions. The unit of measurement for the smallest cycle of all is the *yuga*—the "age." A *yuga* is preceded by a "dawn" and followed by a "dusk," which fill the intervals between the successive "ages." A complete cycle or *mahayuga* is composed of four "ages" of unequal duration, the longest appearing at the beginning of a cycle and the shortest at the end of it. The names of these *yuga* are borrowed from the names of the "throws" in the game of dice. *Krita yuga* (from the verb *kri*, to "make" or to "accomplish") means the "perfect age"; in dice-play, the throw that

SOURCE: *IS*/62–67, 71–73; cf. *Y*/200–207, 269–73.

turns up the side with four pips is the winning throw. For in the Indian tradition, the number four symbolizes totality, plenitude, or perfection. The *krita yuga* is the perfect age, and therefore it is also called the *satya yuga*; that is, the "real," true, or authentic age. From every point of view it is the golden age, the beatific epoch ruled by justice, happiness and prosperity. During the *krita yuga* the moral order of the Universe, the *dharma*, is observed in its entirety. What is more, it is observed spontaneously, without constraint, by all beings, for during the *krita yuga* the *dharma* is in some sort identified with human existence. The perfect man of the *krita yuga* incarnates the cosmic norm, and therefore the moral law. He leads an exemplary, archetypal existence. In other, non-Indian traditions, this golden age is equivalent to the primordial, paradisiac epoch.

The succeeding age, the *treta yuga* or triad, so named after the die with three pips, marks the beginning of a regression. Human beings no longer observe more than three-quarters of the *dharma*. Work, suffering and death are now the lot of mankind. Duty is no longer performed spontaneously, but has to be learnt. The customs proper to the four castes begin to be altered.

With the *dvapara yuga* (the age symbolized by "two"), only half of the *dharma* survives on earth. Vices and evils increase, human life becomes of still shorter duration. And in *kali yuga*, the "evil age," only a quarter of the *dharma* remains. The term *kali* designates the die marked with one pip only, which is also the "losing throw" (personified, moreover, as an evil spirit): *kali* signifies also "dispute, discord" and, in general, the most evil of any group of beings or objects. In *kali yuga* man and society reach the extreme point of disintegration. According to the *Vishnu Purana* (IV, 24) the syndrome of *kali yuga* is marked by the fact that it is the only age in which property alone confers social rank; wealth becomes the only motive of the virtues, passion and lust the only bonds between the married, falsehood and deception the first condition of success in life, sexuality the sole means of enjoyment, while external, merely ritualistic religion is confused with spirituality. For several thousand years, be it understood, we have been living in *kali yuga*.

The figures 4, 3, 2 and 1 denote both the decreasing length of each *yuga* and the progressive diminution of the *dharma* subsisting in it; to which, moreover, corresponds a shortening of the length of human life, accompanied as we saw by a progressive relaxation of morals and a continuous decline of intelligence. Certain Hindu schools like the *Pancaratra* connect the theory of cycles with a doctrine about the "decline of knowledge" (*jnana bhramsa*).

The relative duration of each of these four *yugas* may be calculated in different ways, depending upon the values ascribed to the years—whether they are regarded as human years, or as divine "years," each comprising 360 years. To take a few examples: according to certain sources (*Manu* I, 69 *et seq.*, *Mahabharata III*, 12, 826), the *krita yuga* lasts for 4,000 years, plus 400 years of "dawn" and as many of "dusk"; then come the *treta yuga* of 3,000 years, the *dvapara* of 2,000 years and *kali yuga* of 1,000—all, of course, with their corresponding periods of "dawn" and "dusk." A complete cycle, a *mahayuga*, therefore comprises 12,000 years. The passage from one *yuga* to another takes place during a twilight interval, which marks a decline even within each *yuga*, every one of them terminating in a phase of darkness. As we are approaching the end of the cycle—that is, the fourth and last *yuga*, the darkness deepens. The final *yuga*, that in which we find ourselves now, is also regarded, more than any other, as the "age of darkness"; for, by a play upon words, it has become associated with the goddess Kali—the "black." Kali is one of the multiple names of the Great Goddess, of Shakti the spouse of the god Shiva; and this name of the Great Goddess has naturally been connected with the Sanskrit word *kala*, "time": Kali thus becomes not only "the Black," but also the personification of Time. But, etymology apart, the association between *kala*, "time," the goddess Kali and *kali yuga* is structurally justifiable: Time is "black" because it is irrational, hard and pitiless; and Kali, like all the other Great Goddesses, is the mistress of Time, of all the destinies that she forges and fulfils.

A complete cycle, a *mahayuga*, ends in a "dissolution" or *pralaya*, and this is repeated in a still more radical way at the *mahapralaya*, or "Great Dissolution," at the end of the thousandth cycle. For later speculation has amplified and multiplied this primordial rhythm of "creation-destruction-creation" *ad infinitum* by projecting the unit of measure—the *yuga*—into vaster and vaster cycles. The 12,000 years of one *mahayuga* have been counted as "divine years" of 360 years each, which gives a total of 4,320,000 years for a single cosmic cycle. A thousand of such *mahayugas* constitute one *kalpa* (or "form"); 14 *kalpas* make up one *manvantara* (so called because each such period is supposed to be governed by a Manu, or mythical ancestor-king). One *kalpa* is equal to one day in the life of Brahma, and another *kalpa* to one night. A hundred of these "years" of Brahma, say 311 thousand billion human years, make up the life of the god. But even this considerable length of Brahma's life does not exhaust the whole of Time, for the gods are not eternal, and the cosmic creations and destructions go on without end.

All we need retain from this cataract of numbers, is the cyclic character of cosmic Time. In fact, what we have here is the repetition to infinity of the same phenomenon (creation-destruction-new creation) prefigured in each *yuga* ("dawn" and "dusk") but completely realised in a *mahayuga*. The life of Brahma thus comprises 2,560,000 of these *mahayugas*, each going through the same stages (*krita*, *treta*, *dvapara*, *kali*) and concluding with a *pralaya*, with a *ragnarok* (the "definitive" destruction, or total dissolution of the cosmic Egg takes place in the *mahapralaya* at the end of each *kalpa*). The *mahapralaya* implies the regression of all forms and all modes of existence into the original, undifferentiated *prakriti*. On the mythical plane nothing remains but the primordial Ocean, on the surface of which the great god Vishnu sleeps.

Besides the metaphysical depreciation *of human life as history*— which, by and in proportion to its duration, causes an *erosion* of all forms, an exhaustion of their ontological substance—and besides the myth of the *perfection of the beginnings*, a universal tradition which recurs here too (paradise is lost gradually in this case, simply because it is *realized*, because it takes *form* and *duration*)—besides these, what most merits our attention in this orgy of figures is the *eternal repetition* of the fundamental rhythm of the Cosmos: its periodical destruction and re-creation. From this cycle without beginning or end, which is the cosmic manifestation of *maya*, man can extricate himself only by an act of spiritual freedom (for all Indian soteriological systems are reducible to a previous deliverance from the cosmic illusion, and to spiritual freedom).

The two great heterodoxies, Buddhism and Jainism, accept the same Indian doctrine of cyclic time, in its general outlines, and liken it to a wheel of twelve spokes (an image that occurs earlier in the Vedic texts, in the *Atharva Veda*, X, 8, 4 and *Rig Veda*, I, 164, 115, etc.). Buddhism adopted the *kalpa* (in Pali *kappa*) as the unit of measurement for the cosmic cycles, dividing it into a variable number of what the texts call "incalculables" (*asam-kheya*, in Pali *a-sam-kheyya*). The Pali sources generally mention 4 *asankheyyas* and 100,-000 *kappa* (for example *Jataka* I, p. 2). In the Mahayana literature the number of "incalculables" varies between 3, 7 and 33, and they are related to the career of the Bodhisattva in the different Cosmoses. The progressive decadence of man is marked, in the Buddhist tradition, by a constant diminution of the length of human life. Thus, according to the *Dighanikaya* II, 2–7, during the epoch of the first Buddha, Vipassi, who lived 91 *kappa* ago, the length of human life was 80,000 years; during that of the second Buddha, Sikhi, 31 *kappa* ago, it was 70,000, and so on. The seventh Buddha, Gautama, made his appearance when human life was no longer than 100 years; that is, when it had been reduced to its absolute minimum. (We find the same idea in the Iranian apocalypses.) However, in Buddhism and in Indian speculation as a whole, time is unlimited; the Bodhisattvas will reincarnate, in order to proclaim the good news of salvation to all beings, for all eternity. The sole possibility of escape from time, of breaking out of the iron ring of existences, is to abolish the human condition and attain Nirvana. Moreover, all the "incalculables" and all the countless aeons also have a soteriological function: the mere contemplation of such a panorama terrifies man, compelling him to realize that he will have to recommence this same transitory existence billions of times over, and endure the same sufferings without end; the effect of which is to stir up his will to escape—that is, to impel him to transcend his condition as an "existant" once and for all.

* * *

The myth of cyclic Time, of the cosmic cycles repeating themselves *ad infinitum*, is not an invention of Indian speculation. . . . The traditional societies—whose representations of Time are so difficult to grasp just because they are conveyed in symbols and rituals whose deeper meaning sometimes remains inaccessible to us—these traditional societies conceive man's temporal existence not only as an infinite repetition of certain archetypes and exemplary gestures, but also as an *eternal recommencement*. Indeed, symbolically and ritually, the world is periodically re-created: the cosmogony is repeated at least once a year—and the cosmogonic myth serves also as the model for a great many actions—marriage, for instance, and healing.

What is the meaning of all these myths and all these rites? That the world is born, disintegrates, perishes and is reborn in a very rapid rhythm. Chaos and the cosmogonic act that puts an end to chaos by a new creation are periodically re-enacted. The year—or what we understand by that term—is equivalent to the creation, duration and destruction of a world, of a Cosmos. It is quite probable that this conception of the periodic creation and destruction of the world, although it may have been confirmed by the spectacle of the periodical death and resurrection of vegetation is, for all that, *not* a creation of the agricultural societies. It is also found in the mythologies of pre-agricultural societies, and is very likely a lunar conception. The moon, indeed, measures the most conspicuous periodicities, and it was terms relating to the moon that were first used for the measurement of time. The lunar rhythm regularly presents a "creation" (the new moon), followed by a growth (to full moon), a diminution and a "death" (the three moonless nights). It was very probably the image of the eternal birth and death of the moon which helped to crystallize the earliest human intuitions about the alternations of Life and Death, and suggested, later on, the myth of the periodic creation and destruction of the world. The most ancient myths of the deluge disclose a lunar structure and origin. After every deluge a mythic Ancestor gives birth to a new humanity; and it generally happens that this mythical Ancestor takes on the aspect of a lunar animal. (In ethnology, those animals are called lunar whose life shows a certain alternation; notably that of periodical appearances and disappearances.)

For the "primitive," therefore, Time is cyclic; the world is successively created and destroyed, and the lunar symbolism of "birth-death-resurrection" is present in a great many myths and rites. It was out of such an immemorial heritage that the pan-Indian doctrine of the ages of the world and of the cosmic cycles was elaborated. Of course the archetypal image of the eternally repeated birth, death and resurrection of the moon was appreciably modified by Indian thought. As for the astronomical aspect of the *yuga*, it is probable that this was influenced by the cosmological and astrological speculations of the Babylonians. But these contingent historical influences of Mesopotamia upon India must not now detain us. The important point for us to note is that the Indians, in magnifying ever more audaciously the duration and the numbers of the cosmic cycles, had a soteriological aim in view. Appalled by the endless number of

births and rebirths of Universes accompanied by an equally vast number of human births and rebirths ruled by the law of *karma*, the
Indian was in a sense *obliged* to seek a way out of this cosmic rota-
tion and these infinite transmigrations. The mystical doctrines and
techniques that are directed towards the deliverance of man from
sorrow and from the frightful successions of "life, death and rebirth,"
take over the mythic images of cosmic cycles, amplify and utilize
them for their proselytizing purpose. By the Indians of the post-
Vedic epoch—that is, by the Indians who had discovered the "suffering of existence"—the "eternal return" was equated with the infinite cycle of transmigration ruled by *karma*. This present illusory
and transitory world, the world of *samsara*, of sorrow and ignorance,
is the world that unfolds itself under the sign of Time. Deliverance
from this world, and the attainment of salvation, are equivalent to deliverance from cosmic Time.

26. CHRISTIANITY: IRREVERSIBLE TIME

... The revelation that Judaeo-Christianity alone received in a historical time which is never repeated, and which issues in the making
of an irreversible history, was already preserved by archaic humanity
in mythic form; nevertheless, the mystical experience of the "primitives" as well as the mystical life of Christians expresses itself through
this same archetype—the re-entry into the original Paradise. We can
clearly see that history—in this case, Sacred History—has brought
no innovation. Among the primitives as among Christians, it is always
a paradoxical return *in illud tempus*, a "leap backwards" abolishing
time and history, that constitutes the mystical re-entry into Paradise.
Consequently, although Biblical and Christian symbolism is charged
with a historical and—in the last analysis—a "provincial" content
(since every local history is provincial in relation to universal history
conceived in its totality), it remains nevertheless universal, like every
coherent symbolism. We may even wonder whether the accessibility
of Christianity may not be attributable in great measure to its symbolism, whether the universal Images that it takes up in its turn have
not considerably facilitated the diffusion of its message. For, to the

non-Christian, one question occurs first of all: how can a local history—that of the Jewish people and of the first Judæo-Christian communities—how can this claim to have become the pattern for all divine manifestation in concrete, historical Time? I believe we have pointed to the answer: this sacred history, although in the eyes of an alien observer it looks like a local history, is also an exemplary history, because it takes up and perfects these trans-temporal Images.

How, then, are we to account for the irresistible impression, felt by non-Christians especially, that Christianity is an *innovation* in relation to all previous religious life? To a Hindu who is sympathetic to Christianity, the most striking innovation (apart from the message and the divinity of Christ) is its valorization of Time—in the final reckoning, its *redemption* of Time and of History. Renouncing the reversibility of cyclic Time, it posits a Time that is irreversible, because the hierophanies manifested in it are no longer repeatable: it is once only that the Christ has lived, has been crucified and has been resurrected. Hence a complete fulfillment of the momentary: Time itself is ontologized: Time is made to *be*, which means that it ceases to become, it transforms itself into eternity. But let this be said at once—it is not *any* temporal moment that opens out into eternity, but only the "favorable moment," the instant that is transfigured by a revelation (whether or not we call this "favorable moment" *kairos*). Time becomes a value, insofar as God manifests himself through it, filling it with a trans-historical meaning and a soteriological intention: for, with each new intervention of God in history, has there not always been a question of the salvation of man—that is, of something which has nothing to do with history? Time turns into pleroma by the very fact of the incarnation of the divine Word: but this fact itself transfigures history. How could it be empty and meaningless—that Time which *saw* Jesus come to birth, suffer, die and rise again? How could it be reversible or repeatable *ad infinitum*?

From the standpoint of the history of religions, Judaeo-Christianity presents us with the supreme hierophany: the *transfiguration of the historical event into hierophany*.[1] This means something more than the "hierophanizing" of Time, for sacred Time is familiar to all religions. But here it is *the historical event* as such which displays the maximum of trans-historicity: God not only intervenes in his-

1. *Hierophany*: manifestation of the sacred. Eds.

tory, as in the case of Judaism; he is incarnated in a historic being, in order to undergo a historically conditioned existence. Jesus of Nazareth is, to all appearances, in no way distinguished from his contemporaries in Palestine. Superficially, the Divine is completely concealed in history. Nothing about the physiology, psychology or the "culture" of Jesus gives one any glimpse of God the Father. Jesus eats, digests, suffers from thirst or from the heat, like any other Jew of Palestine. But, in reality, this "historical event" constituted by the existence of Jesus is a total theophany;[2] what it presents is like an audacious effort to *save the historical event* in itself, by endowing it with the maximum of being.

In spite of the value it accords to Time, Judaeo-Christianity does not lead to historicism, but to a theology of history. It is not for its own sake that an event is valued, but only for the sake of the revelation it embodies—a revelation that precedes and transcends it. Historicism as such is a product of the decomposition of Christianity: it could only have come about insofar as we had lost faith in the trans-historical reality of the historical event.

One fact, however, remains: Christianity strives to *save* history; first, because it accords a value to historic time; and also because, for the Christian, the historical event, while remaining just what it is, becomes capable of transmitting a trans-historical message. For, since the incarnation of the Christ, the Christian is supposed to look for the interventions of God not only in the Cosmos (with the aid of the cosmic hierophanies, of the Images and symbols), but also in historical events. This is not always an easy undertaking; we may, without too much difficulty, read the "signs" of the divine presence in the Cosmos; but the corresponding "signs" in History are much more disguised.

Indeed, the Christian admits that, after the Incarnation, miracles are no longer easy to recognize; the greatest of all miracles having been, in fact, the Incarnation itself, all that *which was clearly manifested as miraculous* before Jesus Christ is of no further use or meaning *after* his coming. There is, of course, an uninterrupted series of miracles that the Church accepts, but they have all been validated insofar as they were dependent upon Christ and not for the sake of

2. Theophany: manifestation of a diety. Eds.

their intrinsically "miraculous" quality. (We know that the Church carefully distinguishes miracles due to "magic" or to "demons" from those vouchsafed by grace.) The existence and the validity of the miracles accepted by the Church, however, leave open the great problem of the *unrecognizability* of the marvelous in the Christian world; for one may very well find oneself very near to Christ, and *imitate* him, without showing any visible sign of it: one may be *imitating the Christ living his life in history* which, apparently, resembled everybody's existence. Altogether, the Christian is led to approach every historical event with "fear and trembling," since for him even the most commonplace historical event, while continuing to be *real* (that is, historically conditioned) may conceal some new intervention of God in history; in any case it may have a trans-historical meaning, may be charged with a message. Consequently, for the Christian, historical life itself can become glorious—as the life of Christ and the saints bear witness. With the coming of Christianity, it is no longer the Cosmos and the Images only that are able to prefigure and reveal—there is also History, especially that of "everyday life," that which is constituted by events apparently without significance.

Undoubtedly. And yet it must not be lost sight of, that Christianity entered into History in order to abolish it: the greatest hope of the Christian is the second coming of Christ, which is to put an end to all History. From a certain point of view, for every Christian individually, this end, and the eternity to follow it—the paradise regained—may be attained *from this moment. The time to come* announced by the Christ is already accessible, and for him who has regained it, history ceases to be. The transformation of Time into Eternity commenced with the first believers. But this paradoxical transformation of Time into Eternity is not the exclusive property of Christianity. We have met with the same conception and the same symbolism in India. . . . *Ksana* corresponds to *kairos;*[3] the one like the other may become the "favorable moment" through which one passes out of time and rejoins eternity . . . The Christian is, in the

---

3. *Ksana*: "the instant, the present moment . . . in Sanskrit" (*IS*/81); *kairos*: the decisive, significance-laden moment in Greek (opposed, in theology, to *chronos*, time as simple sequentiality). Eds.

final reckoning, required to become the contemporary of the Christ: and this implies a concrete existence in history, as well as contemporaneity with the preaching, the agony and the resurrection of the Christ.

27. HISTORICAL TIME AND LITURGICAL TIME

In proclaiming the Incarnation, Resurrection, and Ascension of the Word, the Christians themselves did not consider that they were putting forth a *new* myth. Actually, they were employing the categories of mythical thought. Obviously they could not recognize this mythical thought in the desacralized mythologies of the pagan scholars who were their contemporaries. But it is clear that for Christians of all creeds the center of religious life is constituted by the drama of Jesus Christ. Although played out in History, this drama first established the possibility of salvation; hence there is only one way to gain salvation—to reiterate this exemplary drama ritually and to imitate the supreme model revealed by the life and teaching of Jesus. Now, this type of religious behavior is integral with genuine mythical thought.

It must at once be added that, *by the very fact that it is a religion*, Christianity had to keep at least one mythical aspect—liturgical Time, that is, the periodical recovery of the *illud tempus* of the "beginnings." "The religious experience of the Christian is based upon an *imitation* of the Christ as *exemplary pattern*, upon the liturgical repetition of the life, death, and resurrection of the Lord, and upon the *contemporaneity* of the Christian with *illud tempus* which begins with the Nativity at Bethlehem and ends, provisionally, with the Ascension." Now, as we have seen, "the imitation of a transhuman model, the repetition of an exemplary scenario and the breakaway from profane time through a moment which opens out into the Great Time, are the essential marks of 'mythical behavior'—that is, the behavior of the man of the archaic societies, who finds the very source of his existence in the myth."[1]

Source: *MR*/168–70.
1. M. Eliade, *MDM*/30–31.

However, though liturgical Time is a circular Time, Christianity, as faithful heir to Judaism, accepts the linear Time of History: the World was created only once and will have only one end; the Incarnation took place only once, in historical Time, and there will be only one Judgment. From the very first, Christianity was subjected to various and conflicting influences, especially those from Gnosticism,[2] Judaism, and "paganism." The Church's reaction was not always the same. The Fathers fought relentlessly against the acosmism and esotericism of the Gnosis; yet they kept the Gnostic elements found in the Gospel of John, in the Pauline Epistles, and in certain primitive texts. But, despite persecutions, Gnosticism was never wholly extirpated, and certain Gnostic myths, in more or less camouflaged form, reappeared in the oral and written literatures of the Middle Ages.

As for Judaism, it gave the Church not only an allegorical method of interpreting the Scriptures, but, most importantly, the outstanding model for "historicizing" the festivals and symbols of the cosmic religion. The "Judaization" of primitive Christianity is equivalent to its "historicization," that is, to the decision of the first theologians to connect the history of Jesus' preaching and of the earliest Church to the Sacred History of the people of Israel. But Judaism had "historicized" a certain number of seasonal festivals and cosmic symbols by connecting them with important events in the history of Israel (cf. the Feast of Tabernacles, Passover, the Hanukkah Feast of Lights, etc.). The Church Fathers took the same course: they "Christianized" Asianic and Mediterranean rites and myths by connecting them with a "Sacred History." Obviously, this "Sacred History" exceeded the bounds of the Old Testament and now included the New Testament, the preaching of the Apostles, and, later, the history of the Saints. A certain number of cosmic symbols— Water, the Tree and the Vine, the plow and the ax, the ship, the chariot, etc.—had already been assimilated by Judaism, and they could easily be incorporated into the doctrine and practice of the Church by being given a sacramental or ecclesiological meaning.

---

2. Gnosticism: a religious system of late-Hellenism emphasizing secret "knowledge" (*gnosis*) as the path to salvation. Eds.

28. "COSMIC CHRISTIANITY"

The real difficulties arose later, when the Christian missionaries were faced, especially in Central and Western Europe, by *living* popular religions. Willy-nilly, they ended by "Christianizing" the "pagan" divine Figures and myths that resisted extirpation. A large number of dragon-slaying Gods or Heroes became St. Georges; storm Gods were transformed into St. Eliases; the countless fertility Goddesses were assimilated to the Virgin or to female Saints. It could even be said that a part of the popular religion of pre-Christian Europe survived, either camouflaged or transformed, in the feasts of the Church calendar and in the cult of the Saints. For more than ten centuries the Church was obliged to fight the continual influx of "pagan" elements—that is, elements belonging to the cosmic religion—into Christian practices and legends. The success of this intensive struggle was not very great, especially in the South and Southeast of Europe. In the folklore and religious practices of the rural populations at the end of the nineteenth century there still survived figures, myths, and rituals from earliest antiquity, or even from protohistory.

The Orthodox and Roman Catholic Churches have been criticized for accepting so many pagan elements. It is a question if these criticisms were always justified. On the one hand, "paganism" could survive only in "Christianized" form, even if at times the Christianization was rather superficial. This policy of assimilating the "paganism" that could not be destroyed was nothing new; the primitive Church had already accepted and assimilated a large part of the pre-Christian sacred calendar. On the other hand, the peasants, because of their own mode of existing in the Cosmos, were not attracted by a "historical" and moral Christianity. The religious experience peculiar to the rural populations was nourished by what could be called a "cosmic Christianity." In other words, the peasants of Europe understood Christianity as a cosmic liturgy. The Christological mystery also involved the destiny of the Cosmos. "All Nature sighs, awaiting the Resurrection" is a central motif not only in the Easter liturgy but also in the religious folklore of Eastern Christianity. Mystical empathy with the cosmic rhythms, which was violently attacked

SOURCE: *MR*/170–74.

by the Old Testament prophets and barely tolerated by the Church, is central to the religions of rural populations, especially in Southeastern Europe. For this whole section of Christendom "Nature" is not the World of sin but the work of God. After the Incarnation, the World had been re-established in its original glory; this is why Christ and the Church had been imbued with so many cosmic symbols. In the religious folklore of Southeastern Europe the sacraments sanctify Nature too.

For the peasants of Eastern Europe this in no sense implied a "paganization" of Christianity, but, on the contrary, a "Christianization" of the religion of their ancestors. When the time comes for the history of this "popular theology" to be written on the evidence that can be traced in seasonal festivals and religious folklores, it will be realized that "cosmic Christianity" is not a new form of paganism or a pagan-Christian syncretism. Rather it is an original religious creation, in which eschatology and soteriology are given cosmic dimensions. Even more significantly, Christ, while remaining the Pantocrator, comes down to Earth and visits the peasants, just as, in the myths of archaic peoples, the Supreme Being was wont to do before he became a *deus otiosus*;[1] this Christ is not "historical," since popular thought is interested neither in chronology nor in the accuracy of events and the authenticity of historical figures. This does not mean that, for the rural populations, Christ is only a "God" inherited from the old polytheisms. For, on the one hand, there is no contradiction between the Christ image of the Gospels and the Church and the Christ image of religious folklore. The Nativity, the teaching of Jesus, and his miracles, the Crucifixion and the Resurrection are essential themes in this popular Christianity. On the other hand, it is a *Christian spirit*—not a pagan spirit—that impregnates all these folklore creations; they tell of man's salvation by Christ; of faith, hope, and charity; of a World that is "good" because it was created by God the Father and redeemed by the Son; of a human existence that will not be repeated and that is not without meaning; man is free to choose good or evil, but he will not be judged solely by that choice.

It does not lie within the scope of this book to outline this "popu-

---

1. Pantocrator: the all-powerful ruler; *deus otiosus*: see selection 13, n. 2. Eds.

lar theology." But it is obvious that the cosmic Christianity of the
rural populations is dominated by nostalgia for a Nature sanctified
by the presence of Jesus. It is, in some sort, a nostalgia for Paradise,
the desire to find again a transfigured and invulnerable Nature, safe
from the cataclysms brought by wars, devastation, and conquests.
It is also the expression of the "ideal" of these agricultural societies,
constantly terrorized by allogeneous warrior hordes and exploited
by the various classes of more or less autochthonous "masters." It is
a passive revolt against the tragedy and injustice of History, in the
last analysis against the fact that evil proves to be no longer only
an individual decision but, increasingly, a transpersonal structure of
the historical World.

But to return to our theme, it is clear that this popular Christianity
has kept alive certain categories of mythical thought even down to
our day.

29. ESCHATOLOGICAL MYTHOLOGIES OF THE MIDDLE AGES

In the Middle Ages we witness an upwelling of mythical thought.
All the social classes depend on their mythological traditions.
Knights, artisans, clerks, peasants, accept an "origin myth" for their
condition and endeavor to imitate an exemplary model. These
mythologies have various sources. The Arthurian cycle and the
Grail theme incorporate, under a varnish of Christianity, a number
of Celtic beliefs, especially those having to do with the Other World.
The knights try to follow the example of Lancelot or Parsifal. The
trouvères[1] elaborate a whole mythology of woman and Love, making use of Christian elements but going beyond or contradicting
Church doctrine.

It is especially in certain historical movements of the Middle Ages
that we find the most typical manifestations of mythical thought.
Millennialist exaltation and eschatological myths come to the fore
in the Crusades, in the movements of a Tanchelm and an Eudes de

Source: *MR*/174, 176–77.
1. Trouvères: narrative poets of northern France, from the eleventh to
fourteenth centuries. Eds.

l'Etoile, in the elevation of Frederick II to the rank of Messiah, and in many other collective messianic, utopian, and prerevolutionary phenomena, which have been brilliantly treated by Norman Cohn in his *The Pursuit of the Millennium*. . . .

* * *

. . . The religious prestige and eschatological function of kings [such as Frederick II] survived in Europe to the seventeenth century. The secularization of the concept of eschatological King did not extinguish the hope, deeply rooted in the collective soul, for a universal renewal brought about by the exemplary Hero in one of his new forms—the Reformer, the Revolutionary, the Martyr (in the name of the freedom of peoples), the Party Leader. The role and mission of the Founders and Leaders of the modern totalitarian movements include a considerable number of eschatological and soteriological elements. Mythical thought transcends and discards some of its earlier expressions, outmoded by History, and adapts itself to the new social conditions and new cultural fashions—but it resists extirpation.

As to the Crusade phenomenon, Alphonse Dupront has well demonstrated its mythical structures and eschatological orientation. "At the center of a Crusade consciousness, in the cleric as in the non-cleric, is the duty to free Jerusalem. . . . What is most strongly expressed in the Crusade is a twofold fulfillment: an accomplishment of the times and an accomplishment of human space. In the sense, for space, that the sign of the accomplishment of the times is the gathering of the nations about the sacred mother city, the center of the world, Jerusalem."[2]

The proof that we are here in the presence of a collective spiritual phenomenon, of an irrational drive, is, among other things, the Children's Crusades that suddenly began in Northern France and Germany in the year 1212. The spontaneity of these movements appear to be beyond doubt: "No one urging them, either from foreign lands or from their own," says a contemporary witness.[3] Children

2. Alphonse Dupront, "Croisades et eschatologie," in *Umanesimo e esoterismo*. Atti del V Convegno Internazionale di Studi Umanistici, a cura di Enrico Castelli (Padua, 1960), p. 177.

3. P. Alphandéry and A. Dupront, *La Chrétienté et l'idée de Croisade* (Paris, 1959), 2: 118.

"having at once two characteristics that were signs of the extraordinary, their extreme youth and their poverty, especially little herd-boys,"[4] took the road, and the poor joined them. There were perhaps thirty thousand of them, and they walked in procession, singing. When asked where they were going, they answered: "To God." According to a contemporary chronicler, "their intention was to cross the sea and do what kings and the mighty had not done, to recapture Christ's Sepulchre."[5] The clergy had opposed this rising of children. The French crusade ended in catastrophe. Reaching Marseilles, they embarked in seven large ships, but two of these ran aground in a storm off Sardinia and all the passengers were drowned. As for the other five ships, the two treacherous shipowners took them to Alexandria, where they sold the children to the Saracen leaders and to slave dealers. . . .

30. SURVIVALS OF ESCHATOLOGICAL MYTH

The failure of the Crusades did not put an end to eschatological hopes. In his *De Monarchia Hispanica* (1600), Tomasso Campanella begged the King of Spain to furnish the money for a new Crusade against the Turkish Empire, and, after the victory, to establish the Universal Monarchy. . . .

It is needless to multiply examples. But it is important to stress the continuity between the medieval eschatological conceptions and the various "philosophies of History" produced by the Enlightenment and the nineteenth century. During the last thirty years it has begun to be realized what an exceptional role was played by the "prophecies" of Gioacchino da Fiore in instigating and articulating all these messianic movements that arose in the thirteenth century and continued, in more or less secularized form, into the nineteenth. . . .

We cannot here present the various eschatological movements inspired by Gioacchino. But we must at least refer to some unexpected continuations of the Calabrian prophet's ideas. Thus, for example,

SOURCE: *MR*/178–81.
2. *Ibid.*, p. 119.
3. Reinier, cited *ibid.*, p. 120.

Lessing in his *Education of the Human Race* elaborates the thesis of continual and progressive revelation culminating in a third age. To be sure, Lessing thought of this third age as the triumph of reason through education; but it was none the less, he believed, the fulfillment of Christian revelation, and he refers with sympathy and admiration to "certain enthusiasts of the thirteenth and fourteenth centuries," whose only error lay in proclaiming the "new eternal Gospel" too soon.[1] Lessing's ideas aroused some repercussions and, through the disciples of Saint-Simon, he probably influenced August Comte and his doctrine of the three stages. Fichte, Hegel, Schelling were influenced, though for different reasons, by the Gioacchinian myth of an imminent third age that will renew and complete History. Through them this eschatological myth influenced certain Russian writers, especially Krasinky, with his *Third Kingdom of the Spirit*, and Merejkowsky, author of *The Christianity of the Third Testament*. To be sure, we are now dealing with semiphilosophical ideologies and fantasies and no longer with the eschatological expectation of the reign of the Holy Spirit. But the myth of universal renovation in a more or less imminent future is still discernible in all these theories and fantasies.

31. FREUDIAN "PRIMORDIAL" TIME

We cannot refrain from thinking of the significance that the "return to the past" has acquired in modern therapeutics. Psychoanalysis especially has found out how to use, as its chief curative method, the memory, the recollection of the "primordial events." But, within the horizons of modern spirituality, and in conformity with the Judæo-Christian conception of historic and irreversible Time, the "primordial" could mean only one's earliest childhood, the true individual *initium*. Psychoanalysis, therefore, introduces historical and individual time into therapeutics. The patient is no longer seen as an individual who is suffering only because of contemporary and objective events (accidents, bacteria, etc.) or by the fault of others (heredity), as he was supposed to be in the pre-psychoana-

SOURCES: *MDM*/53–54; *Q*/49; *MR*/78–79.
1. Cf. Karl Löwith, *Meaning in History* (Chicago, 1949), p. 208.

lytic age; he is also suffering the after-effects of a shock sustained in his own temporal duration, some personal trauma that occurred in the *illud tempus* of childhood—a trauma that has been forgotten or, more exactly, has never come to consciousness. And the cure consists precisely in a "return to the past"; a retracing of one's steps in order to re-enact the crisis, to relive the psychic shock and bring it back into consciousness. We might translate the operative procedure into terms of archaic thought, by saying that the cure is to begin living all over again; that is, to repeat the birth, to make oneself contemporary with "the beginning": and this is no less than an imitation of the supreme beginning, the cosmogony. At the level of archaic thought, owing to its cyclic conception of Time, the repetition of the cosmogony presented no difficulty: but for the modern man, personal experience that is "primordial" can be no other than that of infancy. When the psyche comes to a crisis, it is to infancy that he must return in order to relive, and confront anew, the event from which that crisis originated.

Freud's was a most audacious undertaking: it introduced Time and History into a category of phenomena that had previously been approached from without, rather in the way that a naturalist treats his subject. One of Freud's discoveries above all has had portentous consequences, namely, that for man there is a "primordial" epoch in which all is decided—the very earliest childhood—and that the course of this infancy is exemplary for the rest of life. Restating this in terms of archaic thinking, one might say that there was once a "paradise" (which for psychoanalysis is the prenatal period, or the time before weaning), ending with a "break" or "catastrophe" (the infantile trauma), and that whatever the adult's attitude may be towards these primordial circumstances, they are none the less constitutive of his being. One would be tempted to extend these observations to take in Jung's discovery of the collective unconscious, of the series of psychic structures prior to those of the individual psyche, which cannot be said to have been forgotten since they were not constituted by individual experiences. The world of the archetypes of Jung is like the Platonic world of Ideas, in that the archetypes are impersonal and do not participate in the historical Time of the individual life, but in the Time of the species—even of organic Life itself. . . .

* * *

Such an urge to *descensus* corresponds to a general tendency of the Western mind at the beginning of the century. One cannot better describe the psychoanalytical technique elaborated by Freud than to say that it is a *decensus ad inferos*, a descent into the deepest and most dangerous zones of the human psyche. When Jung revealed the existence of the collective unconscious, the exploration of these immemorial treasures—the myths, symbols, and images of archaic humanity—began to resemble the techniques of oceanography and speleology. Just as descents into the depths of the sea or expeditions to the bottoms of the caves had revealed elementary organisms long vanished from the surface of the earth, so analysis retrieved forms of deep psychic life previously inaccessible to study. Speleology presented biologists with Tertiary and even Mesozoic organisms, primitive zoömorphic forms not susceptible of fossilization—in other words, forms that had vanished from the surface of the earth without leaving a trace. By discovering "living fossils," speleology markedly advanced our knowledge of archaic modes of life. Similarly, archaic modes of psychic life, "living fossils" buried in the darkness of the unconscious, now become accessible to study through the techniques developed by Freud and other depth psychologists.

* * *

Two of Freud's ideas are relevant to our subject: (1) the bliss of the "origin" and "beginnings" of the human being, and (2) the idea that through memory, or by a "going back," one can relive certain traumatic incidents of early childhood. The bliss of the "origin" is, we have seen, a quite frequent theme in the archaic religions; it is attested in India, Iran, Greece, and in Judaeo-Christianity. The fact that Freud postulates bliss at the beginning of human existence does not mean that psychoanalysis has a mythological structure or that it borrows an archaic mythical theme or accepts the Judaeo-Christian myth of Paradise and Fall. The only connection that can be made between psychoanalysis and the archaic conception of the bliss and perfection of the origin is based on the fact that Freud discovered the decisive role of the "primordial and paradisal time" of earliest childhood, the bliss before the break (= weaning), that is, before time becomes, for each individual, a "living time."

As for the second Freudian idea relevant to our investigation— that is, the "going back" by which one hopes to reconstitute certain decisive events of earliest childhood—it too supports a comparison with archaic behavior. We have cited a number of examples for the belief that one can reconstitute, and hence relive, the primordial events narrated in the myths. But with a few exceptions (among others, magical cures) these examples illustrate a *collective* "going back." It was the entire community, or a large part of the community, that rituals caused to relive the events reported in the myths. Psychoanalytic technique makes possible an *individual* return to the Time of the origin. Now, this existential going back is also known to archaic societies and plays an important part in certain psychophysiological techniques of the East. . . .

32. SYMBOLISM AND PSYCHOANALYSIS

Symbolic thinking is not the exclusive privilege of the child, of the poet or of the unbalanced mind: it is consubstantial with human existence, it comes before language and discursive reason. The symbol reveals certain aspects of reality—the deepest aspects—which defy any other means of knowledge. Images, symbols and myths are not irresponsible creations of the psyche; they respond to a need and fulfil a function, that of bringing to light the most hidden modalities of being. Consequently, the study of them enables us to reach a better understanding of man—of man "as he is," before he has come to terms with the conditions of History. Every historical man carries on, within himself, a great deal of prehistoric humanity. That, indeed, is a point that was never quite forgotten even in the most inclement days of positivism; for who knows better than a positivist that man is an "animal," defined and ruled by the same instincts as his brothers, the animals? That correct but incomplete description served as an exclusive frame of reference. But today we are beginning to see that the non-historical portion of every human being does not simply merge into the animal kingdom, as in the nineteenth century so many thought it did, nor ultimately into "Life"; but that, on the contrary, it bifurcates and rises right above Life. This non-historical part of the human being wears, like a medal, the imprinted memory of a richer, a more complete and almost beatific existence. When a historically conditioned being—for instance, an Occidental of our own days—allows himself to be invaded by the non-historical part of himself (which happens to him much oftener and more completely than he imagines), this is not necessarily a retrogression towards the animal stage of humanity or a redescent toward the deepest sources of organic life. Often he is re-entering, by means of the images and the symbols that then come into play, a paradisiac stage of primordial humanity (whatever its concrete existence may then have been; for this "primordial man" is admittedly an archetype never fully "realizable" in any human existence at all). In escaping from his historicity, man does not abdicate his status as a human being or abandon himself to "animality": he recovers the language, and sometimes the experience, of a "lost paradise." Dreams, waking dreams, the images of his nostalgias and of his enthusiasms, etc., are so many forces that may project the historically conditioned human being into a spiritual world that is infinitely richer than the closed world of his own "historic moment."

According to the surrealists, any man might become a poet: he need only know how to give himself up to automatic writing. Their poetic technique is fully justifiable from sound psychological doctrine. The "unconscious," as it is called, is far more "poetic"—and, let us add, more "philosophic," more "mythic"—than the conscious. It is not always necessary to know mythology in order to live out the great mythical themes. This is well known to psychologists, who discover the most beautiful mythologies in the "waking dreams" of their patients. For the unconscious is not haunted by monsters only: the gods, the goddesses, the heroes and the fairies dwell there too; moreover, the monsters of the unconscious are themselves mythological, seeing that they continue to fulfil the same functions that they fulfilled in all the mythologies—in the last analysis, that of helping man to liberate himself, to complete his initiation.

The brutal language of Freud and his orthodox disciples has often irritated *bien pensants* readers.[1] In fact, however, that brutality of language arises from a misunderstanding: it is not the sexuality in itself that is annoying, it is the ideology that Freud built upon his "pure sexuality." Fascinated by his mission—he believed himself to be the first Awakened One, whereas he was only the last of the Posi-

1. *Bien pensant*: right-thinking, orthodox. Eds.

tivists—Freud could not bring himself to see that sexuality never
has been "pure," that everywhere and always it is a polyvalent function whose primary and perhaps supreme valency is the cosmological function: so that to translate a psychic situation into sexual terms
is by no means to belittle it; for, except in the modern world, sexuality has everywhere and always been a hierophany, and the sexual
act an integral action (therefore also a means to knowledge).

The attraction that the male infant feels towards its mother, and
its corollary the Oedipus complex, are only "shocking" in so far as
they are analyzed *as such*; instead of being presented as they should
be, *as so much imagery*. For it is the Image of the Mother that is
really in question, and not this or that mother *hic et nunc*, as Freud
gives one to understand. It is the Image of the Mother which reveals
—and which *alone can reveal*—her reality and her functions, at
once cosmological, anthropological and psychological.[2] To "translate" the images into concrete terms is an operation devoid of meaning: the images comprise, it is true, all those allusions to the "concrete" that Freud has brought to light, but the reality that they are
trying to signify cannot be reduced to such "concrete" references.
The "origin" of the Images, also, is a problem that is beside the point;
it is as though one were to dispute the truth of mathematics on the
pretext that the "historical discovery" of geometry emerged from
the great works undertaken by the ancient Egyptians for the canaliza-
tion of the Delta.

Philosophically, these problems of the "origin" and of the "true
interpretation" of the Images are pointless. We need only remember
that the attraction to the mother, if we interpret it on the plane of
the immediate and "concrete"—like the desire to possess one's own
mother—can *never tell us anything more than what it says*; whereas,
if we take account of the fact that what is in question is the Image
of the Mother, this desire means many things at once, for it is the
desire to re-enter into the bliss of living Matter that is still "un-
formed," with all its possible lines of development, cosmological,
anthropological, etc. For, as we have said and as the following pages
will show, Images by their very structure are *multivalent*. If the

2. The greatest merit of C. G. Jung is that he has gone further than Freudian psychoanalysis *on the plane of psychology itself*, and has thus restored
the spiritual significance of the Image.

mind makes use of images to grasp the ultimate reality of things, it is just because reality manifests itself in contradictory ways and therefore cannot be expressed in concepts. (We know what desperate efforts have been made by various theologies and metaphysics, oriental as well as occidental, to give expression to the *coincidentia oppositorum*[3]—a mode of being that is readily, and also abundantly, conveyed by images and symbols.) It is therefore the image as such, as a whole bundle of meanings, that is *true*, and not any *one* of its meanings, nor one alone of its many frames of reference. To translate an image into a concrete terminology by restricting it to any one of its frames of reference is to do worse than mutilate it—it is to annihilate, to annul it as an instrument of cognition.

We are not unaware that in certain cases the psyche may fixate an image on one single frame of reference—that of the "concrete"; but this is already a proof of psychic disequilibrium. No doubt there are cases in which the Image of the Mother is no more than an incestuous desire for the actual mother; but psychologists are in agreement in seeing such a carnal interpretation of the symbol as a sign of psychic crisis. Upon the actual plane of dialectic of the image, any exclusive reduction is an aberration. The history of religions, too, abounds in unilateral and therefore aberrant interpretations of symbols. One could hardly adduce a single great religious symbol whose history is not that of a tragic succession of innumerable "falls." There is no heresy so monstrous or orgy so infernal, no religious cruelty, folly, absurdity, or religious magic so insane, that it may not be "justified" in its very principle by some false—*because partial and incomplete*—interpretation of a grandiose symbolism.

It is not necessary, however, to appeal to the discoveries of depth-psychology or the surrealist techniques of automatic writing in order to prove the subconscious survival, in modern man, of a mythology that is ever abundant and, in our view, of a spiritual authenticity superior to his "conscious" living. We do not need to rely on the poets or psychiatry for confirmation of the actuality and power of images and symbols. The most commonplace existence swarms with images, the most "realistic" man lives by them. Let us repeat—and what follows will richly illustrate this—that symbols never dis-

3. *Coincidentia oppositorum*: coincidence of opposites; see selection 186. Eds.

appear from the *reality* of the psyche. The aspect of them may change, but their function remains the same; one has only to look behind their latest masks. . . .

◆ ◆

Intercommunication

The process of human communication includes symbols and myths today as it did in archaic societies. We, too, have moments when the Past is not The Dead Past, when the Sacred is My Sacred; and Eliade demonstrates homologies between archaic cultures and our own culture in making these revitalizations. Regionally or locally valued symbols and sacred images are capable of being revalued, which may mean the continuation, re-emergence, or depreciation of religious meaning.

In these excerpts, Eliade deals with the interrelations between mythic values and other values, and with the ways myths are treated differently at different stages in a culture—myths "intercommunicate" in so far as they are essentially concerned with the purest manifestations of reality even amidst a process of perpetual transformation.

33. THE MYTHS OF THE MODERN WORLD

It seems unlikely that any society could completely dispense with myths, for, of what is essential in mythical behavior—the exemplary pattern, the repetition, the break with profane duration and integration into primordial time—the first two at least are consubstantial with every human condition. Thus, it is not so difficult to recognize, in all that modern people call instruction, education and didactic culture, the function that is fulfilled by the myth in archaic societies. This is so not only because myths represent both the sum of ancestral traditions and the norms it is important not to transgress, and because their transmission—generally secret, initiatory—is equivalent to the more or less official "education" of a modern society. The homology of the respective functions of the myth and of our public instruction is verified above all when we consider the

SOURCE: *MDM*/31–35.

origins of the exemplary models upheld by European education. In antiquity there was no hiatus between mythology and history: historical personages endeavored to imitate their archetypes, the gods and mythical heroes.

And the lives and deeds of those personages, in their turn, became paradigms for posterity. Livy had already assembled a rich array of models for young Romans to emulate, when Plutarch wrote his *Lives of Famous Men*, a veritable mine of examples for the centuries to come. The moral and civic virtues of these illustrious personages continued to provide the supreme criteria for European pedagogy, especially after the Renaissance. Right to the end of the nineteenth century European education for citizenship was still following the archetypes of classical antiquity, those models which had been made manifest *in illo tempore*, in that privileged interval of time which educated Europeans regarded as the highest point of the Greco-Latin culture.

But they did not think of assimilating the functions of mythology to the process of instruction, because they overlooked one of the chief characteristics of the myth, which is the creation of exemplary models for a whole society. In this, moreover, we recognize a very general human tendency; namely, to hold up one life-history as a paradigm and turn a historical personage into an archetype. This tendency survives even among the most eminent representatives of the modern mentality. As Gide has rightly observed, Goethe was highly conscious of a mission to lead a life that would be exemplary for the rest of humanity. In all that he did he was trying to *create an example*. In his own life he, in his turn, was imitating, if not the lives of the gods and mythical heroes, at least their behaviour. As Paul Valéry wrote in 1932: "He represents for us, *gentlemen of the human race*, one of our best attempts to render ourselves like gods."

But this imitation of model lives is promoted not only by means of school education. Concurrently with official pedagogy, and long after this has ceased to exert its authority, modern man is subjected to the influence of a potent if diffuse mythology that offers him a number of patterns for imitation. Heroes, real and imaginary, play an important part in the formation of European adolescents: the characters in tales of adventure, heroes of war, screen favorites, etc. This mythology is continually enriched with the growing years; we meet, one after another, the exemplary figures thrown up by changes of fashion, and we try to become like them. Critical writers have often pointed out modern versions of, for example, Don Juan, the political or the military hero, the hapless lover; of the cynic, the nihilist, the melancholy poet, and so forth: all these models are carrying on mythological traditions which their topical forms reveal in mythical behavior. The copying of these archetypes betrays a certain discontent with one's own personal history; an obscure striving to transcend one's own local, provincial history and to recover some "Great Time" or other—though it be only the mythic Time of the first surrealist or existentialist manifesto.

But an adequate analysis of the diffuse mythologies of the modern world would run into volumes: for myths and mythological images are to be found everywhere, laicized, degraded, or disguised; one only needs to be able to recognize them. We have referred to the mythological basis of New Year celebrations, and of the festivities that mark any "new beginning"; in which we can discern anew the nostalgia for a *renewal*, the yearning for the world to be renovated; that one might enter upon a new History, in a world reborn; that is, *created afresh*. It would be easy to multiply instances. The myth of the lost paradise still survives in the images of a paradisiac island or a land of innocence; a privileged land where laws are abolished and Time stands still. For it is important to underline this fact—that it is, above all, *by analyzing the attitude of the modern man toward Time that we can penetrate the disguises of his mythological behavior*. We must never forget that one of the essential functions of the myth is its provision of an opening into the Great Time, a periodic re-entry into Time primordial. This is shown by a tendency to a neglect of the present time, of what is called the "historic moment."

The Polynesians, when setting out upon a grandiose maritime adventure, are careful to deny its "novelty," its unprecedentedness, its spontaneity; for them, it is only a case of repeating the voyage that was made by some mythical hero *in illo tempore*, to "show men the way," to set an example. But thus to embark on a present adventure as the reiteration of a mythic saga is as much as to put the present time out of mind. Such disinclination to face historic time, together with an obscure desire to share in some glorious, primordial, *total* Time, is betrayed, in the case of modern people, by a sometimes desperate effort to break through the homogeneity of time, to "get beyond" duration and re-enter a time qualitatively different from that which creates, in its course, their own history. It is with this in mind that we can render the best account of what has become of myths in the world of today. For modern man, too, by means that are multiple, but homologous, is endeavouring to liberate himself from his "history" and to live in a qualitatively different temporal rhythm. And in so doing he is returning, without being aware of it, to the mythical style of life.

One can understand this better if one looks more closely at the two principal ways of "escape" in use by modern people—visual entertainment, and reading. We need not go into all the mythical precedents for our public spectacles; it is enough to recall the ritual origins of bull-fighting, racing and athletic contests; they all have this point in common, that they take place in a "concentrated time," time of a heightened intensity; a residuum of, or substitute for, magico-religious time. This "concentrated time" is also the specific dimension of the theatre and the cinema. Even if we take no account of the ritual origins and mythological structure of the drama or the film, there is still the important fact that these are two kinds of spectacle that make us live in time of a quality quite other than that of "secular duration," in a temporal rhythm, at once concentrated and articulated, which, apart from all aesthetic implications, evokes a profound echo in the spectator.

34. SYMBOLS AND CULTURES

The history of a symbolism is a fascinating study, and one that is also fully justified, since it is the best introduction to what is called the philosophy of culture. Images, archetypes and symbols are variously lived and valued; and the product of these multiple realizations of them is largely constitutive of the different "cultural styles" of life. At Ceram, an island in the Molucca Sea, as at Eleusis, we again hear of the mythical adventures of a primordial young woman—of Hainuwele, as of Kore Persephone.[1] From the struc-

SOURCE: *IS*/172–75.
1. See Ad. E. Jensen, *Hainuwele. Volkserzählungen von der Molukken-Insel Ceram* (Frankfurt-am-Main, 1939); *id.*, *Die Drei Ströme* (Leipzig, 1948), pp. 277 ff.

tural point of view, their myths show resemblances—and yet, what a difference between the Greek and the Ceramian cultures! The morphology of culture, the philosophy of styles, will be chiefly concerned with the particular forms taken on by the image of the Young Woman in Greece and in the Moluccan Isles respectively. But although, regarded as historical formations, these cultures are no longer interchangeable, being already fixed in their own styles, they are still comparable upon the plane of imagery and symbolism. It is just this perennial and universal quality of the archetypes which "saves" cultures in the last resort, and renders possible a philosophy of culture that is more than a morphology or history of styles. All culture is a "fall" into history, and is, by the same token, limited. Let no one be misled by the incomparable beauty, nobility and perfection of Greek culture; even this does not make it universally valid *as a historical phenomenon*. Try, for instance, to reveal the Greek culture to an African or to an Indonesian: it is not the admirable Greek "style" that they will understand; it is the Images that the African or Indonesian will rediscover in classical statuary or literature. What is, for an Occidental, *beautiful* and *true* in the *historic manifestation* of antique culture has no value for an Oceanian; for any culture is limited by its manifestation in the structures and styles conditioned by history. But the Images which precede and inform cultures remain eternally alive and universally accessible. A European will find it difficult to admit that the broadly humanist spiritual value and the profound meaning of such a Greek masterpiece as the Venus of Milo, for instance, does not reside—for three-quarters of the human race—in the formal perfection of that statue but in the image of Woman which it conveys. Nevertheless, if we do not manage to grasp that simple matter of fact, there is no hope of entering into any useful dialogue with a non-European.

After all, it is the presence of the images and symbols that keeps the cultures "open": starting from no matter what culture, the Australian no less than the Athenian, the "limit-situations" of man are fully revealed, owing to the symbols that sustain those cultures. If we neglect this unique spiritual foundation of the various cultural styles, the philosophy of culture will be condemned to remain no more than a morphological and historical study, without any validity for the human condition as such. If the Images were not at the same time an "opening-out" into the transcendent, one would ultimately become suffocated in any culture, however great and admirable one might believe it to be. Starting from any stylistically and historically conditioned creation of the spirit one can regain the vision of the archetype: Kore Persephone, as well as Hainuwele, reveals to us the same pathetic, yet creative destiny of the Young Woman.

The Images provide "openings" into a trans-historical world. That is by no means their least value: thanks to them, the different "histories" can intercommunicate. Much has been said about the unification of Europe by Christianity: and it is never better attested than when we see how Christianity coordinated the popular religious traditions. It was by means of Christian hagiography that the local cults—from Thrace to Scandinavia and from the Tagus to the Dnieper—were brought under a "common denominator." By the fact of their Christianization, the gods and the sacred places of the whole of Europe not only received common names but rediscovered, in a sense, their own archetypes and therefore their universal valencies: a fountain in Gaul, regarded as sacred ever since prehistoric times, but sanctified by the presence of a divine local or regional figure, became sacred *for Christianity as a whole* after its consecration to the Virgin Mary. All the slayers of dragons were assimilated to Saint George or to some other Christian hero; all the Gods of the storm to holy Elijah. From having been regional and provincial, the popular mythology became ecumenical. It is, above all, through the creation of a new mythological language common to all the populations who remained attached to their soil—and therefore in the greater danger of becoming insulated in their own ancestral traditions—that the civilizing mission of Christianity has been so remarkable. For, by Christianizing the ancient European religious heritage, it not only purified the latter, but took up, into the new spiritual dispensation of mankind, all that deserved to be "saved" of the old practices, beliefs and hopes of pre-Christian man. Even today, in popular Christianity, there are rites and beliefs surviving from the neolithic: the boiled grain in honour of the dead, for instance (the *coliva* of Eastern and Aegean Europe). The Christianization of the peasant levels of Europe was effected thanks above all to the Images: everywhere they were rediscovered, and had only to be revalorized, reintegrated and given new names.

Let us not hope, however, for an analogous phenomenon tomor-row, repeated upon the planetary scale. On the contrary, the reac-tion that will be provoked everywhere by the entry of the exotic peoples into history will be a heightening of the prestige of the autoch-thonous religions. As we have said, the West is now compelled to accept a dialogue with the other, the "exotic" or "primitive" cul-tures. It would be regrettable indeed if we entered upon this with-out having learnt anything from all the revelations vouchsafed to us by the study of symbolisms.

35. SYMBOLISM AND HISTORY

Having discussed The Symbolism of "Limit-Situations" (IS/115–19), Eliade turns here to an analogous pattern, the complex hav-ing to do with ritual ascension and magical flight (see also selections 98–100 below).

. . . Though we can discern certain historical relations (filiation, borrowings) between the different beliefs and systems (rituals, mys-ticisms, etc.) which include ascension as one of their essential ele-ments, the morphology of ascension and of the symbolism of flight far surpasses these historic connections. Even should we succeed, some day, in identifying *the* historic source from which all the rit-uals and symbolisms of ascension emanated; even were we there-fore to find ourselves in a position to specify the mechanism and the stages of their diffusion, much would still remain to be explained—the symbolism of the dream of ascension, of waking dreams and aesthetic visions, which are not only centered in the complex of as-cension and flight, but present this complex already organized, and charged with the same values that are revealed in the rituals, the myths and *philosophumena* of ascension. . . . Here, let us be con-tent with the conclusion that we have to do with non-historical ex-pressions of the same archetypal symbolism, manifesting itself in a coherent and systematic manner on the plane of the "unconscious" (of dream, hallucination or waking dream) as well as upon those of the "trans-conscious" and the conscious (aesthetic vision, ritual, mythology and *philosophumena*). And let us emphasize, by the way, that the manifestations of the unconscious and the subconscious present values, and a structure, that are in perfect agreement with those of the conscious manifestations; and that, since the latter are "reasonable," in the sense that their values are logically justifiable, we might speak of a sub- or trans-conscious "logic" which is not always heterogeneous to "normal" logic (meaning thereby classical logic, or that of good sense). Provisionally, then, let us accept the hypothesis that at least a certain zone of the subconscious is ruled by the archetypes which also dominate and organize conscious and trans-conscious experience. Hence we are entitled to regard the multiple variants of the same complexes of symbols (such as those of "ascension" and of "binding") as endless successions of "forms," which, on the different levels of dream, myth, ritual, theology, mysticism, metaphysics, etc., are trying to "realize" the archetype.

These "forms," it is true, are not all spontaneous; not all of them depend directly upon the ideal archetype; a great many of them are "historical" in the sense that they result from the evolution or the imitation of a previously existing form. Certain variants of "binding" by sorcery are rather disconcertingly simian in this respect. They give one the impression of having been copied, on their own limited plane, from pre-existent "historical forms" of magical sovereignty or funerary mythology. But here we must be careful, for it is very commonly the case that pathological variants of religious complexes also have a superficially simian appearance. What seems more reliable is the tendency of every "historical form" to approximate as nearly as possible to its archetype, even when it has been realized at a secondary or insignificant level: this can be verified everywhere in the religious history of humanity. Any local goddess tends to become *the* Great Goddess; any village anywhere *is* the "Center of the World," and any wizard whatever pretends, at the height of his ritual, to be the Universal Sovereign. It is this same tendency toward the archetype, towards the restoration of the *perfect form*—of which any myth or rite or divinity is only a variant, and often rather a pale one—that makes the history of religions possible. Without this, magico-religious experience would be continually creating transitory or evanescent forms of gods, myths, dogmas, etc.; and the student would be faced by a proliferation of ever

new types impossible to set in order. But when once it is "realized"
—"historicized"—the religious form tends to disengage itself from
its conditions in time and space and to become universal, to return
to the archetype. And, finally, the "imperialism" of the victorious
religious forms is also explainable by this tendency of every hierophany or theophany to become *everything*—that is, to sum up in
itself all manifestations of the holy, to incorporate all the immense
morphology of the sacred.

Whatever one may think of these general views, it is probable
that the magico-religious complex of "binding" corresponds closely
to an archetype, or constellation of archetypes (several of which
we have noted—the weaving of the Cosmos, the thread of human
destiny, the labyrinth, the chain of existence, etc.). The ambivalence and heterogeneity of the motives of "binding" and of "knots,"
and also of "deliverance from bonds," show once again how multiple and various are the planes on which these archetypes have been
"realized."[1] This is not, of course, to say that amidst this enormous
mass of data relating to the magico-religious facts in question one
cannot distinguish certain groups that are *historically interconnected*,
or that we have no right to regard them as dependent upon one another, or as all derived from a common source. That is what Gün-
tert, Dumézil and A. Closs have done, from different points of view,
in the Indo-European field. But one hesitates to follow Closs when,
faithful to the principles of the historico-cultural school of Vienna,
he ventures to explain this or that rite or myth of "binding," in
America or Melanesia, as historically dependent upon the same
source as the Indo-European forms. More plausible is his hypothesis of the Caucasian origin of the Indo-European ritual complex of
"binding": the Finno-Ugrians and the Turko-Tatars know nothing of rites and myths of "binding," which does seem to indicate
that the origin of this complex must be looked for in the countries
of the South. Indeed, the nearest parallels to the Georgian rite of
the chains . . . are to be found in India: on the one hand, there is the
iron ring that the sorcerer (Panda) of the Gonds wears round his
neck during the nine days of the feast of Kali-Durga (a festival that
the Gonds call *zvara*, a word derived from the Hindu *javara*, "oats,"
a proof of its agrarian origin); and, on the other hand, there are the

1. On binding and knots, see selection 174. Eds.

rings of iron about the necks of a feminine idol and of the "proto-Shiva," both found at Mohenjo-Daro. It would, of course, be rash to assume that the present rite of the Gonds is directly derived from the proto-historic culture of the Indus, but the correspondences that W. Koppers establishes between these facts are not without interest.[2]

However, the frequency of the motifs of "binding" and of "knots" in the archaic strata of the Mesopotamian religions remains still to be explained. Can this be a lateral variant which (in contrast to what happened among the Indo-Europeans) was unable to organize itself into a theological and ritual system and impose itself upon the religious life as a whole; a variant which then became multiplied to infinity, and was transformed into a divine as well as a demonic magic, annexed by every divinity and exploited by every sorcerer? What we do know is that it is only among Indo-Europeans that the "binding" complex is found organically integrated into the very structure of "terrible" sovereignty, both divine and human; and that it is only among Indo-Europeans—as M. Dumézil's researches especially have shown—that we find a *coherent system*, and one that is generally applicable at the levels of ritual, mythology, theology, etc. And yet—as the preceding pages have tried to show—this *system*, centered in the conception of the Terrible Sovereign, did not exhaust the creative power in the magico-religious forms and symbolisms relative to "binding"; and of that fact we have even tried to find an explanation upon the planes of magic, mythology and of religion itself. It may be due to the very situation of man in the world (spontaneous "origin"), or to more or less servile imitation of already existing forms (historical "genesis"). But whichever explanation one prefers, the complexity of the Indo-European conception of the sovereign and terrible god is henceforth certain. We begin to glimpse the prehistory of it, we are prepared to discern traces of foreign religious traditions. It would perhaps be incorrect to define this conception as an exclusively magical one, although its structure often invites us so to regard it. On the one hand, in India itself, we have underlined the cosmogonic and metaphysical values of the "bindings" of Varuna and Vritra, and,

2. W. Koppers, "Zentralindische Fruchtbarkeitsriten und ihre Beziehungen zur Induskultur," *Geographica Helvetica* 1 (1946), 2: 165–77.

on the other hand, the religious experiences induced by this same complex among the Hebrews prove that a very pure and profound religious life may find nourishment even in "bondage" to a God of terrible and "binding" appearance.

36. THE REVALORIZATION OF MYTHICAL TIME

The relationships between historical occurrences and their mythical elaborations are varied. In Australian Religions *(AR/74–75), Eliade discusses the process by which features of several mythical personages may be integrated into a single divine figure, and the ways in which cultures existing alongside one another may fuse elements of each other's mythology into new combinations. "One has the impression," Eliade writes (AR/75), "that a* specific paradigmatic model is being repeated again and again, as if a certain type of mythological figure and a certain religious function must be continuously reactualized, made present, active, and efficient." *The following excerpt discusses similar modifications and adaptations in other cultures.*[1]

. . . A familiar paradigmatic myth recounts the combat between the hero and a gigantic serpent, often three-headed, sometimes replaced by a marine monster (Indra, Herakles, and others; Marduk). Where tradition is still more or less a living thing, great monarchs consider themselves imitators of the primordial hero: Darius saw himself as a new Thraetaona, the mythical Iranian hero who was said to have slain a three-headed monster; for him—and through him—history was regenerated, for it was in fact the revivification, the reactualization, of a primordial heroic myth. The Pharaoh's adversaries were considered "sons of ruin, wolves, dogs," and so forth. In the *Book of Apophis* the enemies whom the Pharaoh fights are identified with the dragon Apophis, while the Pharaoh himself is assimilated with the god Re, conqueror of the dragon.

SOURCE: *CH*/37–48.
1. The interested reader may wish to read an account of Hopi-Navaho relationships becoming mythicized: Fred Eggan, "From History to Myth: A Hopi Example," *Studies in Southwestern Ethnography* (The Hague, 1967), pp. 33–35, cited by M. Titiev, *The Hopi Indians of Old Oraibi* (Ann Arbor, 1972), p. 356, n. 4. Eds.

The same transfiguration of history into myth, but from another point of view, is found in the visions of the Hebrew poets. In order to "tolerate history," that is, to endure their military defeats and political humiliations, the Hebrews interpreted contemporary events by means of the very ancient cosmogonico-heroic myth, which, though it of course admitted the provisional victory of the dragon, above all implied the dragon's final extinction through a King-Messiah. Thus their imagination gives the Gentile kings (Zadokite Fragments, IX: 19–20) the characteristics of the dragon: such is the Pompey described in the Psalms of Solomon (IX: 29), the Nebuchadrezzar presented by Jeremiah (51: 34). And in the Testament of Asher (VII:3) the Messiah kills the dragon under water (cf. Psalm 74:13).

In the case of Darius and the Pharaoh, as in that of the Hebrew Messianic tradition, we are dealing with the conception of an "elite" who interpret contemporary history by means of a myth. A series of contemporary events is given an articulation and an interpretation that conform with the atemporal model of the heroic myth. For a hypercritical modern, Darius' pretention might signify boasting or political propaganda; the mythical transformation of the Gentile kings into dragons might represent a labored invention on the part of a Hebraic minority unable to tolerate "historical reality" and seeking to console themselves at any cost by taking refuge in myth and wishful thinking. That such an interpretation is erroneous, because it makes no allowance for the structure of archaic mentality, is shown, for one thing, by the fact that popular memory applies a strictly analogous process of articulation and interpretation to historical events and personages. If the transformation into myth of the biography of Alexander the Great may be suspected of having a literary origin, and consequently be accused of artificiality, the objection has no force in regard to the documents to which we shall now refer.

Dieudonné de Gozon, third Grand Master of the Knights of St. John at Rhodes, has remained famous for having slain the dragon of Malpasso. Legend, as was natural, bestowed on him the attributes of St. George, famed for his victorious fight with the monster. Needless to say, the documents of de Gozon's period make no reference to any such combat, and it does not begin to be mentioned until some two centuries after the hero's birth. In other words, by the simple fact that he was regarded as a hero, de Gozon was identified with a category, an archetype, which, entirely disregarding his real exploits, equipped him with a mythical biography from which it was *impossible* to omit combat with a reptilian monster.

Petru Caraman, in a copiously documented study of the genesis of the historical ballad, shows that, of a definitely established historical event—the expedition against Poland by Malkoš Pasha in 1499, in an especially severe winter, which is mentioned in Leunclavius' chronicle as well as in other Polish sources, and during the course of which a whole Turkish army perished in Moldavia—the Romanian ballad that narrates the catastrophic Turkish expedition preserves almost nothing, the historical event having been completely translated into a mythical action (Malkoš Pasha fighting King Winter, etc.).[2]

This "mythicization" of historical personages appears in exactly the same way in Yugoslavian heroic poetry. Marko Kraljević, protagonist of the Yugoslavian epic, became famous for his courage during the second half of the fourteenth century. His historical existence is unquestionable, and we even know the date of his death (1394). But no sooner is Marko's historical personality received into the popular memory than it is abolished and his biography is reconstructed in accordance with the norms of myth. His mother is a *Vila*, a fairy, just as the Greek heroes were the sons of nymphs or naiads. His wife is also a *Vila*; he wins her through a ruse and takes great care to hide her wings lest she find them, take flight, and abandon him—as, by the way, in certain variants of the ballad, proves to be the case after the birth of their first child. Marko fights a three-headed dragon and kills it, after the archetypal model of Indra, Thraetaona, Herakles, and others. In accordance with the myth of the enemy brothers, he too fights with his brother Andrija and kills him. Anachronisms abound in the cycle of Marko, as in all other archaic epic cycles. Marko, who died in 1394, is now the friend, now the enemy of John Hunyadi, who distinguished himself in the wars against the Turks *ca.* 1450. . . .

. . . The historical character of the persons celebrated in epic poetry is not in question. But their historicity does not long resist the

2. Petru Caraman, "Geneza baladei istorice," *Anuarul Arhivei de Folklor* (Bucharest), I–II (1933–34).

corrosive action of mythicization. The historical event in itself, however important, does not remain in the popular memory, nor does its recollection kindle the poetic imagination save insofar as the particular historical event closely approaches a mythical model. In the *bylina*[3] devoted to the catastrophes of the Napoleonic invasion of 1812, the role of Czar Alexander I as head of the army has been forgotten, as have the name and the importance of Borodino; all that survives is the figure of Kutusov in the guise of a popular hero. In 1912, an entire Serbian brigade saw Marko Kraljević lead the charge against the castle of Prilep, which, centuries earlier, had been that popular hero's fief; a particularly heroic exploit provided sufficient occasion for the popular imagination to seize upon it and assimilate it to the traditional archetype of Marko's exploits, the more so because his own castle was at stake.

"Myth is the last—not the first—stage in the development of a hero."[4] But this only confirms the conclusion reached by many investigators (Caraman and others): the recollection of a historical event or a real personage survives in popular memory for two or three centuries at the utmost. This is because popular memory finds difficulty in retaining individual events and real figures. The structures by means of which it functions are different: categories instead of events, archetypes instead of historical personages. The historical personage is assimilated to his mythical model (hero, etc.), while the event is identified with the category of mythical actions (fight with a monster, enemy brothers, etc.). If certain epic poems preserve what is called "historical truth," this truth almost never has to do with definite persons and events, but with institutions, customs, landscapes. Thus, for example, as Murko observes, the Serbian epic poems quite accurately describe life on the Austrian-Turkish and Turkish-Venetian frontier before the Peace of Karlowitz in 1699.[5] But such "historical truths" are not concerned with personalities or events, but with traditional forms of social and political life (the "becoming" of which is slower than the "becoming" of the individual)—in a word, with archetypes.

3. *Bylina*: tales. Eds.
4. H. Munro and N. Chadwick, *The Growth of Literature* (Cambridge, 1932–40), 3: 762.
5. Matthias Murko, *La Poésie populaire épique en Yougoslavie au début du XX*e *siècle* (Paris, 1929), p. 29.

The memory of the collectivity is anhistorical. This statement implies neither a popular origin for folklore nor a collective creation for epic poetry. Murko, Chadwick, and other investigators have brought out the role of the creative personality, of the "artist," in the invention and development of epic poetry. We wish to say no more than that—quite apart from the origin of folklore themes and from the greater or lesser degree of talent in the creators of epic poetry—the memory of historical events is modified, after two or three centuries, in such a way that it can enter into the mold of the archaic mentality, which cannot accept what is individual and preserves only what is exemplary. This reduction of events to categories and of individuals to archetypes, carried out by the consciousness of the popular strata in Europe almost down to our day, is performed in conformity with archaic ontology. We might say that popular memory restores to the historical personage of modern times its meaning as imitator of the archetype and reproducer of archetypal gestures—a meaning of which the members of archaic societies have always been, and continue to be, conscious (as the examples cited in this chapter show), but which has been forgotten by such personages as Dieudonné du Gozon or Marko Kraljević.

Sometimes, though very rarely, an investigator chances to come upon the actual transformation of an event into myth. Just before the last war, the Romanian folklorist Constantin Brailoiu had occasion to record an admirable ballad in a village in Maramures. Its subject was a tragedy of love: the young suitor had been bewitched by a mountain fairy, and a few days before he was to be married, the fairy, driven by jealousy, had flung him from a cliff. The next day, shepherds found his body and, caught in a tree, his hat. They carried the body back to the village and his fiancée came to meet them; upon seeing her lover dead, she poured out a funeral lament, full of mythological allusions, a liturgical text of rustic beauty. Such was the content of the ballad. In the course of recording the variants that he was able to collect, the folklorist tried to learn the period when the tragedy had occurred; he was told that it was a very old story, which had happened "long ago." Pursuing his inquiries, however, he learned that the event had taken place not quite forty years earlier. He finally even discovered that the heroine was still alive. He went to see her and heard the story from her own lips. It was a quite commonplace tragedy: one evening her lover had slipped and fallen over a cliff; he had not died instantly; his cries had been heard by mountaineers; he had been carried to the village, where he had died soon after. At the funeral, his fiancée, with the other women of the village, had repeated the customary ritual lamentations, without the slightest allusion to the mountain fairy.

Thus, despite the presence of the principal witness, a few years had sufficed to strip the event of all historical authenticity, to transform it into a legendary tale: the jealous fairy, the murder of the young man, the discovery of the dead body, the lament, rich in mythological themes, chanted by the fiancée. Almost all the people of the village had been contemporaries of the authentic historical fact; but this fact, as such, could not satisfy them: the tragic death of a young man on the eve of his marriage was something different from a simple death by accident; it had an occult meaning that could only be revealed by its identification with the category of myth. The mythicization of the accident had not stopped at the creation of a ballad; people told the story of the jealous fairy even when they were talking freely, "prosaically," of the young man's death. When the folklorist drew the villagers' attention to the authentic version, they replied that the old woman had forgotten; that her great grief had almost destroyed her mind. It was the myth that told the truth: the real story was already only a falsification. Besides, was not the myth truer by the fact that it made the real story yield a deeper and richer meaning, revealing a tragic destiny?

The anhistorical character of popular memory, the inability of collective memory to retain historical events and individuals except insofar as it transforms them into archetypes—that is, insofar as it annuls all their historical and personal peculiarities—pose a series of new problems, which we are obliged to set aside for the moment. But at this point we have the right to ask ourselves if the importance of archetypes for the consciousness of archaic man, and the inability of popular memory to retain anything but archetypes, do not reveal to us something more than the resistance to history exhibited by traditional spirituality; if this mnemonic lacuna does not reveal the transitoriness, or at least the secondary character, of human individuality as such—that individuality whose creative spontaneity, in the last analysis, constitutes the authenticity and irreversibility of history. In any case, it is remarkable that, on the one hand, popular memory refuses to preserve the personal, historical elements of a hero's biography while, on the other hand, higher mystical experiences imply a final elevation of the personal God to the transpersonal God. It would also be instructive to compare, from this point of view, the conceptions of life after death that have been elaborated by various traditions. The transformation of the dead person into an "ancestor" corresponds to the fusion of the individual into an archetypal category. In numerous traditions (in Greece, for example) the souls of the common dead no longer possess a "memory"; that is, they lose what may be called their historical individuality. The transformation of the dead into ghosts, and so on, in a certain sense signifies their reidentification with the impersonal archetype of the ancestor. The fact that in the Greek tradition only heroes preserve their personality (i.e., their memory) after death, is easy to understand: having, in his life on earth, performed no actions which were not exemplary, the hero retains the memory of them, since, from a certain point of view, these acts were impersonal.

Leaving aside the conceptions of the transformation of the dead into "ancestors," and regarding the fact of death as a concluding of the "history" of the individual, it still seems very natural that the post-mortem memory of that history should be limited or, in other words, that the memory of passions, of events, of all that is connected with the individual strictly speaking, comes to an end at a certain moment of his existence after death. As for the objection that an impersonal survival is equivalent to a real death (inasmuch as only the personality and the memory that are connected with duration and history can be called a survival), it is valid only from the point of view of a "historical consciousness," in other words, from the point of view of modern man, for archaic consciousness accords no importance to personal memories. It is not easy to define what such a "survival of impersonal consciousness" might mean, although certain spiritual experiences afford a glimpse. What is personal and historical in the emotion we feel when we listen to the music of Bach, in the attention necessary for the solution of a mathematical problem, in the concentrated lucidity presupposed by the examination of any philosophical question? Insofar as he allows himself to be influenced by history, modern man feels himself diminished by the possibility of this impersonal survival. But interest in the "irreversible" and the "new" in history is a recent discovery in the life of humanity. On the contrary, archaic humanity, as we shall presently see, defended itself, to the utmost of its powers, against all the novelty and irreversibility which history entails.

37. THE CORRUPTION OF MYTHS[1]

A myth may degenerate into an epic legend, a ballad or a romance, or survive only in the attenuated form of "superstitions," customs, nostalgias, and so on; for all this, it loses neither its essence nor its significance. . . . The "trials," sufferings, and journeyings of the candidate for initiation survived in the tales of the sufferings and obstacles undergone by heroes of epic or drama before they gained their end (Ulysses, Aeneas, Parsifal, certain of Shakespeare's characters, Faust, and so on). All these "trials" and "sufferings" which make up the stories of epic, drama or romance can be clearly connected with the ritual sufferings and obstacles on the "way to the center." No doubt the "way" is not on the same initiatory plane, but, typologically, the wanderings of Ulysses, or the search for the Holy Grail, are echoed in the great novels of the nineteenth century, to say nothing of paperback novels, the archaic origins of whose plots are not hard to trace. If today, detective stories recount the contest between a criminal and a detective (the good genie and wicked genie, the dragon and fairy prince of the old stories), whereas a few generations back, they preferred to show an orphan prince or innocent maiden at grips with a "villain," while the fashion of a hundred and fifty years ago was for "black" and turgid romances with "black monks," "Italians," "villains," "abducted maidens," "masked protectors," and so on, such variations of detail are due to the different coloring and turn of popular sentiment; the theme does not change.

Obviously, every further step down brings with it a blurring of the conflict and characters of the drama as well as a greater num-

Source: *PCR*/431–34; cf. *Z*/67–68, on the transformation of Zalmoxis; *AR*/181 f., on the fusion of Jesus, Noah, and cargo planes.

1. Cf. also *PCR*/440 ff., on "The Degradation of Symbols"; there Eliade traces the sequence of reinterpretation of magico-religious stones. What were originally *signs* or *emblems* of deities or metaphysical abstractions become material *objects* worn on the bodies of priests or worshippers. Eds.

ber of additions supplied by "local color." But the patterns that have come down from the distant past never disappear; they do not lose the possibility of being brought back to life. They retain their point even for the "modern" consciousness. To take one of a thousand examples: Achilles and Søren Kierkegaard. Achilles, like many other heroes, did not marry, though a happy and fruitful life had been predicted for him had he done so; but in that case he would have given up becoming a *hero*, he would not have realized his unique success, would not have gained immortality. Kierkegaard passed through exactly the same existential drama with regard to Regina Olsen; he gave up marriage to remain himself, unique, that he might hope for the eternal by refusing the path of a happy life with the general run of men. He makes this clear in a fragment of his private Journal:[2] "I should be happier, in a finite sense, could I drive out this thorn I feel in my flesh; but in the infinite sense, I should be lost." In this way a mythical pattern can still be realized and is in fact realized, on the plane of existential experience, and, certainly in this case, with no thought of or influence from the myth.

The archetype is still creative even though sunk to lower and lower levels. So, for instance, with the myth of the Fortunate Islands or that of the Earthly Paradise, which obsessed not only the imagination of the secular mind, but nautical science too right up to the great age of seafaring discoveries. Almost all navigators, even those bent on a definite economic purpose (like the Indian route), *also* hoped to discover the Islands of the Blessed or the Earthly Paradise. And we all know that there were many who thought they had actually found the Island of Paradise. From the Phoenicians to the Portuguese, all the memorable geographical discoveries were the result of this myth of the land of Eden. And these voyages, searches, and discoveries were the only ones to acquire a spiritual meaning, to create culture. If the memory of Alexander's journey to India never faded it was because, being classed with the great myths, it satisfied the longing for "mythical geography"—the only sort of geography man could never do without. The Genoese commercial ventures in Crimea and the Caspian Sea, and the Venetian

2. VIII, A 56.

in Syria and in Egypt, must have meant a very advanced degree of nautical skill, and yet the mercantile routes in question "have left no memory in the history of geographical discovery."[3] On the other hand, expeditions to discover the mythical countries did not only create legends: they also brought an increase of geographical knowledge.

These islands and these new lands preserved their mythical character long after geography had become scientific. The "Isles of the Blessed" survived till Camoens, passed through the age of enlightenment and the romantic age, and have their place even in our own day. But the mythical island no longer means the garden of Eden: it is Camoens' Isle of Love, Daniel Defoe's island of the "good savage," Eminescu's Island of Euthanasius, the "exotic" isle, a land of dreams with hidden beauties, or the island of liberty, or perfect rest—or ideal holidays, or cruises on luxury steamers, to which modern man aspires in the mirages offered to him by books, films or his own imagination. The *function* of the paradisal land of perfect freedom remains unchanged; it is just that man's view of it has undergone a great many displacements—from Paradise in the biblical sense to the exotic paradise of our contemporaries' dreams. A decline, no doubt, but a very prolific one. At all levels of human experience, however ordinary, archetypes still continue to give meaning to life and to create "cultural values": the paradise of modern novels and the isle of Camoens are as significant culturally as any of the isles of medieval literature.

In other words man, whatever else he may be free of, is forever the prisoner of his own archetypal intuitions, formed at the moment when he first perceived his position in the cosmos. The longing for Paradise can be traced even in the most banal actions of the modern man. Man's concept of the *absolute* can never be completely uprooted: it can only be debased. And primitive spirituality lives on in its own way not in action, not as a thing man can effectively accomplish, but as a *nostalgia* which creates things that become values in themselves: art, the sciences, social theory, and all the other things to which men will give the whole of themselves.

3. Olschki, *Storia letteraria delle scoperte geografiche* (Florence, 1937), p. 195.

38. INFANTILIZATION OF SYMBOLIC MEANING

. . . It is often a question of variants "popular" in appearance but learned in origin—in the last case metaphysical (cosmological, etc.) —which can be easily recognized (as with the snake-stone) and bear all the marks of a process of infantilization. This process might also take place in a good many other ways. Two of the commonest are either for a "learned" symbolism to end up by being used in lower social strata so that its original meaning degenerates, or for the symbol to be taken in a childish way, over concretely, and apart from the system it belongs to . . .

For the second sort of infantilization of symbols (where there is not necessarily any "history," and "descent" from a scholarly to a popular level), there are a great many examples in Lévy-Bruhl's excellent book, *L'Expérience mystique et les symboles chez les primitifs.* Most of the evidence given by the French scholar shows the symbol as a substitute for the sacred object or as a means of establishing a relationship with it, and with this sort of substitution there must inevitably be a process of infantilization—and that not only among "primitives," but even in the most developed societies. . . .

For the moment, let us simply note the fact of the coexistence in primitive as well as developed societies of a coherent symbolism alongside an infantilized one. We will lay aside the problem of what causes this infantilization and the question whether it may be simply the effect of the human condition as such. Here we need only realize clearly that, whether coherent or degenerate, the symbol always has an important part to play in all societies. Its function remains unchanged: it is to transform a thing or an action into *something other* than that thing or action appears to be in the eyes of profane experience. . . .

39. ARCHAISM AND SURVIVAL OF IMAGES AND SYMBOLS

We must not let ourselves be led astray by the "contemporaneousness" of folklore: it very often happens that beliefs and customs

Source: *PCR*/444–45.
Source: Z/188–89.

still alive in certain eminently conservative parts of Europe (among which Romania and the Balkans must always be reckoned) reveal strata of culture more archaic than the one represented, for example, by the "classic" Greek and Roman mythologies. The fact is especially evident in regard to everything to do with the customs and magico-religious behavior of hunters and herders. But even among the agriculturalists of contemporary central Europe it has been possible to show to what an extent considerable fragments of prehistoric myths and rituals have been preserved. Systematic research in the field of Romanian and Balkan paleoethnology is still to be undertaken; but it is already established that a certain number of pre-Indo-European cultural elements have been better preserved there than anywhere else in Europe (perhaps with the exception of Ireland and the Pyrenees).

It is not always possible to reconstruct all the phases through which a religious concept passed before it crystallized into folk artistic creations. Then too, as we have already said, it is not here that the chief interest of the investigation lies. It is far more important to arrive at a thorough understanding of the original spiritual universe in which such primordial religious conceptions arose—for they are conceptions that, despite the numerous religious reevaluations they have undergone (of which the last, Christianity, was also the most radical), have nevertheless survived, at least in the form of "superstitions," of folk beliefs imbued with extremely ancient images and symbols. The fidelity of a people to one or another mythical scenario, to one or another exemplary image, tells us far more about its deeper soul than many of its historical accomplishments. . . .

40. THE DESACRALIZATION OF NATURE

. . . For religious man nature is never only natural. Experience of a radically desacralized nature is a recent discovery; moreover, it is an experience accessible only to a minority in modern societies, especially to scientists. For others, nature still exhibits a charm, a mystery, a majesty in which it is possible to decipher traces of an-

Source: SP/151-55.

cient religious values. No modern man, however irreligious, is entirely insensible to the charms of nature. We refer not only to the esthetic, recreational, or hygienic values attributed to nature, but also to a confused and almost indefinable feeling, in which, however, it is possible to recognize the memory of a debased religious experience.

A definite example of these changes and deteriorations in the religious values of nature will not be without value. We have taken our example from China, for two reasons. (1) In China, as in the West, the desacralization of nature is the work of a minority, especially of the literati; (2) nevertheless in China and in the entire Far East, the process of desacralization has never been carried to its final extreme. Even for the most sophisticated men of letters, "aesthetic contemplation" still retains an aura of religious prestige.

From the seventeenth century, arranging gardens in pottery bowls became the fashion among Chinese scholars. The bowls were filled with water, out of which rose a few stones bearing dwarf trees, flowers, and often miniature models of houses, pagodas, bridges, and human figures; they were called "Miniature Mountains" in Annamese and "Artificial Mountains" in Sino-Annamese. These names themselves suggest a cosmological signification; for, as we have seen, the mountain is a symbol of the universe.

But these miniature gardens, which became objects valued by esthetes, had a long history, or even a prehistory, which reveals a profound religious feeling for the world. Their ancestors were bowls whose perfumed water represented the sea and their cover the mountain. The cosmic structure of these objects is obvious. The mystical element was also present, for the mountain in the midst of the sea symbolized the Isles of the Blessed, a sort of Paradise in which the Taoist Immortals lived. So that we have here *a world apart*, a world in miniature, which the scholar set up in his house in order to partake in its concentrated mystical forces, *in order, through meditation, to re-establish harmony with the world*. The mountain was ornamented with grottoes, and the folklore of caves played an important role in the construction of these miniature gardens. Caves are secret retreats, dwellings of the Taoist Immortals and places of initiation. They represent a paradisal world and hence are difficult to enter (symbolism of the "narrow gate"). . . .

But this whole complex—water, trees, mountain, grotto—which

had played such a considerable role in Taoism was only the development of a still older religious idea: that of the *perfect place*, combining *completeness* (mountain and water) with *solitude*, and thus *perfect* because at once the world in miniature and Paradise, source of bliss and place of immortality. But the perfect landscape—mountain and water—was only the immemorial sacred place where, in China, at every returning spring, youths and girls met to intone alternating ritual chants and for amorous encounters. It is possible to divine the successive valorizations of the primordial sacred place. In the earliest times it was a privileged space, a closed, sanctified world, where the youths and girls met periodically to participate in the mysteries of life and cosmic fecundity. The Taoists took over this archaic cosmological schema—mountain and water—and elaborated it into a richer complex (mountain, water, grotto, trees), but reduced to the smallest scale; it was a paradisal universe in miniature, which was charged with mystical forces because apart from the profane world and in contemplation of which the Taoists sank into meditation.

The sanctity of the closed world is still discernible in the covered bowls of perfumed water symbolizing the sea and the Isles of the Blessed. This complex still served for meditation, just as the miniature gardens did in the beginning, before the fashion for them among scholars in the seventeenth century transformed them into art objects.

Yet it is worth noting that in this example we never witness a complete desacralization of the world, for in the Far East what is called the "aesthetic emotion" still retains a religious dimension, even among intellectuals. But the example of the miniature gardens shows us in what direction and by what means the desacralization of the world is accomplished. We need only imagine what an aesthetic emotion of this sort could become in a modern society, and we shall understand how the experience of cosmic sanctity can be rarefied and transformed until it becomes a purely human emotion —that, for example, of art for art's sake.

41. MYTHOLOGY, ONTOLOGY, AND HISTORY

The great mythologies—those consecrated by such poets as Homer and Hesiod and the anonymous bards of the Mahabharata, or elaborated by ritualists and theologians (as in Egypt, India, and Mesopotamia)—are more and more inclined to narrate the *gesta*[1] of the Gods. And at a certain moment in History—especially in Greece and India but also in Egypt—an elite begins to lose interest in this *divine history* and arrives (as in Greece) at the point of no longer believing in the *myths* while claiming still to believe in the *Gods*.

The history of religions here finds the first example of a conscious and definite process of "demythicization." To be sure, even in the archaic cultures a myth would sometimes be emptied of religious meaning and become a legend or a nursery tale; but other myths remained in force. In any case, there was no question here, as there was in Pre-Socratic Greece and Upanishadic India, of a cultural phenomenon of the first importance, whose consequences have proved to be incalculable. For after this "demythicization" process the Greek and Brahmanic mythologies could no longer represent for the respective elites of those countries what they had represented for their forefathers.

For these elites the "essential" was no longer to be sought in the history of the Gods but in a "primordial situation" preceding that history. We witness an attempt to go beyond mythology as divine history and to reach a primal source from which the real had flowed, to identify the womb of Being. It was in seeking the source, the principle, the *arche*, that philosophical speculation for a short time coincided with cosmogony; but it was no longer the cosmogonic myth, it was an ontological problem.

The "essential" is reached, then, by a prodigious "going back" —no longer a *regressus* obtained by ritual means, but a "going back" accomplished by an effort of thought. In this sense it could be said that the earliest philosophical speculations derive from mythologies: systematic thought endeavors to identify and understand the "absolute beginning" of which the cosmogonies tell, to

SOURCE: *MR*/110–13.
1. *Gesta*: primal sacred acts. Eds.

unveil the mystery of the Creation of the World, in short, the mystery of the appearance of Being.

But we shall see that the "demythicization" of Greek religion and the triumph, with Socrates and Plato, of strict and systematic philosophy, did not finally do away with mythical thought. Then too, it is difficult to imagine a radical outmoding of mythological thought as long as the prestige of the "origins" remains intact and as long as *forgetting* what took place *in illo tempore*—or in a transcendental World—is regarded as the chief obstacle to knowledge or salvation. We shall see to what an extent Plato is still a partisan of this archaic mode of thought. And venerable mythological themes still survive in the cosmology of Aristotle.

In all probability, the Greek genius left to itself and its own devices could not have exorcised mythical thought, even if the last God had been dethroned and his myths brought down to the level of children's tales. For, on the one hand, the Greek philosophical genius accepted the essence of mythical thought, the eternal return of things, the cyclic vision of cosmic and human life, and, on the other hand, the Greek mind did not consider that History could become an object of knowledge. Greek physics and metaphysics developed some basic themes of mythical thought: the importance of the origin, the *arche*; the essential that precedes human existence; the determinative role of memory, and so on. This, of course, does not mean that there is no solution of continuity between Greek myth and philosophy. But we can easily understand that philosophical thought could employ and continue the mythical vision of cosmic reality and human existence.

It is only through the discovery of History—more precisely by the awakening of the historical consciousness in Judaeo-Christianity and its propagation by Hegel and his successors—it is only through the radical assimilation of the new mode of being represented by human existence in the World that myth could be left behind. But we hesitate to say that mythical thought has been abolished. As we shall soon see, it managed to survive, though radically changed (if not perfectly camouflaged). And the astonishing fact is that, more than anywhere else, it survives in historiography!

42. SOLAR THEOLOGY AND ELITIST SECULARIZATION

"Sun" heroes appear pretty much throughout the world. Eliade cautions us, however, against "reducing sun heroes to solar phenomena in the way 'naturalist' mythology does" (PCR/150). Rejecting a naturalist explanation, he notes the "imperialist" nature of myths and religious forms: "Every form that gains the ascendancy tends to seek to be all, to extend its power over the whole of religious experience" (ibid.). Solar myths, therefore, include many religious themes, but the focus in selection 42 is upon the relationship between solar theologies and the rationalization of solar beliefs by rulers and then philosophers.

. . . It is worth underlining the close connection between solar theology and the elite—whether of kings, initiates, heroes or philosophers. Unlike other nature hierophanies, sun hierophanies tend to become the privilege of a closed circle, of a minority of the elect. The result is the hastening of the process of rationalization. In the Greco-Roman world the sun, having become the "fire of intelligence," ended by becoming a "cosmic principle"; from a *hierophany* it turned into an *idea* by a process rather similar to that undergone by various of the sky gods (Iho, Brahman, etc.). Even Heraclitus says that "the sun is new each day." To Plato it was the image of the good as expressed in visible things,[1] to the Orphics it was the intellect of the world. Rationalization and syncretism advanced together. Macrobius[2] relates all theology to sun-worship, and sees in the sun Apollo, Liber-Dionysos, Mars, Mercury, Aesculapius, Hercules, Serapis, Osiris, Horus, Adonis, Nemesis, Pan, Saturn, Adad, and even Jupiter. The Emperor Julian in his treatise *On the Sun King*, and Proclus in his *Hymn to the Sun*, offers their own syncretist and rationalist interpretations.

These last honours paid to the sun in the twilight of antiquity are not entirely devoid of significance; they are like palimpsests in which traces of the old writing can still be seen under the new—they still reveal traces of the true, primitive hierophanies: the de-

---

SOURCE: *PCR*/150–51; cf. Also *PCR*/125–26 on rationalization of solar hierophanies, and selection 35, above.

1. *Rep.*, 508 b, c.
2. *Saturnalia*, I, 17–23.

pendence of the sun on God which recalls the very early myth of the solarized demiurge, its connections with fecundity and plant life and so on. But generally speaking, we find there only the palest shadow of what the sun hierophanies once meant, and constant rationalization makes it paler still. The philosophers, last among the "elect," thus at last completed the secularization of what was one of the mightiest of all the cosmic hierophanies.

43. FRAGMENTS OF FORGOTTEN TRUTH

In selections 43 through 47, Eliade shows that he is not just concerned with documentation, but also with the way "myth" and "history" represent different approaches to the world, and also with the role of the professional analyst of religions. Instead of merely assembling data, the historian of religions has the responsibility to consider the cultural assimilation of his data. He will seek to learn from cultures other than our own, ignoring neither their own contexts nor our own cultural complexities, but presenting a sympathetic listening.

Certain peoples, both ancient and modern, have preserved myths or more or less fragmentary mythological memories concerning their "origins." Revered by romantic historiography, these fabulous traditions were later "demythicized" by historians of the critical and rationalistic school. Far be it from us to minimize the results of their scrupulously careful investigations. But whatever purpose they may have served in the nineteenth century, we may ask if such exercises in "demythicization" are still worth pursuing. Further efforts to prove the nonhistoricity of one or another legendary tradition would be a waste of time. There is agreement today that the myth and the legend are "true" in another sense than the "truth" of, say, a historical reality. "Myth" and "history" represent two different modes of existing in the World, two different approaches of the mind to the interpretation of the data of reality—modes of being and activities of the mind that, in any case, are not mutually

SOURCE: Z/131–32; cf. IS/161–64, on history adding new meanings to myths; examples: PCR/26–30, 52–54, 109–11.

exclusive. A people, as well as an individual, can be conscious of its responsibilities in history and courageously assume them, while at the same time continuing to enjoy the ancient myths and legends and to create new ones; for they account for other dimensions of human existence.

. . . What is of primary interest to us is to discover the meanings of the legend and to comprehend the system of spiritual values in which similar legends could arise and flourish. Though we must enter into the problem of the origin and dissemination of our mythical theme, let us make it clear from the beginning that we do not consider it crucial. The question that can elucidate the function of a legendary story in the life of a people is not: "Whence does the legend come?" Assuming that it really does come from somewhere, we must ask: "Why was precisely this legend adopted, and what was made of it after it was assimilated?"

44. THE FALLACY OF DEMYSTIFICATION

It would be useless, because ineffectual, to appeal to some reductionist principle and to demystify the behavior and ideologies of *homo religiosus* by showing, for example, that it is a matter of projections of the unconscious, or of screens raised for social, economic, political, or other reasons. Here we touch a rather thorny problem that comes again to each generation with new force.

. . . In a number of traditional archaic cultures the village, temple, or house is considered to be located at the "Center of the World." There is no sense in trying to "demystify" such a belief by drawing the attention of the reader to the fact that there exists no Center of the World and that, in any case the multiplicity of such centers is an absurd notion because it is self-contradictory. On the contrary, it is only by taking this belief seriously, by trying to clarify all its cosmological, ritual, and social implications, that one succeeds in comprehending the existential situation of a man who believes that he is at the Center of the World. All his behavior, his understanding of the world, the values he accords to life and to his own existence, arise and become articulated in a "system"

SOURCE: Q/68–71.

on the basis of this belief that his house or his village is situated near the *axis mundi*.[1]

We have cited this example in order to recall that demystification does not serve hermeneutics.[2] Consequently, whatever may be the reason for which human activities in the most distant past were charged with a religious value, the important thing for the historian of religions remains the fact that these activities *have had* religious values. This is to say that the historian of religions recognizes a spiritual unity subjacent to the history of humanity; in other terms, in studying the Australians, Vedic Indians, or whatever other ethnic group or cultural system, the historian of religions does not have a sense of moving in a world radically "foreign" to him. Certainly, the unity of the human species is accepted *de facto* in other disciplines, for example, linguistics, anthropology, sociology. But the historian of religions has the privilege of grasping this unity at the highest levels—or the deepest—and such an experience is susceptible of enriching and changing him. Today history is becoming truly universal for the first time, and so culture is in the process of becoming "planetary." The history of man from paleolithic to present times is destined to occupy the center of humanist education, whatever the local or national interpretations. The history of religions can play an essential role in this effort toward a *planétisation* of culture; it can contribute to the elaboration of a universal type of culture.

Certainly, all this will not come tomorrow. But the history of religions will be able to play this role only if the historians of religions become conscious of their responsibility, in other words, if they break free of the inferiority complexes, timidity, and immobility of the last fifty years. To remind historians of religions that they are supposed to contribute creatively to culture, that they do not have the right to produce only *Beiträge*[3] but also some *cultural values* does not mean to say that one invites them to make facile syntheses and hasty generalizations. It is on the example of an E. Rohde, a Pettazzoni, a van der Leeuw that one ought to meditate and not on that of some successful journalist. But it is the attitude of the historian of religions vis-à-vis his own discipline

1. Cf. selections 148–49. Eds.
2. Hermeneutics: the theory of interpretation. Eds.
3. *Beiträge*: "supplements," i.e., learned monographs. Eds.

that ought to change if he wants to hope for an early renewal of
this discipline. In the measure that historians of religions will not
attempt to integrate their researches in the living stream of contemporary culture, the "generalizations" and "syntheses" will be
made by dilettantes, amateurs, journalists. Or, what is no happier,
instead of a creative hermeneutics in the perspective of the history
of religions, we shall continue to submit to the audacious and irrele-
vant interpretations of religious realities made by psychologists,
sociologists, or devotees of various reductionist ideologies. And for
one or two generations yet we shall read books in which the religious realities will be explained in terms of infantile traumatisms, social organization, class conflict, and so on. Certainly such books,
including those produced by dilettantes as well as those written by
reductionists of various kinds, will continue to appear, and probably
with the same success. But the cultural milieu will not be the same
if, beside this production, appear some responsible books signed by
historians of religions. (This on the condition, understandably, that
these books of synthesis are not improvised, at the demand of a
publisher, as happens sometimes even with very respectable scholars. Obviously, "synthesis," like "analysis," is not amenable to im-
provization.)

It seems to me difficult to believe that, living in a historical moment like ours, the historians of religions will not take account of
the creative possibilities of their discipline. How to assimilate *culturally* the spiritual universes that Africa, Oceania, Southeast Asia
open to us? All these spiritual universes have a religious origin and
structure. If one does not approach them in the perspective of the
history of religions, they will disappear as spiritual universes; they
will be reduced to *facts* about social organizations, economic re-
gimes, epochs of precolonial and colonial history, etc. In other
words, they will not be grasped as spiritual creations; they will not
enrich Western and world culture—they will serve to augment
the number, already terrifying, of *documents* classified in archives,
awaiting electronic computers to take them in charge.

It may be, of course, that this time also the historians of religions
will sin through an excessive timidity and leave to other disciplines
the task of interpreting these spiritual universes (alas! already changing vertiginously, perhaps even disappearing). It may also be that,
for various reasons, the historians of religions will prefer to remain

in the subordinate situation that they have previously accepted. In this case we must expect a slow but irrevocable process of decomposition, which will end in the disappearance of the history of religions as an autonomous discipline. Thus, in one or two generations, we shall have some Latinist "specialists" in the history of Roman religion, Indianist "specialists" in one of the Indian religions, and so on. In other words, the history of religions will be endlessly fragmented and the fragments reabsorbed in the different "philologies," which today still serve it as documentary sources nourishing its own hermeneutics.

As for the problems of more general interest—for example, myth, ritual, religious symbolism, conceptions of death, initiation, etc.— they will be treated by sociologists, anthropologists, philosophers (as was done, moreover, from the beginnings of our studies, although never exclusively). But this leads us to say that the problems that preoccupy the historians of religions today *will not in themselves disappear*; it is to say only that they will be studied in other perspectives, with different methods, and in the pursual of different objectives. The void left by the disappearance of the history of religions as an autonomous discipline will not be filled. But the gravity of our responsibility will remain the same.

45. RESISTANCE TO HISTORICO-RELIGIOUS PEDAGOGY

. . . The history of religions affirms itself as both a "pedagogy," in the strong sense of that term, for it is susceptible of changing man, and a source of creation of "cultural values," whatever may be the expression of these values, historiographic, philosophic, or artistic. It is to be expected that the assumption of this function by the history of religions will be suspected, if not frankly contested, by the scientists as well as by the theologians. The former are suspicious of any effort to revalorize religion. Satisfied with the vertiginous secularization of Western societies, the scientists are inclined to suspect obscurantism or nostalgia in authors who see in the different forms of religion something other than superstition, ignorance, or, at the most, psychological behavior, social institutions, and rudimentary ideologies fortunately left behind by the progress of

SOURCE: Q/66–68.

scientific thought and the triumph of technology. Such a suspicion does not belong exclusively to the scientists in the strict sense of the term; it is equally shared by a large number of sociologists, anthropologists, and social scientists who conduct themselves, not as humanists, but as naturalists with respect to their object of study. But it is necessary to accept such resistance gracefully; it is inevitable in any culture that can still develop in complete freedom.

As for the theologians, their hesitations are explained by various reasons. On the one hand, they are rather suspicious of historico-religious hermeneutics that might encourage syncretism or religious dilettantism or, worse yet, raise doubt about the uniqueness of the Judaeo-Christian revelation. On the other hand, the history of religions envisages, in the end, cultural *creation* and the *modification* of man. The humanist culture poses an embarrassing problem for theologians and for Christians in general: What do Athens and Jerusalem have in common? We do not intend to discuss here this problem that still obsesses certain theologians. But it would be futile to ignore the fact that nearly all the contemporary philosophies and ideologies recognize that man's specific mode of being in the universe inevitably forces him to be a creator of culture. Whatever the point of departure for an analysis that seeks a definition of man, whether one utilizes the psychological, sociological, or existentialist approach, or some criterion borrowed from classical philosophies, one comes, explicitly or implicitly, to characterize man as a creator of culture (i.e., language, institutions, techniques, arts, etc.). And all the methods of liberation of man—economic, political, psychological—are justified by their final goal: to deliver man from his chains or his complexes in order to open him to the world of the spirit and to render him *culturally creative*. Moreover, for the unbelievers or the irreligious all that a theologian, indeed, simply a Christian, considers heterogeneous in the sphere of culture—the mystery of faith, the sacramental life, etc.—is included in the sphere of "cultural creations." And one cannot deny the character of "cultural facts," at least to the *historical expressions* of the Christian religious experience. Many contemporary theologians have already accepted the presuppositions of the sociology of religion and are ready to accept the inevitability of technology. The fact that there are some theologies of culture indicates the direction in which contemporary theological thought is moving.

But for the historian of religions the problem is posed differently, although not necessarily in contradiction with the theologies of culture. The historian of religions knows that what one calls "profane culture" is a comparatively recent manifestation in the history of the spirit. In the beginning, every cultural creation—tools, institutions, arts, ideologies, etc.—was a religious expression or had a religious justification or source. This is not always evident to a nonspecialist, particularly because he is used to conceiving "religion" according to the forms familiar in Western societies or in the great Asian religions. It is conceded that dance, poetry, or wisdom were, in their beginning, religious; one has difficulty in imagining that alimentation or sexuality, an essential work (hunting, fishing, agriculture, etc.), the tools employed, or a habitation, equally participate in the sacred. And yet one of the embarrassing difficulties for the historian of religions is that the nearer he approaches to "origins," the greater becomes the number of "religious facts." This is so much so that in certain cases (for example, in archaic or prehistoric societies) one asks himself what is *not* or has not once been "sacred" or connected with the sacred. . . .

46. "DEMYSTIFICATION IN REVERSE"

In the Western world, initiation in the traditional and strict sense of the term has disappeared long ago. But initiatory symbols and scenarios survive on the unconscious level, especially in dreams and imaginary universes. It is significant that these survivals are studied today with an interest difficult to imagine fifty or sixty years ago. Freud has shown that certain existential tendencies and decisions are not conscious. Consequently, the strong attraction toward literary and artistic works with an initiatory structure is highly revealing. Marxism and depth psychology have illustrated the efficacy of the so-called demystification when one wants to discover the *true* —or the *original*—significance of a behavior, an action, or a cultural creation. In our case, we have to attempt a demystification in reverse; that is to say, we have to "demystify" the apparently profane worlds and languages of literature, plastic arts, and cinema in order to disclose their "sacred" elements, although it is, of course, an ignored, camouflaged, or degraded "sacred." In a desacralized world such as ours, the "sacred" is present and active chiefly in the imaginary universes. But imaginary experiences are part of the total human being, no less important than his diurnal experiences. This means that the nostalgia for initiatory trials and scenarios, nostalgia deciphered in so many literary and plastic works, reveals modern man's longing for a total and definitive renewal, for a *renovatio* capable of radically changing his existence.

It is for this reason that the recent research which we have rapidly reviewed does not represent only contributions interesting to such disciplines as history of religions, ethnology, orientalism, or literary criticism; they can also be interpreted as characteristic expressions in the cultural configuration of modern times.

47. COSMIC RELIGIOSITY

Contemporary man seems to be areligious, in comparison with humans of earlier cultures. Eliade discusses this areligiosity, and suggests that modern artists represent one force in our society where the areligiosity is now balanced by a return to more primary origins, archetypal configurations, and indeed a nonsectarian "cosmic religiosity."

. . . Man in Western society . . . wants to be, and declares himself to be areligious—completely rid of the sacred. On the level of everyday consciousness, he is perhaps right; but he continues to participate in the sacred through his dreams and his daydreams, through certain attitudes (his "love of nature," for example), through his distractions (reading, theater), through his nostalgias and his impulses. That is to say, modern man has "forgotten" religion, but the sacred survives, buried in his unconscious. One might speak, in Judaeo-Christian terms, of a "second fall." According to the biblical tradition, man lost after the fall the possibility of "encountering" and "understanding" God; but he kept enough intelligence to rediscover the traces of God in nature and in his own consciousness. After the "second fall" (which corresponds to the death of God as proclaimed by Nietzsche) modern man has lost the possibility of experiencing the sacred at the conscious level, but he continues to be nourished and guided by his unconscious. And, as certain psychologists never stop telling us, the unconscious is "religious" in the sense that it is constituted of impulses and images charged with sacrality.

We are not about to develop these few remarks about the religious situation of modern man here. But if what we are saying is true of Western man in general, it is *a fortiori* still more true of the artist. And this is for the simple reason that the artist does not act passively either in regard to the Cosmos or in regard to the unconscious. Without telling us, perhaps without knowing it, the artist penetrates—at times dangerously—into the depths of the world and his own psyche. From cubism to tachism, we are witnessing a desperate effort on the part of the artist to free himself of the "surface" of things and to penetrate into matter in order to lay bare its ultimate structures. To abolish form and volume, to descend into the interior of substance while revealing its secret or larval modalities—these are not, according to the artist, operations undertaken for the purpose of some sort of objective knowledge; they are ventures provoked by his desire to grasp the deepest meaning of his plastic universe.

In certain instances, the artist's approach to his material recovers and recapitulates a religiosity of an extremely archaic variety that disappeared from the Western world thousands of years ago. Such, for example, is Brancusi's attitude towards stone, an attitude comparable to the solicitude, the fear, and the veneration addressed by a neolithic man towards certain stones that constituted hierophanies —that is to say, that revealed simultaneously the sacred and ultimate, irreducible reality.[1]

1. Professor Eliade reflects on Brancusi's work in "The Sacred and the Modern Artist," *Criterion* 4, no. 2 (Divinity School of the University of Chicago, Spring, 1965): 22–27.
His own involvement in the arts is seen in his reputation on the Continent as a novelist (several articles in J. M. Kitagawa and C. H. Long, eds., *Myths and Symbols: Studies in Honor of Mircea Eliade* [Chicago, 1969], pp. 343–406, discuss his fiction). The only English translations available are *Two Tales of the Occult*, trans. W. A. Coates (New York, 1970), two short stories in Eric Tappe, ed., *Fantastic Tales* (London, 1969), pp. 10–75, and another story, "With the Gypsy Girls," *Denver Quarterly* 8, no. 2 (Spring, 1973): 13–58. Eds.

The two specific characteristics of modern art, namely the destruction of traditional forms and the fascination for the formless, for the elementary modes of matter, are susceptible to religious interpretation. The hierophanization of matter, that is to say the discovery of the sacred manifested through the substance itself, characterizes that which has been called "cosmic religiosity," that type of religious experience which dominated the world before the advent of Judaism and which is still alive in "primitive" and Asiatic societies. To be sure, this cosmic religiosity was forgotten in the West in the wake of the triumph of Christianity. Emptied of every religious value or meaning, nature could become the "object" *par excellence* of scientific investigation. From a certain viewpoint, Western science can be called the immediate heir of Judaeo-Christianity. It was the prophets, the apostles, and their successors the missionaries who convinced the Western world that a rock (which certain people have considered to be sacred) was only a rock, that the planets and the stars were only cosmic *objects*—that is to say, that they were not (and could not be) either gods or angels or demons. It is as a result of this long process of the desacralization of Nature that the Westerner has managed to *see* a natural object where his ancestors saw hierophanies, sacred presences.

But the contemporary artist seems to be going beyond his objectivizing scientific perspective. Nothing could convince Brancusi that a rock was only a fragment of inert matter; like his Carpathian ancestors, like all neolithic men, he sensed a presence in the rock, a power, an "intention" that one can only call "sacred." But what is particularly significant is the fascination for the infrastructures of matter and for the embryonic modes of life. In effect we might say that for the past three generations we have been witnessing a series of "destructions" of the world (that is to say, of the traditional artistic universe) undertaken courageously and at times savagely for the purpose of recreating or recovering another, new, and "pure" universe, uncorrupted by time and history. We have analyzed elsewhere the secret significance of this will to demolish formal worlds made empty and banal by the usage of time and to reduce them to their elementary modes, and ultimately to their original *materia prima*. This fascination for the elementary modes of matter betrays a desire to deliver oneself from the weight of mortal form, the nostalgia to immerse oneself in an auroral world.

The public has evidently been particularly struck by the icono-clastic and anarchistic furor of contemporary artists. But in these vast demolitions one can always read like a watermark the hope of creating a new universe, more viable because it is more true, that is, more adequate to the actual situation of man.

However, one of the characteristics of "cosmic religion" both among the primitives and among the peoples of the Ancient Near East is precisely this need for periodically annihilating the world, through the medium of ritual, in order to be able to recreate it. The annual reiteration of the cosmogony implies a provisory reac-tualization of chaos, a symbolic regression of the world to a state of virtuality. Simply because it has been going on, the world has wilted, it has lost its freshness, its purity and its original creative power. One cannot "repair" the world; one must annihilate it in order to recreate it.

There is no question of homologizing this primitive mythico-ritual scenario to modern artistic experiences. But it is not without interest for us to note a certain convergence existing between, on the one hand, repeated efforts at destroying traditional artistic lan-guage and attraction towards the elementary modes of life and mat-ter and, on the other hand, the archaic conceptions which we have tried to evoke. From a structural point of view, the attitude of the artist in regard to the cosmos and to life recalls to a certain extent the ideology implicit in "cosmic religion."

It may be, furthermore, that the fascination for matter may be only a precursory sign of a new philosophical and religious orienta-tion. Teilhard de Chardin, for example, proposes to "carry Christ . . . to the heart of the realities reputed to be the most dangerous, the most naturalistic, the most pagan." For the Father wanted to be "the evangelist of Christ in the universe."

2

Rites—Birth, Renewal, Religious Experience, and Technique

Introduction

The relationship between myths and rituals is a matter of great debate among scholars. Generally, one can say that the old hegemony of the "ritual dominant" school is broken: we no longer think that we have to demonstrate a ritual performance underlying every myth, or show relationship to a hypothetical "New Year's festival" for each Ancient Near Eastern myth. But some intimate relationship between *many* myths and *many* rituals would be affirmed today by just about every scholar.

We have opted, in designing this book, for a mechanical separation of myths and rituals, following convenience of design rather than Eliade. In this second chapter, then, we have selected materials on rituals that are often discussed by Eliade in conjunction with mythic counterparts. Surely one of the strengths of his approach has been its focus upon rituals as well as myths, and we are pleased that the design of this book allows a fairly strong emphasis upon the ritual aspects.

The selections begin with Eliade's own methodological remarks about the interrelationships of myths and rituals; we will see below that he considers rituals to have the same divine prototypes as all activities of societies, but we are especially concerned with religious rites, and so the discussion soon moves on to analysis of the ways in which ritual means are used to distinguish the "sacred" from the "profane," a distinction that has been widely discussed by Eliade's followers and opponents.[1]

The third major section demonstrates the various types of rituals that societies use to express, mold, or inform religious experience, and includes specific materials on such topics as initiations, death rituals, circumcision, marriage. Also treated are the more elaborate corporate rituals of societies, such as the periodic renewal rituals known as New Year's festivals, modern cargo cults, and the whole series of sacrifice motifs.

The medicine man and the shaman—both religious specialists—are of interest in that the mythic beliefs of a people are often demonstrated most dramatically in the careers of their sacred tech-

1. See, for example, L. E. Shiner, "Sacred Space, Profane Space, Human Space," *Journ. Amer. Acad. Religion* 40 (1972): 425–36.

nicians; this is a field where Eliade's name is highly respected, and we have given representative selections on these topics.

Finally, we have given considerable space to discussion of the role of religious societies and religious mysticism—again an area in which Eliade is well known, and an area that discloses in concrete practices the religious belief systems of various peoples.

◆ ◆

Ritual Performance, Mythic Archetype

Rituals are given sanctification and rationalization in a culture by being referred to supposedly divine prototypes. Rituals periodically reconfirm the sacredness of their origins and re-establish "sacred" (as opposed to "profane") time for the community performing the rituals.

◆

THE RELATION BETWEEN MYTHS AND RITUALS

48. DIVINE MODELS OF RITUALS

Every ritual has a divine model, an archetype; this fact is well enough known for us to confine ourselves to recalling a few examples. "We must do what the gods did in the beginning" (*Satapatha Brahmana*, VII, 2, 1, 4). "Thus the gods did; thus men do" (*Taittiriya Brahmana*, I, 5, 9, 4). This Indian adage summarizes all the theory underlying rituals in all countries. We find the theory among so-called primitive peoples no less than we do in developed cultures. The aborigines of southeastern Australia, for example, practice circumcision with a stone knife because it was thus that their ancestors taught them to do; the Amazulu Negroes do likewise because Unkulunkulu (civilizing hero) decreed *in illo tempore*: "Let men circumcise, that they may not be boys."[1] The hako ceremony of the Pawnee Indians was revealed to the priests by Tirawa, the

SOURCE: *CH*/21–23.

1. A. W. Howitt, *The Native Tribes of South-East Australia* (London, 1904), pp. 645 ff.; Henry Callaway, *The Religious System of the Amazulu* (London, 1869), p. 58.

supreme God, at the beginning of time. Among the Sakalavas of Madagascar, "all domestic, social, national, and religious customs and ceremonies must be observed in conformity with the *lilin-draza*, i.e., with the established customs and unwritten laws inherited from the ancestors . . ."[2] It is useless to multiply examples; all religious acts are held to have been founded by gods, civilizing heroes, or mythical ancestors.[3] It may be mentioned in passing that, among primitives, not only do rituals have their mythical model but any human act whatever acquires effectiveness to the extent to which it exactly *repeats* an act performed at the beginning of time by a god, a hero, or an ancestor. . . .

However, as we said, such a "theory" does not justify ritual only in primitive cultures. In the Egypt of the later centuries, for example, the power of rite and word possessed by the priests was due to imitation of the primordial gesture of the god Thoth, who had created the world by the force of his word. Iranian tradition knows that religious festivals were instituted by Ormazd to commemorate the stages of the cosmic Creation, which continued for a year. At the end of each period—representing, respectively, the creation of the sky, the waters, the earth, plants, animals, and man —Ormazd rested for five days, thus instituting the principal Mazdean festivals (cf. *Bundahisn*, I, A 18ff.). Man only repeats the act of the Creation; his religious calendar commemorates, in the space of a year, all the cosmogonic phases which took place *ab origine*. In fact, the sacred year ceaselessly repeats the Creation; man is contemporary with the cosmogony and with the anthropogony because ritual projects him into the mythical epoch of the beginning. A bacchant, through his orgiastic rites, imitates the drama of the suffering Dionysos; an Orphic, through his initiation ceremonial, repeats the original gestures of Orpheus.

The Judaeo-Christian Sabbath is also an *imitatio dei*. The Sabbath rest reproduces the primordial gesture of the Lord, for it was on the seventh day of the Creation that God ". . . rested . . . from all his work which he had made" (Genesis 2:2). The message of the Saviour is first of all an example which demands imitation. After

2. Arnold van Gennep, *Tabou et totémisme à Madagascar* (Paris, 1904), pp. 27 ff.

3. Cf. Gerardus van der Leeuw, *Phänomenologie der Religion* (Tübingen, 1933), pp. 349 ff., 360 ff.

washing his disciples' feet, Jesus said to them: "For I have given you an example, that ye should do as I have done to you" (John 13:15). Humility is only a virtue; but humility practiced after the Saviour's example is a religious act and a means of salvation: ". . . as I have loved you, that ye also love one another" (John 13:34; 15:12). This Christian love is consecrated by the example of Jesus. Its actual practice annuls the sin of the human condition and makes man divine. He who believes in Jesus can do what He did; his limitations and impotence are abolished. "He that believeth on me, the works that I do shall he do also . . ." (John 14:12). The liturgy is precisely a commemoration of the life and Passion of the Saviour. . . . This commemoration is in fact a reactualization of those days. . . .

49. MYTHIC PROTOTYPES

It would be tedious, as well as purposeless . . . to mention the mythical prototypes of all human activities. The fact that human justice, for example, which is founded upon the idea of "law," has a celestial and transcendent model in the cosmic norms (*tao, artha, rta, tzedek, themis,* etc.) is too well known for us to insist upon it. That "works of human art are imitations of those of divine art" (*Aitareya Brahmana,* VI, 27)[1] is likewise a leitmotiv of archaic aesthetics, as Ananda K. Coomaraswamy's studies have admirably shown.[2] It is interesting to observe that the state of beatitude itself, *eudaimonia,* is an imitation of the divine condition, not to mention the various kinds of *enthousiasmos* created in the soul of man by the repetition of certain acts realized by the gods *in illo tempore* (Dionysiac orgy, etc.): "The Working of the Gods, eminent in blessedness, will be one apt for Contemplative Speculation: and of all human Workings that will have the greatest capacity for Happiness which is nearest akin to this" (Aristotle, *Nicomachean Ethics,* 1178*b,* 21);[3] "to become as like as possible to God" (Plato, *Theaetetus,* 176*e*); "haec hominis est perfectio, similitudo Dei" (St. Thomas Aquinas).

SOURCE: *CH*/31–32.
1. Cf. Plato, *Laws,* 667–69; *Statesman,* 306*d,* etc.
2. See especially Coomaraswamy, "The Philosophy of Mediæval and Oriental Art," *Zalmoxis* (Paris and Bucharest), I (1938): 20–49, and *Figures of Speech or Figures of Thought* (London, 1946), pp. 29–96.
3. Trans. D. P. Chase, *The Ethics of Aristotle,* (London, 1934).

We must add that, for the traditional societies, all the important acts of life were revealed *ab origine* by gods or heroes. Men only repeat these exemplary and paradigmatic gestures *ad infinitum*. . . .

50. REITERATING THE CREATIVITY OF THE DREAM TIME

The religious actuality of Ungud and the Wondjina [in Australia] is demonstrated particularly by their powers as the source of rain and of fertility. In northern Kimberley, if a rock painting is touched by a man from the proper totemic clan, rain will fall and the spirit children will become available for incarnation. Likewise, repainting the animal and vegetal images is said to increase the respective species. "In one part of Northern Kimberley the man who finds a spirit-child, must go to the gallery and touch up the painting of the rainbow-serpent, and even paint a representation of a spirit-child, so that the former will be able to keep up the supply."[1]

These spirit children are pre-existent; while unborn, they sojourn in well-defined sites. "The pre-existent spirits for the most part came into existence during the long-past dream time as a result of some activity of a hero; according to some beliefs, however, they are made from time to time or brought into being by a creative hero whose activity was not confined to the past but is continuous."[2] Among the Ungarinyin, Petri found only the belief that the spirit-child is found by the father in a dream; cohabitation is considered merely to be a pleasure.[3] Similar conceptions are attested among many neighboring tribes of the Ungarinyin. And, as is well known, all over central Australia procreation is not directly associated with sexual intercourse.

The "increase" of the animal and vegetal species by repainting the rock figures is not a magic act but a religious one.[4] The men are *reactivating their contact with the source of life*. Thus the cre-

SOURCE: *AR*/80–83.

1. A. B. Elkin, *The Australian Aborigines*, 3d ed. (Sydney, 1954), p. 201; cf. Elkin, "Rock Paintings of North-West Australia," *Oceania* I (1930): 262.
2. Elkin, *The Australian Aborigines*, p. 198.
3. Helmut Petri, *Sterbende Welt in Nordwest-Australien* (Braunschweig, 1954), p. 163.
4. *Ibid.*, pp. 197 ff., 215–16; Elkin, *Aborigines*, pp. 199 ff.

ativity of the Dream Time is again reiterated on earth. The same principle informs the "increase ceremonies" (*intichiuma* or, to use the more general Aranda term, *mbanbiuma*) of the central Australians, so abundantly described by Spencer and Gillen. The ceremonies are carried out at spots associated with the mythical history of the tribe: that is, the sites where the totemic Heroes performed the rituals for the first time. Each actor represents a mythical Ancestor; as a matter of fact, he reincarnates that Ancestor. Each ceremony lasts only a few minutes, and while it is being performed the audience chants a song narrating the mythical episode in process of re-enactment. At the conclusion of each ritual, the old men explain its meaning and the meaning of the decorations and symbols to the newly initiated youth.[5] As Strehlow puts it, the chorus of old men "chant those verses of the traditional song which commemorate the original scene in the life of the ancestor which has been dramatized in the ceremony witnessed by them."[6]

Among the Karadjeri, notes Piddington, the increase ceremonies take place at specific centers, founded during the *bugari* ("dream") time, where the spirits of the species had been left in abundance. Sometimes the performers chant a song associated with the mythical origin of the community.[7]

Thus the increase of a natural species is brought about through a reactivation of the contact with the Dream Time Heroes, and *such a reactivation can be brought about by refreshing the rock paintings (Wondjina), by re-enacting the original creative act, or by chanting the myth* in which this episode is narrated.

51. ARCHETYPES OF PROFANE ACTIVITIES

. . . We might say that the archaic world knows nothing of "profane" activities: every act which has a definite meaning—hunting, fishing, agriculture; games, conflicts, sexuality in some way par-

Source: *CH*/27–29.
5. Baldwin Spencer and F. J. Gillen, *Native Tribes of the Northern Territory of Australia* (London, 1914), pp. 318 ff.
6. T. G. H. Strehlow, *Aranda Traditions* (Melbourne, 1947), pp. 56–57.
7. Ralph Piddington, "Totemic System of the Karadjeri Tribe," *Oceania* II (1932): 377–78.

ticipates in the sacred. . . . The only profane activities are those
which have no mythical meaning, that is, which lack exemplary
models. Thus we may say that every responsible activity in pursuit
of a definite end is, for the archaic world, a ritual. But since the
majority of these activities have undergone a long process of desacralization and have, in modern societies, become profane, we
have thought it proper to group them separately.

Take the dance, for example. All dances were originally sacred;
in other words, they had an extrahuman model. The model may in
some cases have been a totemic or emblematic animal, whose motions were reproduced to conjure up its concrete presence through
magic, to increase its numbers, to obtain incorporation into the animal on the part of man. In other cases the model may have been
revealed by a divinity (for example the pyrrhic, the martial dance
created by Athena) or by a hero (cf. Theseus' dance in the Labyrinth). The dance may be executed to acquire food, to honor the
dead, or to assure good order in the cosmos. It may take place
upon the occasion of initiations, of magico-religious ceremonies, of
marriages, and so on. But all these details need not be discussed here.
What is of interest to us is its presumed extrahuman origin (for
every dance was created *in illo tempore*, in the mythical period,
by an ancestor, a totemic animal, a god, or a hero). Choreographic
rhythms have their model outside of the profane life of man;
whether they reproduce the movements of the totemic or emblematic animal, or the motions of the stars; whether they themselves
constitute rituals (labyrinthine steps, leaps, gestures performed with
ceremonial instruments)—a dance always imitates an archetypal gesture or commemorates a mythical moment. In a word, it is a repetition, and consequently a reactualization, of *illud tempus*, "those
days." . . .

52. RECOVERING SACRED TIME

*Rituals periodically reconfirm myths—which establish what
mythic man believes to be real by referring to the transmundane
and transhuman level.*

Source: MR/140; cf. SP/99–102, on the imitatio dei; PCR/319–21, on ritual
contests.

This "transcendent" world of Gods, the Heroes, and the mythical Ancestors is accessible because archaic man does not accept the irreversibility of Time. As we have repeatedly seen, ritual abolishes profane, chronological Time and recovers the sacred Time of myth. Man becomes contemporary with the exploits that the Gods performed *in illo tempore.* On the one hand, this revolt against the irreversibility of Time helps man to "construct reality"; on the other, it frees him from the weight of dead Time, assures him that he is able to abolish the past, to begin his life anew, and to re-create his world. . . .

53. WHAT "KNOWING THE MYTHS" MEANS

Australian totemic myths usually consist in a rather monotonous narrative of peregrinations by mythical ancestors or totemic animals. They tell how, in the "Dream Time" (*alcheringa*)—that is, mythical time—these Supernatural Beings made their appearance on earth and set out on long journeys, stopping now and again to change the landscape or to produce certain animals and plants, and finally vanished underground. But knowledge of these myths is essential for the life of the Australians. The myths teach them how to repeat the creative acts of the Supernatural Beings, and hence how to ensure the multiplication of such-and-such an animal or plant.

These myths are told to the neophytes during their initiation. Or rather, they are "performed," that is, re-enacted. "When the youths go through the various initiation ceremonies, [their instructors] perform a series of ceremonies before them; these, though carried out exactly like those of the cult proper—except for certain characteristic particulars—do not aim at the multiplication and growth of the totem in question but are simply intended to show those who are to be raised, or have just been raised, to the rank of men the way to perform these cult rituals."[1]

We see, then, that the "story" narrated by the myth constitutes a

Source: *MR*/14–15.

1. C. Strehlow, *Die Aranda-und-Loritja-Stämme in Zentral-Australien*, vol. 3, pp. 1–2; L. Lévy-Bruhl, *La mythologie primitive* (Paris, 1935), p. 123; cf. *CH*/4 ff.

"knowledge" which is esoteric, not only because it is secret and is handed on during the course of an initiation but also because the "knowledge" is accompanied by a magico-religious power. For knowing the origin of an object, an animal, a plant, and so on is equivalent to acquiring a magical power over them by which they can be controlled, multiplied, or reproduced at will. . . .

54. CREATING NEW PERSPECTIVES

. . . The imitation of the paradigmatic acts of the Gods, the Heroes, and the mythical Ancestors [however] does not produce an "eternal repetition of the same thing," a total cultural immobility. Ethnology knows of no single people that has not changed in the course of time, that has not had a "history." At first sight the man of the archaic societies seems only to repeat the same archetypal act forever. But actually he is tirelessly conquering the World, organizing it, transforming the landscape of nature into a cultural milieu. For by virtue of the exemplary model revealed by the cosmogonic myth, man, too, becomes creative. Though the myths, by presenting themselves as sacrosanct models, would seem to paralyze human initiative, actually they stimulate man to create, they are constantly opening new perspectives to his inventiveness. . . .

◆

The Sacred and the Profane

To the religious mind, all of nature is available for being made "sacred," including geographical areas, localized spaces within buildings, animals, and people, and even time itself. Examples here illustrate the actual process of making something sacred, and center around Eliade's concept of "hierophany"—the act of manifestation of the sacred, as he explains in the first excerpt.

55. WHEN THE SACRED MANIFESTS ITSELF

Man becomes aware of the sacred because it manifests itself, shows itself, as something wholly different from the profane. To designate

Source: *MR*/140–41.
Source: *SP*/11–13; cf. *SP*/63–65, on religious man's quest for Being.

the *act of manifestation* of the sacred, we have proposed the term *hierophany*. It is a fitting term, because it does not imply anything further; it expresses no more than is implicit in its etymological content, *i.e.*, that *something sacred shows itself to us*.[1] It could be said that the history of religions—from the most primitive to the most highly developed—is constituted by a great number of hierophanies, by manifestations of sacred realities. From the most elementary hierophany—*e.g.*, manifestation of the sacred in some ordinary object, a stone or a tree—to the supreme hierophany (which, for a Christian, is the incarnation of God in Jesus Christ) there is no solution of continuity. In each case we are confronted by the same mysterious act—the manifestation of something of a wholly different order, a reality that does not belong to our world, in objects that are an integral part of our natural "profane" world.

The modern Occidental experiences a certain uneasiness before many manifestations of the sacred. He finds it difficult to accept the fact that, for many human beings, the sacred can be manifested in stones or trees, for example. But . . . what is involved is not a veneration of the stone in itself, a cult of the tree in itself. The sacred tree, the sacred stone are not adored as stone or tree; they are worshipped precisely because they are *hierophanies*, because they show something that is no longer stone or tree but the *sacred*, the *ganz andere*.[2]

It is impossible to overemphasize the paradox represented by every hierophany, even the most elementary. By manifesting the sacred, any object becomes *something else*, yet it continues to remain *itself*, for it continues to participate in its surrounding cosmic milieu. A *sacred* stone remains a *stone*; apparently (or, more precisely, from the profane point of view), nothing distinguishes it from all other stones. But for those to whom a stone reveals itself as sacred, its immediate reality is transmuted into a supernatural reality. In other words, for those who have a religious experience all nature is capable of revealing itself as cosmic sacrality. The cosmos in its entirety can become a hierophany.

The man of the archaic societies tends to live as much as possible *in* the sacred or in close proximity to consecrated objects. The ten-

---

1. Cf. *PCR*/7 ff.
2. *Ganz andere*: totally other. Eds.

dency is perfectly understandable, because, for primitives as for the man of all premodern societies, the *sacred* is equivalent to a *power*, and, in the last analysis, to *reality*. The sacred is saturated with *being*. Sacred power means reality and at the same time enduringness and efficacity. The polarity sacred-profane is often expressed as an opposition between *real* and *unreal* or pseudoreal. (Naturally, we must not expect to find the archaic languages in possession of this philosophical terminology, *real-unreal*, etc.; but we find the *thing*.) Thus it is easy to understand that religious man deeply desires *to be*, to participate in *reality*, to be saturated with power. . . .

. . . It should be said at once that the *completely* profane world, the wholly desacralized cosmos, is a recent discovery in the history of the human spirit. It does not devolve upon us to show by what historical processes and as the result of what changes in spiritual attitudes and behavior modern man has desacralized his world and assumed a profane existence. For our purpose it is enough to observe that desacralization pervades the entire experience of the non-religious man of modern societies and that, in consequence, he finds it increasingly difficult to rediscover the existential dimensions of religious man in the archaic societies.

56. TWO MODES OF BEING IN THE WORLD

The abyss that divides the two modalities of experience—sacred and profane—[becomes apparent when one considers] sacred space and the ritual building of the human habitation, or the varieties of the religious experience of time, or the relations of religious man to nature and the world of tools, or the consecration of human life itself, the sacrality with which man's vital functions (food, sex, work and so on) can be charged. Simply calling to mind what the city or the house, nature, tools, or work have become for modern and non-religious man will show with the utmost vividness all that distinguishes such a man from a man belonging to any archaic society, or even from a peasant of Christian Europe. For modern consciousness, a physiological act—eating, sex, and so on—is in sum only an organic phenomenon, however much it may still be encumbered

Source: *SP*/14.

by taboos (imposing, for example, particular rules for "eating properly" or forbidding some sexual behavior disapproved by social morality). But for the primitive, such an act is never simply physiological; it is, or can become, a sacrament, that is, a communion with the sacred.

The reader will very soon realize that *sacred* and *profane* are two modes of being in the world, two existential situations assumed by man in the course of his history. . . .

57. HOMOGENEITY OF SPACE AND HIEROPHANY

For religious man, space is not homogeneous; he experiences interruptions, breaks in it; some parts of space are qualitatively different from others. "Draw not nigh hither," says the Lord to Moses; "put off thy shoes from off thy feet, for the place whereon thou standest is holy ground" (Exodus, 3, 5). There is, then, a sacred space, and hence a strong, significant space; there are other spaces that are not sacred and so are without structure or consistency, amorphous. Nor is this all. For religious man, this spatial nonhomogeneity finds expression in the experience of an opposition between space that is sacred—the only *real* and *real-ly* existing space—and all other space, the formless expanse surrounding it.

It must be said at once that the religious experience of the non-homogeneity of space is a primordial experience, homologizable to a founding of the world. It is not a matter of theoretical speculation, but of a primary religious experience that precedes all reflection on the world. For it is the break effected in space that allows the world to be constituted, because it reveals the fixed point, the central axis for all future orientation. When the sacred manifests itself in any hierophany, there is not only a break in the homogeneity of space; there is also revelation of an absolute reality, opposed to the nonreality of the vast surrounding expanse. The manifestation of the sacred ontologically founds the world. In the homogeneous and infinite expanse, in which no point of reference is possible and hence no *orientation* can be established, the hierophany reveals an absolute fixed point, a center.

SOURCE: *SP*/20–24.

So it is clear to what a degree the discovery—that is, the revelation—of a sacred space possesses existential value for religious man; for nothing can begin, nothing can be *done*, without a previous orientation. . . . The profane experience, on the contrary, maintains the homogeneity and hence the relativity of space. No *true* orientation is now possible, for the fixed point no longer enjoys a unique ontological status; it appears and disappears in accordance with the needs of the day. Properly speaking, there is no longer any world, there are only fragments of a shattered universe, an amorphous mass consisting of an infinite number of more or less neutral places in which man moves, governed and driven by the obligations of an existence incorporated into an industrial society.

Yet this experience of profane space still includes values that to some extent recall the nonhomogeneity peculiar to the religious experience of space. There are, for example, privileged places, qualitatively different from all others—a man's birthplace, or the scenes of his first love, or certain places in the first foreign city he visited in youth. Even for the most frankly nonreligious man, all these places still retain an exceptional, a unique quality; they are the "holy places" of his private universe, as if it were in such spots that he had received the revelation of a reality *other* than that in which he participates through his ordinary daily life. . . .

58. SACRED PLACES AND THEIR SIGNS

Every sacred space implies a hierophany, an irruption of the sacred that results in detaching a territory from the surrounding cosmic milieu and making it qualitatively different. When Jacob in his dream at Haran saw a ladder reaching to heaven, with angels ascending and descending on it, and heard the Lord speaking from above it, saying: "I am the Lord God of Abraham," he awoke and was afraid and cried out: "How dreadful is this place: this is none other but the house of God, and this is the gate of heaven." And he took the stone that had been his pillow, and set it up as a monument, and poured oil on the top of it. He called the place Beth-el, that is, house of God (Genesis, 28, 12–19). The symbolism implicit in the

SOURCE: *SP*/26–29.

expression "gate of heaven" is rich and complex; the theophany that occurs in a place consecrates it by the very fact that it makes it open above—that is, in communication with heaven, the paradoxical point of passage from one mode of being to another. We shall soon see even clearer examples—sanctuaries that are "doors of the gods" and hence places of passage between heaven and earth.

Often there is no need for a theophany or hierophany properly speaking; some *sign* suffices to indicate the sacredness of a place. "According to the legend, the *marabout*[1] who founded El Hamel at the end of the sixteenth century stopped to spend the night near a spring and planted his stick in the ground. The next morning, when he went for it to resume his journey, he found that it had taken root and that buds had sprouted on it. He considered this a sign of God's will and settled in that place."[2] In such cases the *sign*, fraught with religious meaning, introduces an absolute element and puts an end to relativity and confusion. *Something* that does not belong to this world has manifested itself apodictically[3] and in so doing has indicated an orientation or determined a course of conduct.

When no sign manifests itself, it is *provoked*. For example, a sort of *evocation* is performed with the help of animals; it is they who *show* what place is fit to receive the sanctuary or the village. This amounts to an evocation of sacred forms or figures for the immediate purpose of establishing an *orientation* in the homogeneity of space. A *sign* is asked, to put an end to the tension and anxiety caused by relativity and disorientation—in short, to reveal an absolute point of support. For example, a wild animal is hunted, and the sanctuary is built at the place where it is killed. Or a domestic animal—such as a bull—is turned loose; some days later it is searched for and sacrificed at the place where it is found. Later the altar will be raised there and the village will be built around the altar. In all these cases, the sacrality of a place is revealed by animals. This is as much as to say that men are not free to *choose* the sacred site, that they only seek for it and find it by the help of mysterious signs.

These few examples have shown the different means by which

---

1. *Marabout*: hermit. Eds.
2. René Basset, in *Revue des Traditions Populaires* (1907), 22: 287.
3. Apodictically: once for all, determinatively. Eds.

religious man receives the revelation of a sacred place. In each case the hierophany has annulled the homogeneity of space and revealed a fixed point. But since religious man cannot live except in an atmosphere impregnated with the sacred, we must expect to find a large number of techniques for consecrating space. As we saw, the sacred is pre-eminently the *real*, at once power, efficacity, the source of life and fecundity. Religious man's desire to live *in the sacred* is in fact equivalent to his desire to take up his abode in objective reality, not to let himself be paralyzed by the never-ceasing relativity of purely subjective experiences, to live in a real and effective world, and not in an illusion. This behavior is documented on every plane of religious man's existence, but it is particularly evident in his desire to move about only in a sanctified world, that is, in a sacred space. This is the reason for the elaboration of techniques of *orientation* which, properly speaking, are techniques for the *construction* of sacred space. But we must not suppose that *human* work is in question here, that it is through his own efforts that man can consecrate a space. In reality the ritual by which he constructs a sacred space is efficacious in the measure in which *it reproduces the work of the gods.* . . .

59. HISTORICAL AND UNIVERSAL ASPECTS

All the definitions given up till now of the religious phenomenon have one thing in common: each has its own way of showing that the sacred and the religious life are the opposite of the profane and the secular life. But as soon as you start to fix limits to the notion of the sacred you come upon difficulties—difficulties both theoretical and practical. . . . Almost everywhere the religious phenomena we see are complex, suggesting a long historical evolution. . . .

We are faced with rites, myths, divine forms, sacred and venerated objects, symbols, cosmologies, theologoumena, consecrated men, animals and plants, sacred places, and more. And each category has its own morphology—of a branching and luxuriant richness. We have to deal with a vast and ill-assorted mass of material, with a Melanesian cosmogony myth or Brahman sacrifice having as much

Source: *PCR*/1–4.

right to our consideration as the mystical writings of a St. Teresa or a Nichiren, an Australian totem, a primitive initiation rite, the symbolism of the Borobudur temple, the ceremonial costumes and dances of a Siberian shaman, the sacred stones to be found in so many places, agricultural ceremonies, the myths and rites of the Great Goddesses, the enthroning of an ancient king or the superstitions attaching to precious stones. Each must be considered as a hierophany in as much as it expresses in some way some modality of the sacred and some moment in its history; that is to say, some one of the many kinds of experience the sacred man has had. Each is valuable for two things it tells us: because it is a hierophany, it reveals some modality of the sacred; because it is a historical incident, it reveals some attitude man has had toward the sacred. . . .

The fact that a hierophany is always a historical event (that is to say, always occurs in some definite situation) does not lessen its universal quality. Some hierophanies have a purely local purpose; others have, or attain, world-wide significance. The Indians, for instance, venerate a certain tree called *ashvattha*; the manifestation of the sacred in that particular plant species has meaning only for them, for only to them is the *ashvattha* anything more than just a tree. Consequently, that hierophany is not only of a certain time (as every hierophany must be), but also of a certain place. However, the Indians also have the symbol of a cosmic tree (*Axis Mundi*), and this mythico-symbolic hierophany is universal, for we find Cosmic Trees everywhere among ancient civilizations. But note that the *ashvattha* is venerated because it embodies the sacred significance of the universe in constant renewal of life; it is venerated, in fact, because it embodies, is part of, or symbolizes the universe as represented by all the Cosmic Trees in all mythologies.[1] But although the *ashvattha* is explained by the same symbolism that we find in the Cosmic Tree, the hierophany which turns a particular plant-form into a sacred tree has a meaning only in the eyes of that particular Indian society.

To give a further example—in this case a hierophany which was left behind by the actual history of the people concerned: the Semites at one time in their history adored the divine couple made up of Ba'al, the god of hurricane and fecundity, and Belit, the goddess of

1. Cf. *PCR*/section 99.

fertility (particularly the fertility of the earth). The Jewish prophets held these cults to be sacrilegious. From their standpoint—from
the standpoint, that is, of those Semites who had, as a result of the
Mosaic reforms, reached a higher, purer and more complete conception of the Deity—such a criticism was perfectly justified. And yet
the old Semitic cult of Ba'al and Belit *was* a hierophany: it showed
(though in unhealthy and monstrous forms) the religious value of
organic life, the elementary forces of blood, sexuality and fecundity. This revelation maintained its importance, if not for thousands,
at least for hundreds of years. As a hierophany it held sway till the
time when it was replaced by another, which—completed in the
religious experience of an elite—proved itself more satisfying and
of greater perfection. The "divine form" of Yahweh prevailed
over the "divine form" of Ba'al; it mainfested a more perfect holiness, it sanctified life without in any way allowing to run wild the
elementary forces concentrated in the cult of Ba'al, it revealed a
spiritual economy in which man's life and destiny gained a totally
new value; at the same time it made possible a richer religious experience, a communion with God at once purer and more complete.
This hierophany of Yahweh had the final victory; because it represented a universal modality of the sacred, it was by its very nature open to other cultures; it became, by means of Christianity, of
world-wide religious value. It can be seen, then that some hierophanies are, or can in this way become, of universal value and significance, whereas others may remain local or of one period—they
are not open to other cultures, and fall eventually into oblivion even
in the society which produced them.

60. KRATOPHANIES (MANIFESTATIONS OF POWER)

. . . This ambivalence of the sacred is not only in the psychological order (in that it attracts or repels), but also in the order of values; the sacred is at once "sacred" and "defiled." Commenting on
Virgil's phrase *auri sacra fames*, Servius[1] remarks quite rightly that
sacer can mean at the same time accursed and holy. Eustathius[2]

SOURCE: *PCR*/14–18.
1. *Ad. Aen.*, III, 75.
2. *Ad Iliadem*, XXIII, 429.

notes the same double meaning with *hagios*, which can express at once the notion "pure" and the notion "polluted." And we find this same ambivalence of the sacred appearing in the early Semitic world and among the Egyptians.

All the negative valuations of "defilement" (contact with corpses, criminals and so on) result from this ambivalence of hierophanies and kratophanies. It is dangerous to come near any defiled or consecrated object in a profane state—without, that is, the proper ritual preparation. What is called taboo—from a Polynesian word that the ethnologists have taken over—means just that: it is the fact of things, or places, or persons, being cut off, or "forbidden," because contact with them is dangerous. Generally speaking, any object, action or person which either has naturally, or acquires by some shift of ontological level, force of a nature more or less uncertain, is, or becomes, taboo. The study of the nature of taboos and of things, persons or actions that are taboo, is quite a rich one. You can get some idea of this by glancing through Part II of Frazer's *The Golden Bough, Taboo and the Perils of the Soul*, or Webster's huge catalogue in his book *Taboo*. Here I will simply quote a few examples from Van Gennep's monograph, *Tabou et totémisme à Madagascar*.[3] The Malagasy word that corresponds to *taboo* is *fady, faly*, which means what is "sacred, forbidden, out of bounds, incestuous, ill-omened"[4]—really, in other words, what is dangerous.[5] *Fady* were "the first horses brought on to the island, rabbits brought by the missionaries, all new merchandise, above all, European medicines" (salt, iodine, rum, pepper and so on).[6] Here again, you see, we find the unusual and the new transformed into kratophanies. They are generally mere lightning-flashes, for such taboos are not lasting in their nature; as soon as things are known and handled, fitted into the primitive cosmos, they lose all power to upset the order of things. Another Malagasy term is *loza*, which the dictionaries tell us means: "All that is outside, or runs counter to, the natural order; any public calamity, or unusual misfortune, sin against the natural law, or incest."[7]

3. (Paris, 1904).
4. *Ibid.*, p. 12.
5. *Ibid.*, p. 23.
6. *Ibid.*, p. 37.
7. *Ibid.*, p. 36.

Clearly death and sickness are phenomena that also come within the category of the unusual and frightening. Among the Malagasy and elsewhere the sick and the dead are sharply cut off from the rest of the community by "interdicts." It is forbidden to touch a dead man, to look at him, or to mention his name. There is another series of taboos applying to women, to sex, to birth, and to certain special situations: for instance, a soldier may not eat a cock that has died in a battle, nor any animal whatever killed by a *sagaie*; one must not slay any male animal in the house of a man who is armed or at war.[8] In each case the interdict is a provisional one due to a temporary concentration of powers in some person or thing (a woman, a corpse, a sick man), or to someone's being in a dangerous situation (a soldier, huntsman, fisherman, and so on). But there are also permanent taboos: those attaching to a king or a holy man, to a name or to iron, or to certain cosmic regions (the mountain of Ambondrome which none dares approach,[9] lakes, rivers, or even whole islands).[10] In this case the taboos are based on the specific mode of being of the person or thing tabooed. A king is an absolute power-house of forces simply because he *is* a king, and one must take certain precautions before approaching him; he must not be directly looked at or touched; nor must he be directly spoken to, and so on. In some areas the ruler must not touch the ground, for he has enough power in him to destroy it completely; he has to be carried, or to walk on carpets all the time. The precautions considered necessary when dealing with saints, priests and medicine men come from the same kind of fear. As for the "tabooing" of certain metals (iron, for instance), or certain places (islands and mountains), there may be various causes: the novelty of the metal, or the fact that it is used for secret work (by sorcerers and smelters, for instance); the majesty or the mystery of certain mountains, or the fact that they cannot be fitted, or have not as yet been fitted, into the local universe, and so on.

However, the elements of the taboo itself are always the same: certain things, or persons, or places belong in some way to a different order of being, and therefore any contact with them will produce an upheaval at the ontological level which might well prove

8. *Ibid.*, pp. 20 ff.
9. *Ibid.*, p. 194.
10. *Ibid.*, pp. 195 ff.

fatal. You will find the fear of such an upheaval—ever present because of this difference in the order of being between what is profane and what is hierophany or kratophany—even in people's approach to consecrated food, or food thought to contain certain magico-religious powers. "Certain food is so holy that it must not be eaten at all, or be eaten in small portions only."[11] That is why in Morocco people visiting the sanctuaries or celebrating feasts eat only very little of the dishes they are offered. When the wheat is on the threshing-floor one tries to increase its "power" (*baraka*), yet if too much power accumulates it may become harmful.[12] For the same reason, if honey is too rich in *baraka* it is dangerous.[13]

. . . What can be noted now is the self-contradictory attitude displayed by man in regard to all that is sacred (using the word in its widest sense). On the one hand he hopes to secure and strengthen his own reality by the most fruitful contact he can attain with hierophanies and kratophanies; on the other, he fears he may lose it completely if he is totally lifted to a plane of being higher than his natural profane state; he longs to go beyond it and yet cannot wholly leave it. This ambivalence of attitude towards the sacred is found not only where you have negative hierophanies and kratophanies (fear of corpses, of spirits, of anything defiled), but even in the most developed religious forms. Even such theophanies as are revealed by the great Christian mystics repel the vast majority of men as well as attracting them (the repulsion may appear under many forms—hatred, scorn, fear, wilful ignorance, or sarcasm).

As I have said, manifestations of the unaccustomed and the extraordinary generally provoke fear and withdrawal. Some particular examples of taboos, and of actions, things and persons tabooed have shown us the workings by which kratophanies of the unusual, the disastrous, the mysterious, and so on, are set apart from the round of ordinary experience. This setting-apart sometimes has positive effects; it does not merely isolate, it elevates. Thus ugliness and deformities, while marking out those who possess them, at the same time make them sacred. So, among the Ojibwa Indians, "many receive the name of witches without making any pretension to the

11. Westermarck, *Pagan Survivals in Mahommedan Civilization* (London, 1933), p. 125.

12. *Ibid.*, p. 126.

13. *Ibid.*

art, merely because they are deformed or ill-looking." All esteemed witches or wizards among these Indians are, as a rule, "remarkably wicked, of a ragged appearance and forbidding countenance." Reade states that in the Congo all dwarfs and albinos are elevated to the priesthood. "There is little doubt that the awe with which this class of men is generally regarded, in consequence of their outward appearance, also accounts for the belief that they are endowed with secret powers."[14]

That shamans, sorcerers and medicine men are recruited for preference from among neuropaths and those who are nervously unbalanced is due to this same value set upon the unaccustomed and the extraordinary. Such stigmata indicate a choice; those who have them must simply submit to the divinity or the spirits who have thus singled them out, by becoming priests, shamans, or sorcerers. Obviously natural external qualities of this sort (ugliness, weakness, nervous disorder, etc.) are not the only means by which the choice is made; the religious calling often comes as a result of certain ritual practices to which the candidate submits willingly or otherwise, or of a selection carried out by the fetish-priest.[15] But in every case a choice has been made.

61. SACRED PLACES: REPEATING THE HIEROPHANY

Every kratophany and hierophany whatsoever transforms the place where it occurs: hitherto profane, it is thenceforward a sacred area. Thus, for the Kanakas of New Caledonia "an innumerable number of rocks and stones with holes in them in the bush have some special meaning. One crevice is helpful if you want rain, another is the dwelling of a totem, one place is haunted by the vengeful spirit of a murdered man. In this way the whole landscape is alive and its smallest details all mean something; nature is rich with human history."[1] To put it more precisely, nature undergoes a

SOURCE: *PCR*/367–69.

14. G. Landtmann, quoted by N. Söderblom, *The Living God* (Oxford, 1933), p. 15.

15. *Ibid.*, pp. 13 f.

1. M. Leenhardt, *Notes d'archéologie néocalédonienne* (Paris, 1930), pp. 23–24.

transformation from the very fact of the kratophany or hierophany, and emerges from it charged with myth. Basing himself on the observations of A. R. Radcliffe-Brown and A. P. Elkin, L. Lévy-Bruhl very rightly stressed the hierophanic nature of sacred places: "To these natives, a sacred spot never presents itself to the mind in isolation. It is always part of a complexus of things which includes the plant or animal species which flourish there at various seasons, as well as the mythical heroes who lived, roamed or created something there and who are often embodied in the very soil, the ceremonies which take place there from time to time, and all the emotions aroused by the whole."[2]

According to Radcliffe-Brown, the cardinal point in this complexus is "the local totem center," and in most cases one can discern a direct bond—a "participation," to use Lévy-Bruhl's word—between the totem centers and certain figures of myth who lived at the beginning of time and created totem centers then. It was in these places of hierophany that the primal revelations were made; it was there that man was taught how to nourish himself and to ensure a constant supply of food. And all the rituals connected with food celebrated within the limits of the sacred area, of the totem center, are simply an imitation and reproduction of the things done *in illo tempore* by mythical beings. "Bandicoots, oppossum, fish and bees were pulled out of their holes in this way by the heroes of olden (*bugari*) times."[3]

In fact the idea of a sacred place involves the notion of repeating the primeval hierophany which consecrated the place by marking it out, by cutting it off from the profane space around it. . . . A similar idea of repetition underlies the idea of sacred time, and is the basis of innumerable ritual systems as well as, in general, of the hopes all religious men entertain in regard to personal salvation. A sacred place is what it is because of the permanent nature of the hierophany that first consecrated it. That is why one Bolivian tribe, when they feel the need to renew their energy and vitality, go back to the place supposed to have been the cradle of their ancestors.[4] The hierophany therefore does not merely sanctify a given seg-

2. *L'Expérience mystique et les symboles chez les primitifs* (Paris, 1938), p. 183.
3. *Ibid.*, p. 186.
4. *Ibid.*, pp. 188–89.

ment of undifferentiated profane space; it goes so far as to ensure that sacredness will continue there. *There*, in *that* place, the hierophany repeats itself. In this way the place becomes an inexhaustible source of power and sacredness and enables man, simply by entering it, to have a share in the power, to hold communion with the sacredness. This elementary notion of the place's becoming, by means of a hierophany, a permanent "center" of the sacred, governs and explains a whole collection of systems often complex and detailed. But however diverse and variously elaborated these sacred spaces may be, they all present one trait in common: there is always a clearly marked space which makes it possible (though under very varied forms) to communicate with the sacred.

The continuity of hierophanies is what explains the permanence of these consecrated spots. That the Australian aboriginals went on visiting their traditional secret places was not because of any pressure of economic circumstances, for, as Elkin points out, once they had entered the service of the white men, they depended on them for their food and their whole economy.[5] What they sought from these places was to remain in mystical union with the land and with the ancestors who founded the civilization of the tribe. The need the aboriginals felt to preserve their contact with those scenes of hierophany was essentially a religious one; it was nothing more than the need to remain in direct communion with a "center" producing the sacred. And these centers were only with the greatest difficulty robbed of their importance—they were passed on like an heirloom from tribe to tribe, from religion to religion. The rocks, springs, caves and woods venerated from the earliest historic times are still, in different forms, held as sacred by Christian communities today. A superficial observer might well see this aspect of popular piety as a "superstition," and see in it a proof that all community religious life is largely made up of things inherited from prehistoric times. But what the continuity of the sacred places in fact indicates is the autonomy of hierophanies; the sacred expresses itself according to the laws of its own dialectic and this expression comes to man *from without*. If the "choice" of his sacred places were left to man himself, then there could be no explanation for this continuity.

5. *Ibid.*, pp. 186–87.

62. THE CONSECRATION OF SPACE

In actual fact, the place is never "chosen" by man; it is merely discovered by him;[1] in other words, the sacred place in some way or another reveals itself to him. The "revelation" is not necessarily effected by means of anything directly hierophanic in nature (*this* place, *this* spring, *this* tree); it is sometimes effected through the medium of a traditional technique originating out of and based upon a system of cosmology. One such process used to "discover" these sites was the *orientatio*.

. . . It was not only for sanctuaries that spaces must be consecrated. The building of a house also involves a transformation of profane space. But, in every case, the spot is always indicated by something *else*, whether that something be a dazzling hierophany, or the principles of cosmology underlying *orientatio* and geomancy, or perhaps, simplest, of all, by a "sign" expressing a hierophany, generally some animal. Sartori assembled a great deal of evidence[2] on the animal signs thought to ratify places chosen for human dwellings. The presence or absence of ants or mice may be a decisive sign of a hierophany. Sometimes a domestic animal, a bull for instance, is let loose; in a few days' time a search is made for it, and it is sacrificed on the spot where it is found, which is recognized as the place for building the town.

"All sanctuaries are consecrated by a theophany," wrote Robertson Smith.[3] But this does not mean that *only* sanctuaries are so consecrated. The remark can be extended to cover the dwellings of hermits or saints, and, in general, all human habitations. . . . All the places where saints lived, prayed, or were buried are, in turn, sanctified, and are therefore cut off from the profane space around them by an enclosure or an embankment of stones. . . . Piles of stones mark places where men died violent deaths (by lightning, snake-bite and so on); in that case the violent death possesses the value of a kratophany or hierophany.

SOURCE: *PCR*/369–71.
1. Van der Leeuw, *Religion in Essence and Manifestation* (London, 1938), pp. 393–94.
2. "Über das Bauopfer," *Zeitschrift für Ethnologie* (1898), 30: 4, n.
3. *Lectures on the Religion of the Semites*, 3d ed. (London, 1946), p. 436.

The enclosure, wall, or circle of stones surrounding a sacred place—these are among the most ancient of known forms of man-made sanctuary. They existed as early as the early Indus civilization . . . and the Aegean civilization. The enclosure does not only imply and indeed signify the continued presence of a kratophany or hierophany within its bounds; it also serves the purpose of preserving profane man from the danger to which he would expose himself by entering it without due care. The sacred is always dangerous to anyone who comes into contact with it unprepared, without having gone through the "gestures of approach" that every religious act demands. . . . Hence the innumerable rites and prescriptions (bare feet, and so on) relative to entering the temple, of which we have plentiful evidence among the Semites and other Mediterranean peoples. The ritual importance of the thresholds of temple and house is also due to this same separating function of limits, though it may have taken on varying interpretations and values over the course of time.

The same is the case with city walls: long before they were military erections, they were a magic defense, for they marked out from the midst of a "chaotic" space, peopled with demons and phantoms (see further on), an enclosure, a place that was organized, made cosmic, in other words, provided with a "center." That is why in times of crisis (like a siege or an epidemic), the whole population would gather to go round the city walls in procession and thus reinforce their magico-religious quality of limits and ramparts. This procession round the city, with all its apparatus of relics and candles, was sometimes purely magico-symbolic in form: the patron saint of the town was offered a coiled waxen taper as long as the perimeter of the wall. All these defense measures were extremely widespread in the Middle Ages, but are to be found in other times and in other places as well. In northern India, for instance, in time of epidemic, a circle is described around the village to stop the demons of the illness from entering its enclosure.[4] The "magic circle," in such favor in so many magico-religious rituals, is intended to set up a partition between the two areas of different kinds.

4. W. Crooke, *Popular Religion and Folklore of Northern India* (London, 1894), 1: 103–42.

63. THE SACRED GROUND (AUSTRALIA)

Details of actually preparing a temporarily sacred area can be studied in the archaic ceremonies of the Australian puberty ceremonies.

. . . Preparations for an initiation festival require a long time. Several months pass between the time when the older men decide to assemble the tribes and the beginning of the ceremony proper. The headman of the inviting tribe sends messengers, carrying bull-roarers (long, thin, narrow pieces of wood attached to a string; when whirled through the air, they make a roaring sound), to the other headmen, to whom they announce the decision. Since the Australian tribes are divided into two intermarrying "classes," class A undertakes the initiation of the youths of class B, and vice versa. In short, the novices are initiated by their potential fathers-in-law.[1] It is unnecessary to rehearse all the details of the preparation for the "bora," as the ceremony is called among the tribes of eastern Australia. Only one fact requires mention; in everything that is done, the greatest precautions are taken to keep the women from knowing what is afoot.

Broadly speaking, the initiation ceremony comprises the following phases: first, the preparation of the "sacred ground," where the men will remain in isolation during the festival; second, the separation of the novices from their mothers and, in general, from all women; third, their segregation in the bush, or in a special isolated camp, where they will be instructed in the religious traditions of the tribe; fourth, certain operations performed on the novices, usually circumcision, the extraction of a tooth, or subincision, but sometimes scarring or pulling out the hair. Throughout the period of the initiation, the novices must behave in a special way; they undergo a number of ordeals, and are subjected to various dietary taboos and prohibitions. Each element of this complex initiatory scenario has a religious meaning. It is primarily these meanings, and their articulation into a religious vision of the world, that I hope to bring out in these pages.

SOURCE: *RSI*/4–7.
1. H. Webster, *Primitive Secret Societies: A Study in Early Politics and Religion* (New York, 1908), p. 139, n. 2.

As we just saw, the bora always involves the preliminary preparation of a sacred ground. The Yuin, the Wiradjuri, the Kamilaroi,
and some of the Queensland tribes prepare a circular ring of earth,
in which the preliminary ceremonies will later take place, and, at
some distance from it, a small sacred enclosure. These two constructions are connected by a path, along which the men of the inviting tribe set up various images and sacred emblems. As the tribal
contingents arrive, the men are led along the path and shown the
images. There is dancing every night, sometimes continuing for several weeks, until the last contingent arrives.

Mathews gives a quite detailed description of the sacred ground
as prepared by the Kamilaroi. It consists of two circles. The larger,
which is seventy feet in diameter, has a pole three yards high in
the center "with a bunch of emu's feathers tied on the top."[2] In
the smaller circle two young trees are fixed in the ground with
their roots in the air. After the ritual separation from the women,
two older men—sometimes described as wizards—climb these trees
and there chant the traditions of the bora.[3] (These trees, which are
anointed with human blood,[4] have a symbolism that we shall inves-
tigate later.) The two circles are connected by a path. On either
side of the path a number of figures are drawn on the ground or
modeled in clay. The largest, which is fifteen feet in height, is that
of the Supreme Being, Baiamai. A couple represents the mythical
Ancestors, and a group of twelve human figures stands for the
young men who were with Baiamai in his first camp. Other figures
represent animals and nests. The neophytes are not allowed to look
at these images, which will be destroyed by fire before the end of
their initiation. But they can examine them on the occasion of the
next bora.[5] This detail is interesting; it shows that religious instruction does not end with initiation, but continues and has several
degrees.

According to Mathews, the "bora ground represents Baiamai's first
camp, the people who were with him while there and the gifts he

2. R. H. Mathews, "The Bora or Initiation Ceremonies of the Kamilaroi
Tribe," *Journal of the Royal Anthropological Institute* 24 (1895): 411–27; 25
(1896): 318–39.
3. *Ibid.*, 24, p. 422.
4. *Ibid.*, 25, p. 325.
5. *Ibid.*, 24, pp. 414 ff.

presented them with."[6] This is to say that the participants in the initiation ceremony reactualize the mythical period in which the bora was held for the first time. Not only does the sacred ground imitate the exemplary model, Baiamai's first camp, but the ritual performed reiterates Baiamai's gestures and acts. In short, what is involved is a reactualization of Baiamai's creative work, and hence a regeneration of the world. For the sacred ground is at once an image of the world (*imago mundi*) and a world sanctified by the presence of the Divine Being. During the bora the participants return to the mythical, sacred time when Baiamai was present on earth and founded the mysteries that are now being performed. The participants become in some sort contemporaries of the first bora, the bora that took place in the beginning, in the Dream Time (*bugari* or "Alchera times"), to use the Australian expression. This is why the initiation ceremonies are so important in the lives of the aborigines; by performing them, they reintegrate the sacred Time of the beginning of things, they commune with the presence of Baiamai and the other mythical Beings, and, finally, they regenerate the world, for the world is renewed by the reproduction of its exemplary model, Baiamai's first camp.

. . . The sacred ground plays an essential role in Australian initiation ceremonies because it represents the image of the primordial world as it was when the Divine Being was on earth. The women, children, and uninitiated are kept at a distance, and even the novices will acquire merely a superficial knowledge of it. Only as initiates, at the time of the next bora, will they examine the images set along the path between the two circles. Having been taught the mythology of the tribe, they will be able to understand the symbols.

64. THE HETEROGENEOUSNESS OF TIME

Not only nature, but time *itself can be ritually manipulated. This extract, and the following one, demonstrate how time can be sanctified.*

Source: *PCR*/388–91.
6. *Ibid.*, 24, p. 418.

The problem we come to [here] is among the most difficult in all religious phenomenology. The difficulty is not simply that magico-religious time and profane time are different in nature; it is rather more the fact that the actual *experience of time as such* is not always the same for primitive peoples as for modern Western man. Sacred time does differ from profane; but, further, this latter reckoning itself differs in nature according to whether we are speaking of primitive or of modern society. It is not easy, at first, to determine whether this difference arises from the fact that the primitive's experience of profane time has not yet become completely detached from his ideas of mythico-religious time. But certainly this experience of time gives the primitive a kind of permanent "opening" on to religious time. To simplify the explanation and to some extent to anticipate the results of our study of it, we might say that the very nature of the primitive's experience of time makes it easy for him to change the profane into the sacred. But as this problem is primarily of interest to philosophic anthropology and sociology, we shall only consider it in so far as it brings us to a discussion of hierophanic time.

The problem we are dealing with is, in fact, this: in what is sacred time distinguishable from the "profane" duration that comes before and after it? The phrase "hierophanic time," we see at once, covers a collection of widely varying things. It may mean the time during which a ritual takes place and therefore a *sacred time*, a time essentially different from the profane succession which preceded it. It might also mean mythical time, reattained by means of a ritual, or by the mere repetition of some action with a mythical archetype. And, finally, it might also indicate the rhythms of the cosmos (like the hierophanies of the moon) in that those rhythms are seen as revelations—that is, manifestations—of a fundamental sacred power behind the cosmos. Thus, an instant or a fragment of time might *at any moment* become hierophanic: it need only witness the occurrence of a kratophany, hierophany, or theophany to become transfigured, consecrated, remembered because repeated, and therefore repeatable forever. All time of whatever kind "opens" on to sacred time—in other words, is capable of revealing what we may for convenience call the *absolute*, the supernatural, the superhuman, the superhistoric.

To the primitive mind, time is not homogeneous. Even apart from the possibility of its being "hierophanized," time as such appears under different forms, varying in intensity and purpose. L. Lévy-Bruhl, following Hardeland, counted five distinct sorts of time believed by the Dyaks to vary, each by its special quality, the pattern of a single day—in this case a Sunday: (1) Sunrise, favourable for the beginning of any work. Children born at this moment are lucky; but one must never choose this time to set off for hunting, fishing or travelling. One would meet with no success; (2) About nine in the morning: an unlucky moment; nothing begun then will succeed, but if one sets out on the road one need not fear bandits; (3) Midday: a very lucky time; (4) Three in the afternoon: a time of battle, lucky for enemies, bandits, huntsmen and fishermen, unlucky for travellers; (5) About sunset: a shorter "lucky time."[1]

Examples are not hard to find. Every religion has its lucky and unlucky days, its best moments even on the lucky ones, "concentrated" and "diluted" periods of time, "strong" and "weak" times, and so on. One point we must bear in mind from now on is the realization that time was seen as not being homogeneous even apart from all the valuations it came to receive in the framework of any given ritual system: certain periods are lucky and certain the reverse. In other words, time can be seen to have a new dimension that we may call hierophanic, as a result of which succession, by its very nature, takes on not only a particular cadence, but also varying "vocations," contradictory "dynamisms." Obviously this hierophanic dimension of time can be displayed, can be "caused," by the rhythms of nature, as with the Dyaks' five sorts of time, or the crises of the solstice, the phases of the moon and the rest; it may equally well be "caused" by the actual religious life of human societies, under such forms as those winter festivals which center around the dead season of agricultural life, and so on.

Various authors have lately pointed out the social origins of the rhythms of sacred time (for instance Mauss and Granet); but it cannot be denied that the rhythms of the cosmos also played a leading role in the "revelation" and ordering of these systems of reckoning. . . . It has been said[2] that the social "origin" of the reck-

1. *Le Surnaturel et la nature dans la mentalité primitive* (Paris, 1931), pp. 18–19.

2. Hubert and Mauss, "La Représentation du temps dans la religion et la magie," *Mélanges d'histoire des religions*, 1909, pp. 213 ff.

oning of sacred time is borne out by the discrepancies between religious calendars and the rhythms of nature. In point of fact this
divergence in no way disproves the link between man's systems of
reckoning and the rhythms of nature; it simply proves on the one
hand the inconsistency of primitive reckoning and chronometry,
and on the other the non-"naturalist" character of primitive piety,
whose feasts were not directed to any natural phenomenon in itself
but to the religious aspect of that phenomenon.

Plant hierophanies [bring] home to us how very movable in the
calendar the spring festival was. . . . What characterized this spring
festival was the metaphysical and religious significance of the *rebirth* of Nature and the *renewal* of life, rather than the "natural"
phenomenon of spring as such. It was not because a calendar did
not accord with astronomical time that sacred time was always
arranged independently of the rhythms of nature. It was simply
that those rhythms were only thought to be of value in so far as
they were hierophanies, and this "hierophanization" of them set
them free from astronomical time which served them rather as a
sort of womb. A "sign" of spring might reveal *spring* before "nature's spring" made itself felt; the sign marked the *beginning* of a
new era and nature's spring would soon come to confirm it—not as
a mere phenomenon of nature but as a complete renewal and recommencement of all cosmic life. Of course the notion of renewal
included a renewal of individuals and of society as well as of the
cosmos.

65. THE UNITY AND CONTIGUITY OF HIEROPHANIC TIME

The heterogeneousness of time, its division into "sacred" and
"profane," does not merely mean periodic "incisions" made in the
profane duration to allow of the insertion of sacred time; it implies,
further, that these insertions of sacred time are linked together so
that one might almost see them as constituting another duration

SOURCE: *PCR*/391–92.

with its own continuity. The Christian liturgy for a given Sunday
is one with the liturgy for the previous Sunday and the Sunday following. The sacred time in which the mystery occurs of the transubstantiation of bread and wine into the Body and Blood of
Christ is different not only in quality from the profane succession from which it is detached like a space enclosed between the
present and the future; not only is this sacred time linked with that
of the Masses preceding and following it, but it can also be looked
on as a continuation of all the Masses which have taken place from
the moment when the mystery of transubstantiation was first established until the present moment. The profane succession, on the
other hand, which flows between two Masses, not being transformed
into sacred time, cannot have any connection with the hierophanic
time of the rite: it runs parallel, so to speak, to sacred time which is
thus revealed to us as a *continuum* which is interrupted by profane
intervals in appearance only.

What is true of time in Christian worship is equally true of time
in all religions, in magic, in myth and in legend. A ritual does not
merely repeat the ritual that came before it (itself the repetition of
an archetype), but is linked to it and continues it, whether at fixed
periods or otherwise. Magic herbs are picked in those critical moments which mark a breaking-through from profane to magico-
religious time—as, for instance, midnight on the feast of St. John.
For a few seconds—as with the "herb of iron" (the Romanian *iarba
fiarelor*), and with ferns—popular belief has it that the heavens
open and magic herbs receive extraordinary powers so that anyone
picking them at that moment will become invulnerable, invisible
and so on.

These instants of hierophany are repeated every year. In the
sense that they form a "succession"—sacred in nature, but a succession none the less—it may be said that they *are continuous*, and go
to make up a single, unique "time" over the years and centuries.
This does not prevent these instants of hierophany from recurring
periodically; we might think of them as momentary openings onto
the Great Time, openings which allow this same paradoxical second of magico-religious time to enter the profane succession of
things. The notions of recurrence and repetition occupy an important place in both mythology and folklore. . . .

◆ ◆

Rituals Expressing, Informing, and
Molding Religious Experience

Rituals are symbols in acted reality; they function to make concrete and experiential the mythic values of a society, and they can
therefore provide clues to the mythic values themselves. Hence
rituals *act*, they perform, modulate, transform. The experience of
death, for instance, can be given positive meaning, and hence become transformed into something less terrifying. Symbolic items
and places in rituals are transformations of the ordinary into the
extraordinary; even as concrete an act as circumcision can be made
to bear symbolic weight that goes beyond its literal happening.

Rituals form the patterns of life, they apply divine models to
human acts such as marriage; and rituals provide periodic re-creation of the world, of potency, as in the New Year's ceremonies. Rituals are also significant as a means of maintaining a sense of the sacred, as a means of sustaining religious devotion and ecstasy for the
individual.

◆

ENTERING THE COSMOS AND THE SOCIETY[1]

66. RITES OF INITIATION

The term initiation in the most general sense denotes a body of
rites and oral teachings whose purpose is to produce a decisive
alteration in the religious and social status of the person to be
initiated. In philosophical terms, initiation is equivalent to a basic
change in existential condition; the novice emerges from his ordeal
endowed with a totally different being from that which he possessed before his initiation; he has become *another*. Among the various categories of initiation, the puberty initiation is particularly important for an understanding of premodern man. These "transition
rites" are obligatory for all the youth of the tribe. To gain the right

SOURCE: *RSI*/x, xii–xv; cf. *Q*/112–15.
    1. See *RSI*, in which the themes of this section are treated in detail; see also
SP/188–92, on the phenomenology of initiation.

to be admitted among adults, the adolescent has to pass through a series of initiatory ordeals: it is by virtue of these rites, and of the revelations that they entail, that he will be recognized as a responsible member of the society. Initiation introduces the candidate into the human community and into the world of spiritual and cultural values. He learns not only the behavior patterns, the techniques, and the institutions of adults but also the sacred myths and traditions of the tribe, the names of the gods and the history of their works; above all, he learns the mystical relations between the tribe and the Supernatural Beings as those relations were established at the beginning of Time. . . .

It is to this traditional knowledge that the novices gain access. They receive protracted instruction from their teachers, witness secret ceremonies, undergo a series of ordeals. And it is primarily these ordeals that constitute the religious experience of initiation—the encounter with the sacred. The majority of initiatory ordeals more or less clearly imply a ritual death followed by resurrection or a new birth. The central moment of every initiation is represented by the ceremony symbolizing the death of the novice and his return to the fellowship of the living. But he returns to life a new man, assuming another mode of being. Initiatory death signifies the end at once of childhood, of ignorance, and of the profane condition. . . .

All the rites of rebirth or resurrection, and the symbols that they imply, indicate that the novice has attained to another mode of existence, inaccessible to those who have not undergone the initiatory ordeals, who have not tasted death. We must note this characteristic of the archaic mentality: the belief that a state cannot be changed without first being *annihilated*—in the present instance, without the child's dying to childhood. It is impossible to exaggerate the importance of this obsession with beginnings, which, in sum, is the obsession with the absolute beginning, the cosmogony. For a thing to be well done, it must be done as it was done *the first time*. But the first time, the thing—this class of objects, this animal, this particular behavior—did not exist: when, in the beginning, this object, this animal, this institution, came into existence, it was as if, through the power of the Gods, being arose from nonbeing.

Initiatory death is indispensable for the beginning of spiritual life. Its function must be understood in relation to what it prepares:

birth to a higher mode of being. As we shall see farther on, initiatory death is often symbolized, for example, by darkness, by cosmic night, by the telluric womb, the hut, the belly of a monster. All these images express regression to a preformal state, to a latent mode of being (complementary to the precosmogonic Chaos), rather than total annihilation (in the sense in which, for example, a member of the modern societies conceives death). These images and symbols of ritual death are inextricably connected with germination, with embryology; they already indicate a new life in course of preparation. Obviously, as we shall show later, there are other valuations of initiatory death—for example, joining the company of the dead and the Ancestors. But here again we can discern the same symbolism of the beginning: the beginning of spiritual life, made possible in this case by a meeting with spirits.

For archaic thought, then, man is *made*—he does not make himself all by himself. . . .

In modern terms we could say that initiation puts an end to the natural man and introduces the novice to culture. But for archaic societies, culture is not a human product, its origin is supernatural. Nor is this all. It is through culture that man re-establishes contact with the world of the Gods and other Supernatural Beings and participates in their creative energies. The world of Supernatural Beings is the world in which things took place for the first time—the world in which the first tree and the first animal came into existence; in which an act, thenceforth religiously repeated, was performed for the first time (to walk in a particular posture, to dig a particular edible root, to go hunting during a particular phase of the moon); in which the Gods or the Heroes, for example, had such and such an encounter, suffered such and such a misadventure, uttered particular words, proclaimed particular norms. The myths lead us into a world that cannot be described but only "narrated," for it consists in the history of acts freely undertaken, of unforeseeable decisions, of fabulous transformations, and the like. It is, in short, the history of everything significant that has happened since the Creation of the world, of all the events that contributed to making man as he is today. The novice whom initiation introduces to the mythological traditions of the tribe is introduced to the sacred history of the world and humanity.

It is for this reason that initiation is of such importance for a knowledge of premodern man. It reveals the almost awesome seriousness with which the man of archaic societies assumed the responsibility of receiving and transmitting spiritual values.

67. INITIATION MYSTERIES IN PRIMITIVE RELIGIONS

. . . The meaning [of the most important type of initiation] is always religious, for the change of existential status in the novice is produced by a religious experience. The initiate becomes another man because he has had a crucial revelation of the world and life. I shall therefore treat this important and difficult problem in the perspective of the history of religion and not, as is usually done, in the perspectives of cultural anthropology or of sociology. Several excellent studies have been written from these points of view; I need only mention two at this time, those of Heinrich Schurtz and Hutton Webster.[1] The historian of religion will always make use—and most profitable use—of the results attained by the ethnologist and the sociologist; but he has to complement these results and give them their due place in a different and broader perspective. The ethnologist is concerned only with the societies that we call primitive, whereas the historian of religion will include the entire religious history of humanity in his field of investigation, from the earliest cults in paleolithic times of which we have no records down to modern religious movements. To understand the meaning and the role of initiation, the historian of religion will cite not only the rituals of primitive peoples but also the ceremonies of the Greco-Oriental mysteries or of Indo-Tibetan Tantrism, the initiation rites of the Scandinavian berserkers or the initiatory ordeals that are still traceable even in the experiences of the great mystics.

The historian of religion parts company with the sociologist too, since his primary concern is to understand the religious experience of initiation and to interpret the deeper meaning of the symbolisms present in initiatory myths and rites. In short, the ambition of the

SOURCE: *RSI*/1–4, 136.
1. Cf. A. van Gennep, *Les Rites de passage* (Paris, 1909) and H. Webster, *Secret Societies: A Study in Early Politics and Religion* (New York, 1908).

historian of religion is to arrive at the existential situation assumed by religious man in the experience of initiation, and to make that primordial experience intelligible to his contemporaries.

Generally speaking, the history of religion distinguishes three categories, or types, of initiations. The first category comprises the collective rituals whose function is to effect the transition from childhood or adolescence to adulthood, and which are obligatory for all members of a particular society. Ethnological literature terms these rituals "puberty rites," "tribal initiation," or "initiation into an age group."

The other two categories of initiations differ from puberty initiations in that they are not obligatory for all members of the community and that most of them are performed individually or for comparatively small groups. The second category includes all types of rites for entering a secret society, a *Bund*, or a confraternity. These secret societies are limited to one sex and are extremely jealous of their respective secrets. Most of them are male and constitute secret fraternities (*Männerbünde*); but there are also some female secret societies. On the level of primitive cultures, societies open to both sexes are extremely rare; where they exist, they usually represent a phenomenon of degeneration. But in the ancient Mediterranean and Near Eastern world, the mysteries were open to both sexes; and although they are a little different in type, we can put the Greco-Oriental mysteries in the category of secret confraternities.

Finally, there is a third category of initiation—the type that occurs in connection with a mystical vocation; that is, on the level of primitive religions, the vocation of the medicine man or the shaman. A specific characteristic of this third category is the importance that personal experience assumes in it. Broadly speaking, we can say that those who submit themselves to the ordeals typical of this third kind of initiation are—whether voluntarily or involuntarily—destined to participate in a more intense religious experience than is accessible to the rest of the community. I said "voluntarily or involuntarily" because a member of a community can become a medicine man or a shaman not only in consequence of a personal decision to acquire religious powers (the process called "the quest") but also through vocation ("the call"), that is, because he is *forced* by Superhuman Beings to become a medicine man or shaman.

I may add that these last two categories—initiation imposed upon entrance to a secret society, and initiation requisite for obtaining a higher religious status—have a good deal in common. They might even be regarded as two varieties of a single class. What principally tends to distinguish them is the element of ecstasy, which is of great importance in shamanic initiations. I may add too that there is a sort of structural common denominator among all these categories of initiation; with the result that, from a certain point of view, all initiations are much alike. But it seemed best to begin by drawing a few guiding lines in this extremely wide field, for without them we might easily get lost. . . .

Initiation represents one of the most significant spiritual phenomena in the history of humanity. It is an act that involves not only the religious life of the individual, in the modern meaning of the word "religion"; it involves his *entire* life. It is through initiation that, in primitive and archaic societies, man becomes what he is and what he should be—a being open to the life of the spirit, hence one who participates in the culture into which he was born. For as we shall soon see, *the puberty initiation represents above all the revelation of the sacred—and, for the primitive world, the sacred means not only everything that we now understand by religion, but also the whole body of the tribe's mythological and cultural traditions.* In a great many cases puberty rites, in one way or another, imply the revelation of sexuality—but, for the entire premodern world, sexuality too participates in the sacred. In short, through initiation, the candidate passes beyond the natural mode— the mode of the child—and gains access to the cultural mode; that is, he is introduced to spiritual values. From a certain point of view it could almost be said that, for the primitive world, it is through initiation that men attain the status of human beings; before initiation, they do not yet fully share in the human condition precisely because they do not yet have access to the religious life. This is why initiation represents a decisive experience for any individual who is a member of a premodern society; it is a fundamental existential experience because through it a man becomes able to assume his mode of being in its entirety.

. . . The puberty initiation begins with an act of rupture—the child or the adolescent is separated from his mother and sometimes the separation is performed in a decidedly brutal way. But the

initiation is not the concern only of the young novices. The ceremony involves the tribe as a whole. A new generation is instructed,
is made fit to be integrated into the community of adults. And on
this occasion, through the repetition, the *reactualization*, of the
traditional rites, the entire community is regenerated. This is why,
in primitive societies, initiations are among the most important of
religious festivals.

* * *

. . . If we can say that initiation constitutes a specific dimension
of human existence, this is true above all because it is only in initiation that death is given a positive value. Death prepares the new,
purely spiritual birth, access to a mode of being not subject to the
destroying action of Time.

68. SCENARIOS OF INITIATORY DEATH

The rites of initiatory death grow longer and more complex,
sometimes becoming real dramatic scenarios. In the Congo and on
the Loango coast, the boys between ten and twelve years old drink
a potion that makes them unconscious. They are then carried into
the jungle and circumcised. Bastian reports that they are buried in
the fetish house, and that when they wake they seem to have forgotten their past life. During their seclusion in the jungle they are
painted white (certainly a sign that they have become ghosts), they
are allowed to steal, are taught the tribal traditions, and learn a new
language.

Characteristic here are death symbolized by loss of consciousness, by circumcision, and by burial; forgetting the past; assimilation of the novices to ghosts; learning a new language. Each of
these motifs recurs in numerous puberty rites of Africa, Oceania,
and North America. As it is impossible to cite them all, I shall confine myself for the moment to a few examples of forgetting the
past after initiation. In Liberia, when the novices—who are supposed to have been killed by the Forest Spirit—are resuscitated to

Source: *RSI*/30–32; cf. *MDM*/227–31, on the significance of initiatory death;
AR/165–72, and *MDM*/201–2.

a new life, tattooed, and given a new name, they seem to have entirely forgotten their past existence. They recognize neither their families nor their friends, they do not even remember their own names, and they behave as if they had forgotten how to perform even the most elementary acts—washing themselves, for example. Similarly, initiates into some Sudanese secret societies forget their language. Among the Makua the novices spend several months in a hut far from the village and are given new names; when they return to the village they have forgotten their family relationships. As Karl Weule puts it: by his stay in the bush, the son is dead in his mother's eyes.[1] Forgetting is a symbol of death, but it can also be interpreted as betokening earliest infancy. Among the Patasiva of western Ceram, for example, the women are shown the bloody lances with which the spirit is supposed to have killed the novices. When the novices come back to the village, they behave like infants—they do not speak, and pick things up by the wrong end. Whatever may be said of their sincerity, these attitudes and types of behavior have a definite purpose—they proclaim to the whole community that the novices are new beings.

The dramatic structure of certain puberty rites comes out more clearly in cases where we have detailed and accurate descriptions. A good example is the Pangwe, whose initiatory rites are the subject of an excellent study by Günther Tessmann. Four days before the ceremony the novices are marked, and the mark is called "consecration to death." On the day of the festival they are given a nauseating potion to drink, and any novice who vomits it up is chased through the village with cries of "You must die!" The novices are then taken to a house full of ants' nests, and are made to remain inside it for some time, during which they are badly bitten; meanwhile their guardians cry, "You will be killed, now you must die!" The tutors then lead the novices to "death" in a cabin in the jungle, where, for a whole month, they will live completely naked and in absolute solitude. They use a xylophone to announce their presence, so that no one will have the bad luck to meet them. At the end of the month they are painted white and are allowed to return to the village to take part in the dances, but they must sleep

---

1. Cited in A. E. Jensen, *Beschneidung und Reifezeremonien bei Naturvölkern* (Stuttgart, 1933), p. 57.

in the cabin in the bush. They are forbidden to let women see them eat because, Tessmann writes, "of course the dead do not eat." They remain in the bush for three months. Among the southern Pangwe, the ceremony is even more dramatic. An excavation representing the grave is covered by a clay figure, usually in the form of a mask. The excavation symbolizes the belly of the cult divinity, and the novices pass over it, thus indicating their new birth.[2]

Here we have a well developed scenario, comprising several moments: consecration to death; initiatory torture; death itself, symbolized by segregation in the bush and ritual nudity; imitation of the behavior of ghosts, for the novices are considered to be in the other world and are assimilated to the dead; finally, the ritual of rebirth and the return to the village. . . .

69. THE MOON AND INITIATION

Death, however, is not final—for the moon's death is not. "As the moon dieth and cometh to life again, so we also, having to die, will again rise," declare the Juan Capistrano Indians of California in ceremonies performed when the moon is new.[1] A mass of myths describe a "message" given to men by the moon through the intermediary of an animal (hare, dog, lizard or another) in which it promises that "as I die and rise to life again, so you shall also die and rise to life again." From either ignorance or ill-will, the "messenger" conveys the exact opposite, and declares that man, unlike the moon, will never live again once he is dead. This myth is extremely common in Africa, but it is also to be found in Fiji, Australia, among the Ainus and elsewhere. It justifies the concrete fact that man dies, as well as the existence of initiation ceremonies. Even within the framework of Christian apologetics, the phases of the

SOURCE: PCR/174–76; see also MDM/193–204, AR/Ch. 3, espec. 84–99, both on initiation in Australia; S/Ch. 4, on shamanic initiation; MDM/210–12, on torture and suffering; S/Ch. 2, on initiatory illness and dreams; FC/151–52, alchemy and initiation; and Q/112–26, on initiation and the modern world.

2. G. Tessmann, Die Pangwe (Berlin, 1913), 2: 39–94.

1. Sir James G. Frazer, The Belief in Immortality and the Worship of the Dead (London, 1913), 1: 68.

moon provide a good exemplar for our belief in resurrection. . . . It is therefore quite easy to understand the role of the moon in initiations, which consist precisely in undergoing a ritual death followed by a "rebirth," by which the initiate takes on his true personality as a "new man."

In Australian initiations, the "dead man" (that is, the neophyte), rises from a tomb as the moon rises from darkness. Among the Koryaks of north-eastern Siberia, the Gilyaks, Tlingits, Tongas and Haidas, a bear—a "lunar animal" because it appears and disappears with the seasons—is present in the initiation ceremonies, just as it played an essential part in the ceremonies of Paleolithic times. The Pomo Indians of Northern California have their candidates initiated by the Grizzly Bear, which "kills" them and "makes a hole" in their backs with its claws. They are undressed, then dressed in new clothes, and they then spend four days in the forest while ritual secrets are revealed to them. Even when no lunar animals appear in the rites and no direct reference is made to the disappearance and reappearance of the moon, we are driven to connect all the various initiation ceremonies with the lunar myth throughout the area of southern Asia and the Pacific, as Gahs has shown in a yet unpublished monograph.

In certain of the shaman initiation ceremonies, the candidate is "broken in pieces" just as the moon is divided into parts (innumerable myths represent the story of the moon being broken or pulverized by God, by the sun and so on). We find the same archetypal model in the osirian initiations. According to the tradition recorded by Plutarch,[2] Osiris ruled for twenty-eight years and was killed on the seventeenth of the month, when the moon was on the wane. The coffin in which Isis had hidden him was discovered by Set when he was hunting by moonlight; Set divided Osiris' body into fourteen and scattered the pieces throughout Egypt.[3] The ritual emblem of the dead god is in the shape of the new moon. There is clearly an analogy between death and initiation. "That is why," Plutarch tells us, "there is such a close analogy between the Greek words for dying and initiating."[4] If mystical initiation is achieved

2. *De Iside.*
3. *Ibid.*, 18.
4. *De Facie*, p. 943 b.

through a ritual death, then death can be looked upon as an initiation. Plutarch calls the souls that attain to the upper part of the moon "victorious," and they wear the same crown on their heads as the initiate and the triumphant.[5]

70. TRADITIONAL TECHNIQUES FOR "GOING BACK"

We have no intention of comparing psychoanalysis with "primitive" or Eastern beliefs and techniques. The point of the comparison we shall make is to show that "going back," of which Freud saw the importance in understanding man and, especially, in healing him, was already practiced in non-European cultures. After all that we have said concerning the hope of renewing the World by repeating the cosmogony, it is not difficult to grasp the basis for these practices: the individual's return to the origin is conceived as an opportunity for renewing and regenerating the existence of him who undertakes it. . . . The "return to the origin" can be effected for a wide variety of purposes and can have many different meanings.

First and foremost, there is the well-known symbolism of initiation rituals implying a *regressus ad uterum*.[1] . . . We will limit ourselves here to some brief indications. From the archaic stages of culture the initiation of adolescents includes a series of rites whose symbolism is crystal clear: through them, the novice is first transformed into an embryo and then is reborn. Initiation is equivalent to a second birth. It is through the agency of initiation that the adolescent becomes both a socially responsible and culturally awakened being. The return to the womb is signified either by the neophyte's seclusion in a hut, or by his being symbolically swallowed by a monster, or by his entering a sacred spot identified with the uterus of Mother Earth.

What concerns us here is that, together with these puberty rites typical of "primitive" societies, initiation rituals involving a *regres-*

SOURCES: *MR*/79–82; cf. *AR*/141–43 and *RSI*/50–51, South Australia; *RSI*/36, 55–56 on initiatory symbols; *FC*/154–56, on the alchemical reduction "back" to primal material; and selection 31, "Freudian 'Primordial' Time."
  5. *Ibid.*, p. 943 d.
  1. *Regressus ad uterum*: return to the womb. Eds.

sus ad uterum also exist in more complex cultures. To confine ourselves, for the present, to India, the motif is discernible in three different types of initiation ceremonies. First there is the *upanayana* ceremony, that is, the boy's introduction to his teacher. The motif of gestation and rebirth is clearly expressed in it: the teacher is said to transform the boy into an embryo and to keep him in his belly for three nights. Whoever has gone through an *upanayana* is "twice born" (*dvi-ja*). Next there is the *diksha* ceremony, obligatory for one preparing to offer the *soma* sacrifice and which, strictly speaking, consists in return to the foetal stage. Finally, the *regressus ad uterum* is similarly central to the *hiranya-garbha* ceremony (literally, "golden foetus"). The person undergoing the ceremony is put in a golden vessel in the shape of a cow, and on emerging from it he is regarded as a newborn infant.

In all these cases the *regressus ad uterum* is accomplished in order that the beneficiary shall be born into a new mode of being or be regenerated. From the structural point of view, the return to the womb corresponds to the reversion of the Universe to the "chaotic" or embryonic state. The prenatal darkness corresponds to the Night before Creation and to the darkness of the initiation hut.

Whether "primitive" or Indian, all these initiation rituals involving a return to the womb have, of course, a mythical model. But even more interesting than the myths relating to initiation rites of *regressus ad uterum* are those that narrate the adventures of Heroes or of Shamans and magicians who accomplished the *regressus* in their flesh-and-blood bodies, not symbolically. A large number of myths feature (1) a hero being swallowed by a sea monster and emerging victorious after breaking through the monster's belly; (2) initiatory passage through a *vagina dentata*, or the dangerous descent into a cave or crevice assimilated to the mouth or the uterus of Mother Earth.[2] All these adventures are in fact initiatory ordeals, after accomplishing which the victorious hero acquires a new mode of being.

The initiation myths and rites of *regressus ad uterum* reveal the following fact: the "return to the origin" prepares a new birth, but the new birth is not a repetition of the first, physical birth. There is properly speaking a mystical rebirth, spiritual in nature—in other

2. Cf. selection 170, "Labyrinth and Toothed Vagina." Eds.

words, access to a new mode of existence (involving sexual maturity, participation in the sacred and in culture; in short, becoming "open" to Spirit). The basic idea is that, to attain to a higher mode of existence, gestation and birth must be repeated; but they are repeated ritually, symbolically. In other words, we here have acts oriented toward the values of Spirit, not behavior from the realm of psycho-physiological activity.

We have found it necessary to dwell on this point to avoid leaving the impression that all myths and rites of "return to the origin" are on the same plane. To be sure, the symbolism is the same; but the contexts differ, and it is the intention shown by the context that gives us the true meaning in each case. As we saw, from the point of view of structure it is possible to homologize the prenatal darkness of the initiation hut with the Night before Creation. And, true enough, the Night from which the Sun is born every morning symbolizes the primordial Chaos, and the rising of the sun is a counterpart to the cosmogony. But obviously this cosmogonic symbolism is enriched with new values in the case of the birth of the mythical Ancestor, the birth of each individual, and initiatory rebirth.

71. CONTEMPLATING ONE'S OWN SKELETON

. . . Even before setting out to acquire one or more helping spirits, which are like new "mythical organs" for any shaman, the Eskimo neophyte must undergo a great initiatory ordeal. Success in obtaining this experience requires his making a long effort of physical privation and mental contemplation directed to gaining *the ability to see himself as a skeleton*. The shamans whom Rasmussen interrogated about this spiritual exercise gave rather vague answers, which the famous explorer summarizes as follows: "Though no shaman can explain to himself how and why, he can, by the power his brain derives from the supernatural, as it were by thought alone, divest his body of its flesh and blood, so that nothing remains but his bones. And he must then name all the parts of his body, mentioning every single bone by name; and in so doing, he must not use ordinary human speech, but only the special and sacred shaman's

SOURCE: *S*/62–64; cf. *S*/145 ff., 434 ff.

language which he has learned from his instructor. By thus seeing himself naked, altogether freed from the perishable and transient flesh and blood, he consecrates himself, in the sacred tongue of the shamans, to his great task, through that part of his body which will longest withstand the action of the sun, wind and weather, after he is dead."[1]

This important exercise in meditation, which is also equivalent to an initiation (for the granting of helping spirits is strictly dependent upon its success) is strangely reminiscent of the dreams of Siberian shamans—with the difference that, in Siberia, reduction to the state of a skeleton is an operation performed by the shaman-ancestors or other mythical beings, while among the Eskimo the operation is mental, attained by asceticism and deliberate personal efforts to establish concentration. In both regions alike the essential elements of this mystical vision are the being divested of flesh and the numbering and naming of the bones. The Eskimo shaman obtains the vision after a long, arduous preparation. The Siberian shamans are, in most instances, "chosen," and passively witness their dismemberment by mythical beings. But in all these cases reduction to the skeleton indicates a passing beyond the profane human condition and, hence, a deliverance from it.

It must be added that this transcendence does not always lead to the same mystical results. . . . In the spiritual horizon of hunters and herdsmen bone represents the very source of life, both human and animal. To reduce oneself to the skeleton condition is equivalent to re-entering the womb of this primordial life, that is, to a complete renewal, a mystical rebirth. On the other hand, in certain Central Asian meditations that are Buddhistic and tantric in origin or at least in structure, reduction to the skeleton condition has, rather, an ascetic and metaphysical value—anticipating the work of time, reducing life by thought to what it really is, an ephemeral illusion in perpetual transformation.

Such contemplations, it should be noted, have remained alive even within Christian mysticism—which once again shows that the ultimates attained by the earliest conscious awareness of archaic man remain unalterable. To be sure, these religious experiences are

1. Knud Rasmussen, *Intellectual Culture of the Iglulik Eskimos* (Copenhagen, 1930), p. 114.

separated by a difference in content, as we shall see in connection
with the process of reduction to a skeleton in use among Central
Asian Buddhist monks. But from a certain point of view all these
contemplative experiences are equivalent; everywhere, we find the
will to transcend the profane, individual condition and to attain a
transtemporal perspective. Whether there is a reimmersion in primordial life in order to obtain a spiritual renewal of the entire being, or (as in Buddhist mysticism and Eskimo shamanism) a deliverance from the illusions of the flesh, the result is the same—a certain
recovery of the very source of spiritual existence, which is at once
"truth" and "life."

72. HERODOTUS 4.94–96

*In this and the following extract, Eliade discusses a passage in the
Greek historian Herodotus'* History *(4.94–96) that tells the story
of Zalmoxis' disappearance into an underground chamber (andreon)
for three years. The story reflects Pythagorean influence and is
also related to ritual banquets of secret religious societies in Thrace
and the Danubian area. Eliade suggests that the original meaning of
the underground chamber was connected with initiatory death.*

In a celebrated passage Herodotus tells us what he had learned
from the Greeks who lived beside the Hellespont and the Black Sea
concerning the religious beliefs of the Getae and, more particularly,
concerning their god Zalmoxis. The Getae, says Herodotus, are
"the bravest and most law-abiding of all Thracians" (4.93). They
"claim to be immortal, [and] this is how they show it: they believe
that they do not die, but that he who perishes goes to the god
[*daimon*] Salmoxis or Gebeleïzis, as some of them call him" (4. 94;
trans. A. D. Godley, in Loeb Classical Library, vol. II). Herodotus
next describes two rituals consecrated to Zalmoxis: the sacrifice of
a messenger, performed every five years, and the shooting of ar-
rows during thunderstorms. We shall examine these rituals later.

SOURCE: Z/21–24; on Zalmoxis, see further selection 101.

For the moment, let us read what else Herodotus had learned from his informants.

"I have been told by the Greeks who dwell beside the Hellespont and Pontus that this Salmoxis was a man who was once a slave in Samos, his master being Pythagoras, son of Mnesarchus; presently, after being freed and gaining great wealth, he returned to his own country. Now the Thracians were a meanly-living and simple-witted folk, but this Salmoxis knew Ionian usages and a fuller way of life than the Thracians; for he had consorted with Greeks, and moreover with one of the greatest Greek teachers, Pythagoras; wherefore he made himself a hall, where he entertained and feasted the chief among his countrymen, and taught them that neither he nor his guests nor any of their descendants should ever die, but that they should go to a place where they would live for ever and have all good things. While he was doing as I have said and teaching this doctrine, he was all the while making him an underground chamber. When this was finished, he vanished from the sight of the Thracians, and descended into the underground chamber, where he lived for three years, the Thracians wishing him back and mourning him for dead; then in the fourth year he appeared to the Thracians, and thus they came to believe what Salmoxis had told them. Such is the Greek story about him. For myself, I neither disbelieve nor fully believe the tale about Salmoxis and his underground chamber; but I think that he lived many years before Pythagoras; and whether there was a man called Salmoxis, or this be the name among the Getae for a god of their country, I have done with him" (4. 95–96; trans. A. D. Godley).

As was only natural, this text made a great impression in the ancient world, from Herodotus' contemporaries to the last Neo-Pythagoreans and Neo-Platonists. It has been minutely commented upon and interpreted by scholars, and continues to be so in our day. . . . For the moment let us single out the most important elements: (a) Herodotus' informants especially emphasized the fact that Zalmoxis had been Pythagoras' slave and that, after being freed, he devoted himself to acquainting the Getae with Greek civilization and his master's teachings; (b) the most essential feature of Zalmoxis' "Pythagorean" doctrine was the idea of immortality, or more precisely of a blissful postexistence; (c) Zalmoxis set forth this doctrine at banquets that he offered to the leading citizens in an *andreon* built for the purpose; (d) during this time he had an underground chamber built, in which he hid for three years; thinking him dead, the Getae mourned him, but he reappeared in the fourth year, thus giving a startling proof that his teaching was true. Herodotus ends his account without committing himself as to the reality of the underground chamber and without deciding if Zalmoxis was a man or a divine being, but stating that, in his opinion, he lived many years before Pythagoras.

Except for one detail that seems incomprehensible—that is, the statement that the Getae mourned Zalmoxis after his disappearance (for how should they have concluded that he was *dead* if they did not find his body?)—the account is consistent: the Hellespontine Greeks, or Herodotus himself, had integrated what they had learned about Zalmoxis, his doctrine, and his cult into a Pythagorean spiritual horizon. That the Hellespontine Greeks, or Herodotus himself, had done this for patriotic reasons (how could such a doctrine possibly have been discovered by barbarians?) is not important. What is important is the fact that the Greeks were struck by the similarity between Pythagoras and Zalmoxis. And this in itself is enough to tell us of what type the doctrine and religious practices of the cult of Zalmoxis were. For the *interpretatio graeca* permitted a considerable number of homologations with Greek gods or heroes. The fact that Pythagoras was named as the source of Zalmoxis' religious doctrine indicates that the cult of the Getic god involved belief in the immortality of the soul and certain rites of the initiatory type. Through the rationalism and the euhemerism of Herodotus, or of his informants, we divine that the cult had the character of a mystery religion. This may be the reason why Herodotus hesitates to give details (if—which is not certain—his sources had informed him); his discretion in regard to the Mysteries is well known. But Herodotus declares that he does not believe in the story of Zalmoxis as the slave of Pythagoras: on the contrary, he is convinced that the Getic *daimon* was by far the earlier of the two, and this detail is important.

73. THE "UNDERGROUND CHAMBER"

The *andreon* that Zalmoxis had built, and in which he received the principal citizens and discoursed on immortality, is reminiscent both of the chamber in which Pythagoras taught at Crotona and the rooms in which the ritual banquets of the secret religious societies took place. Such scenes of ritual banquets are abundantly documented later on monuments found in Thrace and in the Danubian area. As for the underground chamber—if it was not an interpolation by Herodotus, who remembered a legend of Pythagoras that we shall now discuss—it is clear that its function was not understood. According to this legend, preserved in a satirical narrative by Hermippus that has come down to us only incompletely,[1] Pythagoras retires for seven years (the seven years' period is given by Tertullian) into an underground hiding place. Following his instructions, his mother writes a letter, which he learns by heart before sealing it. When he reappears, like a dead man returning from Hades, he goes before the assembly of the people and declares that he can read the tablet without breaking the seal. After this miracle the people of Crotona are convinced that he had been in the underworld and believe all that he tells them about the fate of their relatives and friends. For Pythagoras, however, survival of the soul is only a consequence of the doctrine of metempsychosis, and it is this doctrine that he makes every effort to inculcate.

Ever since Rohde first pointed it out, scholars have recognized that the source of this parody is Herodotus' account of Zalmoxis going into hiding.[2] But it is possible that Hermippus used other sources as well. Furthermore, Iamblichus in his "Life of Pythagoras" repeats the same story but adds details that are not in Herodotus.[3] Whatever is to be made of this, Herodotus' rationalistic ac-

Source: Z/24–27.

1. In abridged form by Diogenes Laertius 8. 41, and by Tertullian *De anima* 28, and the scholiast on *Electra* v. 62—texts reprinted by Isidore Lévy, *Recherches sur les sources de la légende de Pythagore* (Paris, 1926), pp. 37–38. See the discussion of this subject in Lévy, *La légende de Pythagore en Grèce et en Palestine* (Paris, 1927), pp. 129 ff.

2. Erwin Rohde, "Die Quellen des Iamblichus in seiner Biographie des Pythagoras," *Rheinisches Museum*, 26 (1871): 554–76, 557; Armand Delatte, *La vie de Pythagore de Diogène Laërce* (Brussels, 1922), p. 245; Lévy, *La légende de Pythagore*, p. 133.

3. J. S. Morrison, "Pythagoras of Samos," *Classical Quarterly* 50 (1956): 135–56, 140–41.

count, as well as the parodies handed down by Hermippus and his sources, are either blind to, or deliberately distort, the religious significance of the facts that they report. Retiring into a hiding place or descending into an underground chamber is ritually and symbolically equivalent to a *katabasis*, a *descensus ad inferos* undertaken as a means of initiation. Such descents are documented in the more or less legendary biographies of Pythagoras. According to Porphyry (*Vita Pyth.* 16–17), Pythagoras, on a visit to Crete, was initiated into the Mysteries of Zeus in the following manner: he was purified by the *mystae* of the Dactyl Morges by the application of a thunderstone, spent the night wrapped in a black fleece, and went down into the cave of Ida, where he remained for twenty-seven days. Diogenes Laertius (8.3) adds that he went down into the cave in company with Epimenedes, the perfect type of the catharite. Finally, in the *Abaris*, of which story only some fragments have come down to us, Pythagoras descends into Hades accompanied by a supernatural guide.[4]

Though these legends are late, they help us to grasp the original meaning of Zalmoxis' underground chamber. It represents an *initiatory ritual*. This does not necessarily imply that Zalmoxis was a chthonian divinity. . . . Descending into Hades means to undergo "initiatory death," the experience of which can establish a new mode of being. The "disappearance" (occultation) and "reappearance" (epiphany) of a divine or semidivine being (messianic king, prophet, magus, lawgiver) is a mythico-ritual scenario frequently found in the world of the Mediterranean and Asia Minor. Minos, son of Zeus, the exemplary model of the lawgiver in antiquity, retired every nine years to the mountain cave of Zeus and emerged from it with the tables of the law (Strabo 10. 4. 8; 16. 2. 38). It is above all Dionysus who is characterized by his periodic epiphanies and disappearances, by his "death" and his "renascence," and we can still discern his relation to the rhythm of vegetation and, in general, to the eternal cycle of life, death, and rebirth. But in the historical period this fundamental connection between the cosmic rhythms and the presence, preceded and followed by the absence, of supernatural Beings was no longer apparent.

4. Cf. Lévy, *La légende de Pythagore*, pp. 79 ff.; cf. also pp. 46 f., 84 f.

74. CIRCUMCISION, SUBINCISION, SUFFERING, INITIATION

We have already been introduced (in selection 68) to the theme of initiatory suffering. This theme is illustrated by the examples which follow in selections 74–76.

In the parts of Australia where the extraction of an incisor is not practiced, puberty initiations usually include circumcision, followed, after some time, by another operation, subincision. Some ethnologists regard Australian circumcision as a recent cultural phenomenon. According to Wilhelm Schmidt, the custom was brought to Australia by a cultural wave from New Guinea.[1] Whatever the case may be as to its origin, circumcision is the outstanding puberty rite not only throughout Oceania but in Africa too, and it is also documented among some peoples of both North and South America. As an initiatory rite of puberty, circumcision is extremely widespread, we might also say universal. . . . I shall of necessity confine myself to one or two aspects of it, especially to the relations between the rite of circumcision and the revelation of religious realities. . . .

All the data concerning the ritual function of the bull-roarers, circumcision, and the Supernatural Beings who are believed to perform the initiation indicate the existence of a mythico-ritual theme whose essential features can be summarized as follows: (1) mythical Beings, identified with or manifesting themselves through the bull-roarers, kill, eat, swallow, or burn the novice; (2) they resuscitate him, but changed—in short, a new man; (3) these Beings also manifest themselves in animal form or are closely connected with an animal mythology; (4) their fate is, in essence, identical with that of the initiates, for when they lived on earth, they too were killed and resuscitated, but by their resurrection they established a new mode of existence. This entire mythico-ritual theme is of primary importance for an understanding of the phenomena of initiation. . . .

SOURCE: *RST*/21, 24–28; cf. *AR*/90–91 on ritual killing.
1. W. Schmidt, "Die Stellung den Aranda," *Zeitschrift für Ethnologie* (1908): 866 ff., 898–900.

The suffering consequent upon circumcision—sometimes an extremely painful operation—is an expression of initiatory death. However, it must be emphasized that the real terror is religious in nature; it arises from the fear of being killed by Divine Beings. But it is always the Divine Being who resuscitates the novices; and then they do not go back to their childhood life, but share in a higher existence—higher because it is open to knowledge, to the sacred, and to sexuality. The relations between initiation and sexual maturity are obvious. The uninitiated are assimilated to infants and young girls, and hence are supposed to be unable to conceive, or, among some peoples, their children are not accepted into the clan. Among the Magwanda and Bapedi peoples of Africa the master of the initiation addresses the novices in these words: "Until now, you have been in the darkness of childhood; you were like women and you knew nothing!"[2] Very often, especially in Africa and Oceania, the young initiates are allowed great sexual freedom after they have been circumcised. But we must beware of misinterpreting these licentious excesses, for what is in question here is not sexual freedom, in the modern, desacralized sense of the term. In premodern societies, sexuality, like all the other functions of life, is fraught with sacredness. It is a way of participating in the fundamental mystery of life and fertility. Through his initiation, the novice has gained access to the sacred; he now knows that the world, life, and fertility are sacred realities, for they are the work of Divine Beings. Hence, for the novice, his introduction to sexual life is equivalent to sharing in the sacredness of the world and of human life.

In Australia . . . circumcision is followed by subincision. The interval between the two operations varies, from five or six weeks among the Arunta to two or three years among the Karadjeri. . . . I will confine myself to two of the religious meanings of subincision. The first is the idea of bisexuality. The second is the religious value of blood. According to Winthuis, the purpose of subincision is symbolically to give the neophyte a female sex organ, so that he will resemble the divinities, who, Winthuis asserts, are always bisexual.[3] The first thing to be said in this connection is that divine bisexuality is not documented in the oldest Australian cultural strata, for it is

2. Junod, cited in A. E. Jensen, *Beschneidung und Reifezeremonien bei Naturvölkern* (Stuttgart, 1933), p. 55.

3. J. Winthuis, *Das Zweigeschlechterwesen* (Leipzig, 1928).

precisely in these archaic cultures that the gods are called Fathers. Nor is divine bisexuality found in other really primitive religions. The concept of divine bisexuality appears to be comparatively recent; in Australia, it was probably introduced by cultural waves from Melanesia and Indonesia.

However, there is an element of truth in Winthuis' hypothesis, and that is the idea of *divine totality*. This idea, which is found in a number of primitive religions, naturally implies the coexistence of all the divine attributes, and hence also the coalescence of sexes.

As to the symbolic transformation of the initiand into a woman by means of subincision, only a few clear cases of this have been found in Australia. W. E. Roth, for example, observed that the Pitta-Pitta and the Boubia of northwest central Queensland assimilate the wound from subincision to the vulva, and also refer to the novice on whom the operation has recently been performed as "one with a vulva."[4] R. M. Berndt, studying the Kunapipi cult in northern Australia, gives the same interpretation: "Symbolically, then," he writes, "the subincised member represents both the female and the male organs, essential in the process of fructification."[5]

. . . I suggest that the religious meaning of all these customs is this: the novice has a better chance of attaining to a particular mode of being—for example, becoming a man, a woman—if he first symbolically becomes a totality. For mythical thought, a particular mode of being is necessarily preceded by a *total* mode of being. The androgyne is considered superior to the two sexes just because it incarnates totality and hence perfection. For this reason we are justified in interpreting the ritual transformation of novices into women—whether by assuming women's dress or by subincision—as the desire to recover a primordial situation of totality and perfection.

But in Australia and the nearby regions, the primary purpose of initiatory subincision appears to be obtaining fresh blood. Throughout the world, blood is a symbol of strength and fertility. In Australia as elsewhere, the novices are daubed with red ocher—a substitute for blood—or sprinkled with fresh blood. Among the Dieiri, for example, the men open veins and let the blood flow over the

4. W. E. Roth, *Ethnological Studies among the North West-Central Queensland Aborigines* (Brisbane and London, 1897), p. 180.
5. R. M. Berndt, *Kunapipi* (Melbourne, 1951), p. 16.

novices' bodies to make them brave. Among the Karadjeri, the Itch-umundi, and other Australian tribes, the novice also drinks blood. . . .

. . . For our purpose, one fact is of primary interest. The novice is initiated into the mystery of blood—that is, his instructors reveal to him the connections (both mystical and physiological) which still bind him to his mother, and the ritual which will enable him to transform himself into a man. Since female blood is the product of female feeding, the novice, as we saw, is subjected to numerous dietary prohibitions. The mystical interconnection between food, blood, and sexuality constitutes an initiatory pattern that is specifi-cally Melanesian and Indonesian, but which is also found else-where. What we should note is the fact that the novice is radically regenerated as the result of these sanguinary mutilations. In short, all these operations find their explanation and justification on the re-ligious plane, for the idea of regeneration is a religious idea. Hence we must guard against being misled by the aberrant aspect of some initiatory multilations or tortures. We must not forget that, on the level both of primitive and of more developed cultures, the strange and the monstrous are expressions frequently used to emphasize the transcendence of the spiritual.

75. INITIATORY "MURDERS"

The African example now to be given is that of a secret society common to the Mandja and the Banda, but there is reason to believe that the same scenario is found on more archaic levels of culture. The society is named Ngakola and its initiation rituals re-enact the following myth: In times past Ngakola lived on Earth. His body was very black and covered with long hair. No one knew where he came from, but he lived in the bush. He had the power to kill a man and bring him back to life. He said to men: "Send me people, I will eat them and vomit them up renewed!" His advice was obeyed; but since Ngakola gave back only half of those he had swallowed, men decided to destroy him. They gave him "great quantities of manioc to eat in which stones had been mixed; thus they weakened the monster and were able to kill him with knives and assegais." This myth provides the basis for and justifies the rituals of the secret society. A flat sacred stone plays a great part in the ceremonies. According to tradition this sacred stone was taken from Ngakola's belly. The neophyte is put in a hut that symbolizes the monster's body. There he hears Ngakola's dismal voice, there he is whipped and tortured; for he is told that "he is now in Ngakola's belly" and being digested. The other initiates sing in chorus: "Ngakola, take our entrails, Ngakola, take our livers!" After other ordeals the master initiator finally announces that Ngakola, who had eaten the neophyte, has now vomited him up.

As we said, this myth and ritual resemble other African initiations which are archaic in type. For African puberty rituals that include circumcision can be reduced to the following elements: The master initiators incarnate the divine Beasts of Prey and "kill" the novices by circumcising them; this initiatory murder is based on a myth that tells of a primordial Animal that killed men in order to bring them back to life "changed"; the Animal was itself finally killed, and this mythical event is ritually reiterated by the circumcision of the novices; "killed" by the wild beast of prey (represented by the master initiator), the novice later returns to life by putting on its skin.

The mythico-ritual theme can be reconstructed as follows: (1) a Supernatural Being kills men (to initiate them); (2) (not understanding the meaning of this initiatory death) men avenge themselves by slaying him; (3) but afterward they institute secret ceremonies related to this primordial drama; (4) the Supernatural Being is made present at these ceremonies through an image or sacred object supposed to represent his body or his voice.

76. THE BULL-ROARER AND CIRCUMCISION

The first aspect that strikes us, in Australia as elsewhere, is the fact that circumcision is believed to be performed not by men but by divine or "demonic" Beings. Here we have not merely the repetition of an act instituted by the Gods or by civilizing Heroes in mythical times; we have the active presence of these Superhuman

Beings themselves during the initiation. Among the Arunta, when the women and children hear the bull-roarers, they believe that they are hearing the voice of the Great Spirit Twanyirrika, come to take the boys. And when the boys are circumcised, they are given bull-roarers (*churingas*).[1] Hence it is the Great Spirit himself who is supposed to perform the operation. According to Strehlow, the Arunta imagine that the ceremony takes place in the following way. The novice is led before Tuanjiraka, who says to him, "Look at the stars!" When the boy looks up, the Great Spirit cuts off his head. He gives it back to him the next day, when the head begins to decompose, and resuscitates him.[2] Among the Pitjandara, a man comes rushing out of the forest with a "broken flint," circumcises the novices, and immediately disappears. Among the Karadjeri, the novice is circumcised in a sitting position, his eyes blindfolded and his ears stopped up; immediately after the operation, he is shown the bull-roarers, and—after the blood of his wound has dried—the flint instruments with which the operation was performed. The Kukata perform the circumcision while the bull-roarers are whirled and after the women and children have fled in terror. The Anula women think that the noise of the bull-roarers is the voice of the Great Spirit Gnabaia, who swallows the novices and later disgorges them as initiates.

There is no need to multiply examples. To sum up, circumcision appears as a sacred act, performed in the name of Gods or of Superhuman Beings incarnated in, or represented by, the operators and their ritual tools. The whirling of the bull-roarers before or during circumcision expresses the presence of the Divine Beings. It was stated that among the Yuin, the Kurnai, and the other tribes of southeastern Australia, where circumcision is not practiced, the central mystery of the initiation includes, among other things, the revelation of the bull-roarer as the instrument or the voice of the Sky God or of his son or servant. This identification of the noise of the bull-roarer with the voice of the God is an extremely old religious idea; we find it among the Indian tribes of California and among

---

1. B. Spencer and F. J. Gillen, *The Arunta* (London, 1927), 1: 202 ff.; cf. also their *The Northern Tribes of Central Australia* (London, 1904), pp. 334 ff., 342 ff.

2. C. Strehlow, *Die Aranda- und Loritja-Stämme in Zentralaustralien* (Frankfurt-am-Main, 1920), 4: 24 ff.

the Ituri pygmies, that is, in regions that the historico-cultural school regards as belonging to the earliest culture (*Urkultur*). As for the complementary idea that the sound of the bull-roarer represents thunder, it is even more widespread, since it is documented among many peoples in Oceania, Africa, and the two Americas, and also in ancient Greece, where the *rhombos* was held to be the "thunder of Zagreus." Hence it is highly probable that in the theology and mythology of the bull-roarer we have one of mankind's oldest religious conceptions. The fact that in southeastern Australia bull-roarers are present at initiations performed under the sign of the Supreme Being of the sky is yet another proof of the archaism of this form of initiation.

77. THE "MAGICAL HEAT" AND THE "MASTERY OF FIRE"

The theme of "suffering," which we have been exploring, includes suffering due to deliberate exposure to the elements—even to intense cold. The next three extracts are devoted to the heat with which the initiand fights the cold, and as we shall see, the concept of heat begins to show itself as a metaphor of mastery of aspects of the universe (most notably in the smith's mastery in selection 79).

One of the initiatory ordeals of shamanism demands a capacity to endure extreme cold, as well as the heat of embers. Among the Manchurians, for instance, the future shaman has to undergo the following trial: in the winter, nine holes are made in the ice; the candidate has to plunge into one of these holes, swim under the ice and come out at the next one, and so on to the ninth hole. And there are certain Indo-Tibetan initiatory ordeals which consist precisely in testing a disciple's progress by his ability, during a winter night and under falling snow, to dry both his naked body and a number of wet sheets. This "psychic heat" is called in Tibetan *gtum-mo* (pronounced *tumo*). "Sheets are dipped in icy water, each man wraps himself up in one of them and must dry it on his

SOURCE: *MDM*/92–95.

body. As soon as the sheet has become dry, it is again dipped in the water and placed on the novice's body to be dried as before. The operation goes on in that way until daybreak. Then he who has dried the largest number of sheets is acknowledged the winner of the competition."[1]

This *gtum-mo* is an exercise of Tantric yoga well known in the Indian ascetic tradition. . . . Here we are in the presence of a very ancient mystical experience; for a number of primitive traditions represent the magico-religious power as "burning." Moreover, this magico-religious power is not a monopoly of the mystics and magicians; it is also obtained in the "excitement" of initiatory military combats. . . .

The "magical heat" is related to another technique that may be called the "mastery of fire," that which renders its practitioners insensible to the heat of live embers. From almost everywhere in the shamanic world we have accounts of such exploits, reminding us of those of the fakirs. In preparation for his trance, the shaman may play with live coals, swallow them, handle red-hot iron, etc. During the festivities at the "ordination" of an Araucanian shaman, the masters and the novices walk barefoot over fire, without burning themselves or setting fire to their clothes. Throughout Northern Asia the shamans gash their bodies, and they are able to swallow burning coals or to touch red- or white-hot iron. The same feats are attested among the shamans of North America. Among the Zuni, for example, the shamans play all kinds of tricks with fire: they are able to swallow glowing coals, to walk upon fire, touch red-hot iron, etc. Matilda Coxe Stevenson relates, among her personal observations, that a shaman kept hot embers in his mouth for up to sixty seconds. The *wâbêne* of Ojibwa are called "handlers of fire," and they manipulate blazing coals with impunity.

Such exploits are sometimes collective. Thus, in China, the *saikong* leads the march over the fire: the ceremony is called "walking on a road of fire," and takes place in front of a temple; the *saikong* is the first to step out upon the embers, followed by his younger colleagues, and even by the public. . . . The most striking example, which has also been the best observed, of collective walk-

1. Alexandra David-Neel, *With Mystics and Magicians in Tibet*, chap. 6 (London, 1931).

ing upon white-hot stones, is the well-known ceremony of Fiji. Certain families possess this "power" and pass it on to their posterity. During the ceremony a great number of the non-initiated, and even of strangers, walk over the glowing embers with impunity: but for this, it should be noted, a degree of "faith" and respect for a particular ritual symbolism are necessary: at Rarotonga, one of the Europeans, who had turned back after starting on the walk, had his feet burned. Similar ceremonies occur sporadically in India. At Madras, a yogi made this fire-walk possible for a considerable number of spectators who were not only unprepared, but some of them frankly sceptical; among them the Bishop of Madras and his attendants.

The "mastery of fire" is attested, together with other shamanic marvels—ascension, magical flight, disappearances, walking upon water, etc.—among the mystics of Islam. One tradition of the dervishes tells us that "the séyyd, while listening to the teachings of the sheik and understanding the mysteries of them, became so excited that he put both feet into the hearth, and took pieces of glowing coal out of it with his hand . . ."[2] Lastly, let us remember that a collective ritual of walking on fire still survives in some places in Greece: although integrated with popular Christian devotion, this rite is incontestably archaic; not only pre-Christian, but perhaps pre-Indo-European. One point of importance to us is that the insensibility to heat and the incombustibility are obtained by prayer and fasting: "faith" plays the essential part, and sometimes the walk over the embers is achieved in ecstasy.

Thus there exists a perfect continuity of these mystical techniques, from cultures at the paleolithic stage right up to the modern religions. The true meaning of the "magic heat" and the "mastery of fire" is not difficult to guess: these "marvelous powers" indicate the attainment of a known condition of ecstasy, or, upon other cultural levels (in India, for instance), access to a nonconditioned state of perfect spiritual freedom. The "mastery of fire" and the insensibility both to extreme cold and to the temperature of live embers are material expressions of the idea that the shaman or the yogi has surpassed the human condition and already participates in the condition of the "spirits."

2. Cl. Huart, quoted in *S*/361.

78. THE "MAGICAL HEAT"

"Heat," "Fire," "Power," are coalescent realities and symbols that consummate their religious significance in Hindu Tantric Yoga under the name of Kundalini *(i.e., having the form of a coiled and sleeping serpent at the base of the human spinal column).*[1] *As a paradoxical sacred power, however, making for conflict or peace, its practical reality is inseparable from techniques of ecstasy whether yogic or shamanic.*

. . . Not enough emphasis has been laid on the fact that the "powers" of the gods, increased by anger, [are] manifested in the shape of flames. Heat and fire, on the plane of mystical physiology, indicate the awakening of a magico-religious power. In yoga and Tantrism, these phenomena are of rather frequent occurrence. . . . He who awakens the *kundalini* feels an intense warmth; the progression of the *kundalini* through the body reveals itself by the fact that the lower parts become inert and ice-cold like a corpse, while the part of the body traversed by the *kundalini* is burning hot. Other Tantric texts specify that this "magical heat" is obtained by the "transmutation" of the sexual energy. These techniques are not a Tantric innovation. The *Majjhima-nikaya* (I, 244, etc.) refers to the "heat" obtained by control of the respiration; and other Buddhist texts, the *Dhammapada* (387) for example, aver that the Buddha is "burning." The Buddha "burns" with heat because he is practicing asceticism (*tapas*). The original meaning of that term, incidentally, was "extreme heat"; but *tapas* has come to denote the ascetic striving in general. *Tapas* is already enjoined in the *Rig Veda*, and its powers are creative both upon the spiritual and upon the cosmic planes; through *tapas* the ascetic becomes clairvoyant and may incorporate the gods. On their side too, the cosmic god Prajapati creates the world by "heating" himself up to an extreme degree by asceticism: he creates it, indeed, by a magical perspiration, just as do certain gods in the cosmogonies of North American tribes.

Here we touch upon an extremely important problem concern-

Source: *MDM*/146–49.
1. See especially *Y*/245–49 and then *Y*/241–45; and see selections 88–89 below. Eds.

ing not only Indian religion but the history of religions in general: the excess of *power*, the magico-religious *force*, is experienced as a very vivid warmth. This is no longer a question of the *myths* and *symbols* of power, but of an experience which modifies the very physiology of the ascetic. There is every reason to believe that this experience was known by the mystics and magicians of the most ancient times. A great many "primitive" tribes conceive the magico-religious power as "burning" and express it by terms that signify "heat," "burn," "very hot," etc. That is why "primitive" sorcerers and magicians drink salted or peppered water or eat exceedingly hot-flavoured herbs; they think this heightens their inner "heat." In modern India the Muslims think that by communicating with God a man becomes "burning," and one who works miracles is said to be "boiling." By extension of the same idea, all kinds of persons, possessing any kind of magico-religious "power" whatever, are supposed to be "burning." It must be remembered, too, that all over the world shamans and sorcerers are reputedly "masters of fire," and swallow burning embers, handle red-hot iron and walk over fire. On the other hand they exhibit great resistance to cold. The shamans of the Arctic regions, as well as the ascetics of the Himalayas, thanks to their "magical heat," perform feats of a resistance to cold that passes imagination.

. . . The meaning of all these techniques of "mastering fire" lies deeper: they indicate the attainment of a certain ecstatic state, a non-conditioned state of spiritual freedom. But a *sacred power* experienced as an intense warmth is obtained by other means besides shamanic and mystical techniques. It may come from the forces aroused during military initiations. Several terms in the Indo-European "heroic" vocabulary—*furor, ferg, wut, menos*—express just that "extreme warmth" and "choler" which in other spheres of the sacred accompany the incarnation of the "power."[2] Just like a yogi or a young shaman, the young hero grows "hot" during his initiatory combat. The Irish hero Cuchulain emerges from his first exploit (which, as Georges Dumézil has shown, is equivalent to an initiation of the warrior type) so "hot" that three tubs of water are brought to cool him. "They put him in the first tub, and he

2. See the fine books of Georges Dumézil, *Mythes et dieux des Germains* (Paris, 1939), and *Horaces et les Curiaces* (Paris, 1942).

gave the water such a heat that it burst the staves and hoops of the tub as one would crack a nutshell. In the second tub the water boiled up in bubbles as big as your fist. In the third tub the heat was such as some men can bear but others cannot. Then the fury (*ferg*) of the little boy diminished, and they put him into his clothes."[3]

This "fury" which is manifested as an intense warmth is a magico-religious experience; there is nothing "ordinary" or "natural" about it, it belongs to the syndrome of possession by something sacred. Being a *sacred energy*, it can be transformed, differentiated, subtilized by a further process of integration or "sublimation." The Indian word *kratu*, which once used to mean "the energy typical of an ardent warrior, especially of Indra," came to signify "victorious strength, heroic strength and ardour, bravery and love of combat" and then, by extension, "power" and "majesty" in general, and finally was used to denote "the power of the pious man, which makes him able to follow the injunctions of the *rita* and attain to happiness."[4]

As one would expect, however, the "fury" and the "heat" aroused by a violent and excessive access of *power* strike fear into the majority of mortals: power of that kind, in its crude state, is chiefly of interest to magicians and warriors: those who are looking to religion for confidence and equilibrium would rather protect themselves against magical "warmth" and "fire." The term *shanti*, which in Sanskrit means tranquillity and peace of soul, absence of passion and suffering relieved, is derived from the root *Sham*, which originally included such meanings as the extinguishing of "fire," and the cooling-down of anger or, indeed, of the "heat" aroused by demonic *powers*. The Indian of Vedic times felt the danger of magic; he resisted temptations to acquire more power. Let us recall, by the way, that the true yogi, also, has to overcome the tempta-

---

3. *Tâin bô Cuâlnge*, summarized and translated in Dumézil, *Horaces et les Curiaces*, pp. 35 ff.

4. Kasten Rönnow, "Ved. *kratu*, eine wortgeschichtliche Untersuchung" in *Le Monde Oriental* 26 (1932): 1–90; Georges Dumézil, *Naissanc d'archanges* (Paris, 1945), p. 145 ff. In the Gatha, "the meaning of *khratu* is the religious striving of the man of piety, or what might be called the pious bravery of the man in this combat with evil which occupies the whole life of the believer" (Dumézil, *Mythes*, p. 145).

tion of "magical powers" (*siddhi*)—the temptations of acquiring the power to fly, or to become invisible, etc.—if he is to reach the perfectly nonconditioned state of *samadhi*. We must not however draw the conclusion that experience of this "heat" and the obtaining of "the powers" belong exclusively to the sphere of magic: "heat," "burning," "interior fire" and luminous epiphanies, like every other kind of "power," are attested everywhere in the history of religions and in the most highly evolved mysticisms. A saint, a shaman, a yogi or a "hero" are all apt to feel the supernatural warmth to the degree that, *each upon his appointed plane of being*, they surpass the profane human condition and become embodiments of the sacred.

79. "MASTERS OF FIRE"

The alchemist, like the smith, and like the potter before him, is a "master of fire." It is with fire that he controls the passage of matter from one state to another. The first potter who, with the aid of live embers, was successful in hardening those shapes which he had given to his clay, must have felt the intoxication of the demiurge: he had discovered a transmuting agent. That which natural heat—from the sun or the bowels of the earth—took so long to ripen, was transformed by fire at a speed hitherto undreamed of. This demiurgic enthusiasm springs from that obscure presentiment that the great secret lay in discovering how to "perform" faster than Nature, in other words (since it is always necessary to talk in terms of the spiritual experience of primitive man) how, without peril, to interfere in the processes of the cosmic forces. Fire turned out to be the means by which man could "execute" faster, but it could also do something other than what already existed in Nature. It was therefore the manifestation of a magico-religious power which could modify the world and which, consequently, did not belong to this world. This is why the most primitive cultures look upon the specialist in the sacred—the shaman, the medicine-man, the magician—as a "master of fire." . . .

SOURCE: *FC*/79–82; cf. *RSI*/85–87, *S*/474 ff.

. . . To produce fire in one's own body is a sign that one has transcended the human condition. According to the myths of certain primitive peoples, the aged women of the tribe "naturally" possessed fire in their genital organs and made use of it to do their cooking but kept it hidden from men, who were able to get possession of it only by trickery. These myths reflect the ideology of a matriarchal society and remind us, also, of the fact that fire, being produced by the friction of two pieces of wood (that is, by their "sexual union"), was regarded as existing naturally in the piece which represented the female. In this sort of culture woman symbolizes the natural sorceress. But men finally achieved "mastery" over fire and in the end the sorcerers became more powerful and more numerous than their female counterparts. In Dobu the aboriginals believe that both male and female magicians fly by night and traces of the fire which they leave behind them can be seen. . . .

Like the shamans, the smiths were reputed to be "masters of fire." And so in certain cultures, the smith is considered equal, if not superior, to the shaman. "Smiths and shamans come from the same nest," says a Yakut proverb. "The wife of a shaman is worthy of respect, the wife of a smith worthy of veneration," says another. And a third: "The first smith, the first shaman and the first potter were blood brothers. The smith was the eldest and the shaman came in between. This explains why the shaman cannot bring about the death of a smith."[1] According to the Dolganes, the shaman cannot "swallow" the soul of a smith because the latter protects it with fire; but on the other hand, it is possible for the smith to get possession of the soul of a shaman and to burn it in fire.[2] According to the myths of the Yakut, the smith received his trade from the "evil" deity, K'daai Maqsin, the Master-Smith of Hell. He dwells in a house made of iron, surrounded by splinters of fire. K'daai Maqsin is a master of great renown; it is he who mends the broken or amputated limbs of heroes; sometimes he participates in the initiation of celebrated shamans from the next world: he tempers their souls as he tempers iron.[3]

1. A. Popov, "Consecration Ritual for a Blacksmith Novice among the Yakuts," *Journal of American Folklore* 46 (1933): 257–71, 257.

2. *Ibid.*, p. 258.

3. *Ibid.*, pp. 260–61.

80. THE "ROPE-TRICK"

*Another aspect of the initiatory scenarios is found in the theme of
"ascending"—usually into another dimension of reality such as
"heaven." In the following extracts we are shown how an enacted
ritual—the so-called rope trick—is part of this scenario, and how it
is related to the inner meanings of initiation. It is a long way from
these accounts to the shoddy performances that are now performed
for tourists!*

Ashvagosha relates in his poem *Buddhacarita* (XIX, 12–13) that
when the Buddha visited his birthplace, Kapilavastu, for the first
time after his illumination, he demonstrated some "miraculous powers" (*siddhi*). In order to convince his people of his spiritual
strength and prepare them for conversion, he raised himself in the
air and cut his body into pieces, which he dropped to the ground
and then joined together again beneath the astonished eyes of the
spectators. This miracle forms so intimate a part of the tradition of
Indian magic that it has become the typical prodigy of fakirism.
The celebrated "rope-trick" of the fakirs and conjurers creates the
illusion that a rope rises very high in the sky, and the master makes
his pupil climb it until he disappears from view. The fakir then
throws his knife into the air and the young man's limbs fall, one
after another, to the ground. . . .

The rope-trick must have been very well-known in eighth- and
ninth-century India, for Gaudapada and Shankara use it as an example to illustrate the illusions created by *maya*. . . . A mystic of
the importance of Al Hallaj found room for a number of anecdotes
from which it is clear that he went to India in order to learn white
magic, "so that he might draw men to God." L. Massignon summarizes and translates a tale preserved in the *Kitab al Oyoun*,
according to which when Al Hallaj reached India he "sought information about a woman, went to look for her, and talked to her.
She put him off till next day. Then she went out with him to the
seashore with a twisted thread tied in knots like a ladder. Then the
woman said some words and climbed the thread; it supported her

feet, and she mounted so high that she disappeared from our view. And Al Hallaj turned to me and said: 'It is for this woman that I came to India.' "[1]

81. HYPOTHESES

There have been attempts to explain the rope-trick either as collective suggestion, or the extraordinary sleight-of-hand of the conjurers. But A. Jacoby had drawn attention to the fabulous, saga-like character of the majority of parallel European stories.[1] But whichever explanation is advanced, suggestion or sleight-of-hand, the problem of the rope-trick does not seem to us yet to have been solved. Why was this sort of conjuring invented? Why was precisely this scenario chosen—the climbing of a rope, and dismemberment of the pupil followed by his resurrection—to be imposed by suggestion or auto-suggestion on the audience's imagination? In other words, the rope-trick in its present form, of imaginative scenario, fabulous tale, or conjuring trick, has a *history*, and this history can only be elucidated by taking into account the religious rites, symbols and beliefs of archaic peoples.

Two elements must be distinguished: (1) the dismemberment of the pupil, (2) the ascent into the sky by means of a rope. These are two characteristics of shamanic rites and ideology. Let us start by analyzing the first theme. We know that during initiatory dreams, apprentice shamans witness their own dismemberment by the "spirits" or "demons" who play the part of initiatory masters: their heads are cut off, their bodies are chopped to pieces, their bones are cleaned, etc., and in the end the demons "gather together" the bones and cover them with new flesh. Here we find ecstatic experiences of an initiatory type: a symbolic death is followed by a renewal of the organs and the resurrection of the initiate. It is worth remembering that visions and experiences of the same kind are cur-

SOURCE: *TO*/164–65.

1. L. Massignon, *Al Hallaj, martyr mystique de l'Islam* (Paris, 1922), 1: 80–83.

1. A. Jacoby, *Zum Zerstückelung und Wiederbelebungswunder der indischen Fakire*, Archiv für Religionswissenschaft 17 (1914): 455–75, see pp. 464–74 and *passim*.

rent among the Australians, Eskimos, and some American and African tribes, which means that we have here an extremely archaic initiatory technique. Now it is remarkable that a Tantric Himalayan rite, the *tchod*, also contains the symbolic dismemberment of the neophyte: he witnesses his decapitation and tearing to pieces by the *dakinis* or other demons. One can therefore consider the dismemberment of the pupil and his resurrection by the fakir as a shamanic initiation scenario almost entirely desacramentalized.

As for the second shamanic element that we have recognized in the rope-trick: the ascent to Heaven by means of a rope, this presents a more complex problem. There is, on the one hand, the archaic and extremely widespread myth of the tree, the rope, the mountain, and the ladder or bridge which at the beginning of Time connected the Sky with the Earth and assured communication between the world of the Gods and mankind. Owing to a crime of the mythical Ancestor, this communication was broken off; the tree, rope or liana has been cut down. This myth is not limited to the countries dominated by Shamanism in the strict sense, but plays a considerable part in the mythologies and the ecstatic rituals of the Shamans.

82. SIGNIFICANCE AND FUNCTION OF THE ROPE-TRICK

. . . It is above all the cultural function of the rope-trick—or, to be more exact, of the archaic scenarios which made it possible—that seems to us important. We have just seen that these scenarios and the ideology which they imply belong to the milieu of the magicians. The object of the exhibition is to reveal to the spectators an unknown and mysterious world: the sacred world of magic and religion to which only the initiated have access. The images and dramatic themes employed, notably the ascent to Heaven by means of a rope,[1] the disappearance and initiatory dismemberment of the aspirant, not only illustrate the occult powers of the magicians, but reveal also a deeper level of reality, inaccessible to the profane; they illustrate in fact the initiatory death and resurrection,

Source: *TO*/186–87.
1. On the "ascent" motif, see selections 98–100.

the possibility of transcending "this world" and disappearing on to a "transcendental" plane. The images released by the rope-trick are capable of producing both an attachment to an invisible, secret and "transcendental" reality and doubts as to the reality of the familiar and "immediate" world. From this point of view, the rope-trick—like all other displays of magic—has a positive cultural value, for it stimulates the imagination and reflection, one acting on the other, by the questions and problems that it raises and, ultimately, by putting the problem of the "true" reality of the World. It is not fortuitous that Shankara uses the example of the rope-trick to illustrate the mystery of cosmic illusion; from the beginnings of Indian philosophical speculation, *maya* was the supreme magic, and the gods, to the degree that they were "creators," were *mayin* or magicians.

Finally, we must take into account the "dramatic" function of the rope-trick (and similar exploits). The magician is, by definition, a stage-producer. Thanks to his mysterious science the spectators witness a "dramatic action" in which they do not take an active part in the sense of "working" (as happens in other collective dramatic ceremonies). During the magicians' trick the spectators are passive; *they contemplate*. This is an occasion for imagining how things may be done without "working," simply by "magic," by the mysterious power of thought and will. It is also an occasion for imagining the creative power of the Gods, who do not create by working with their hands, but by the force of their words or thought. To be brief, a whole moral is pointed: that spiritual science is all-powerful, that man is free and that it is possible for him to transcend his familiar Universe. All these thoughts are raised by the contemplation of the "spectacle," by the fact that man discovers the function of a "contemplative."

◆

FORMING AND RECREATING

As we have seen, rituals cause the world to be present to man—they "form" its contours, and identify concretely what the myths relate. The first set of extracts in this section reports on matrimonial rites, which are supposedly based on divine models of creation of the world in many areas, and which are the basis of rites and interpretations of sexuality. Tantrism represents the high point of such interpretations, and Eliade shows that tantric sexuality is a means of experiencing the sacred in the most physical of man's inter-relationships.

83. DIVINE MODELS OF RITUALS

Marriage rites have a divine model, and human marriage reproduces the hierogamy, more especially the union of heaven and earth. "I am Heaven," says the husband, "thou art Earth" (*dyaur aham, pritivi tvam; Brihadaranyaka Upanishad*, VI, 4, 20). Even in Vedic times, husband and bride are assimilated to heaven and earth (*Atharva Veda*, XIV, 2, 71), while in another hymn (*Atharva-Veda*, XIV, 1) each nuptial gesture is justified by a prototype in mythical times: "Wherewith Agni grasped the right hand of this earth, therefore grasp I thy hand . . . Let god Savitar grasp thy hand . . . Tvashtar disposed the garment for beauty, by direction of Brihaspati, of the poets; therewith let Savitar and Bhaga envelop this woman, like Surya, with progeny (48, 49, 52)."[1] In the procreation ritual transmitted by the *Brihadaranyaka Upanishad*, the generative act becomes a hierogamy of cosmic proportions, mobilizing a whole group of gods: "Let Vishnu make the womb prepared! Let Tvashtri shape the various forms! Prajapati—let him pour in! Let Dhatri place the germ for thee!" (VI, 4, 21).[2] Dido celebrates her marriage with Aeneas in the midst of a violent storm (Virgil, *Aeneid*, VI, 160); their union coincides with that of the elements; heaven embraces its bride, dispensing fertilizing rain. In Greece, marriage rites imitated the example of Zeus secretly uniting himself with Hera (Pausanias, II, 36, 2). Diodorus Siculus tells us that the Cretan hierogamy was imitated by the inhabitants of that island; in other words, the ceremonial union found its justification in a primordial event which occurred *in illo tempore*.

What must be emphasized is the cosmogonic structure of all these matrimonial rites: it is not merely a question of imitating an exemplary model, the hierogamy between heaven and earth; the

SOURCE: *CH*/23–27.

1. W. D. Whitney and C. R. Lanman, trans., *Atharva-Veda* (Harvard Oriental Series, VIII, Cambridge, Mass., 1905), pp. 750–51.
2. R. E. Hume, trans., *The Thirteen Principal Upanishads* (Oxford, 1931).

principal consideration is the result of that hierogamy, i.e., the cosmic Creation. This is why, in Polynesia, when a sterile woman wants to be fecundated, she imitates the exemplary gesture of the Primordial Mother, who, *in illo tempore*, was laid on the ground by the great god, Io. And the cosmogonic myth is recited on the same occasion. In divorce proceedings, on the contrary, an incantation is chanted in which the "separation of heaven and earth" is invoked. The ritual recitation of the cosmogonic myth on the occasion of marriages is current among numerous peoples; we shall return to it later. For the moment let us point out that the cosmic myth serves as the exemplary model not only in the case of marriages but also in the case of any other ceremony whose end is the restoration of integral wholeness; this is why the myth of the Creation of the World is recited in connection with cures, fecundity, childbirth, agricultural activities, and so on. The cosmogony first of all represents Creation.

Demeter lay with Iasion on the newly sown ground, at the beginning of spring (*Odyssey*, V, 125). The meaning of this union is clear: it contributes to promoting the fertility of the soil, the prodigious surge of the forces of telluric creation. This practice was comparatively frequent, down to the last century, in northern and central Europe—witness the various customs of symbolic union between couples in the fields. In China, young couples went out in spring and united on the grass in order to stimulate "cosmic regeneration" and "universal germination." In fact, every human union has its model and its justification in the hierogamy, the cosmic union of the elements. Book IV of the *Li Chi*, the "Yüeh Ling" (book of monthly regulations), specifies that his wives must present themselves to the emperor to cohabit with him in the first month of spring, when thunder is heard. Thus the cosmic example is followed by the sovereign and the whole people. Marital union is a rite integrated with the cosmic rhythm and validated by that integration.

The entire Paleo-Oriental symbolism of marriage can be explained through celestial models. The Sumerians celebrated the union of the elements on the day of the New Year; throughout the ancient East, the same day receives its luster not only from the myth of the hierogamy but also from the rites of the king's union with the goddess. It is on New Year's day that Ishtar lies with Tammuz, and the king reproduces this mythical hierogamy by consummating ritual union with the goddess (i.e., with the hierodule who represents her on earth) in a secret chamber of the temple, where the nuptial bed of the goddess stands. The divine union assures terrestrial fecundity; when Ninlil lies with Enlil, rain begins to fall. The same fecundity is assured by the ceremonial union of the king, that of couples on earth, and so on. The world is regenerated each time the hierogamy is imitated, i.e., each time matrimonial union is accomplished. The German *Hochzeit* is derived from *Hockgezît*, New Year festival. Marriage regenerates the "year" and consequently confers fecundity, wealth, and happiness.

The assimilation of the sexual act to agricultural work is frequent in numerous cultures. In the *Shatapatha Brahmana* (VII, 2, 2, 5) the earth is assimilated to the female organ of generation (*yoni*) and the seed to the *semen virile*. "Your women are your tilth, so come into your tillage how you choose" (*Qur'ân*, II, 223).[3] The majority of collective orgies find a ritual justification in fostering the forces of vegetation: they take place at certain critical periods of the year, e.g., when the seed sprouts or the harvests ripen, and always have a hierogamy as their mythical model. Such, for example, is the orgy practiced by the Ewe tribe (West Africa) at the time when the barley begins to sprout; the orgy is legitimized by a hierogamy (young girls are offered to the python god). We find this same legitimization among the Oraons; their orgy takes place in May, at the time of the union of the sun god with the earth goddess. All these orgiastic excesses find their justification, in one way or another, in a cosmic or biocosmic act: regeneration of the year, critical period of the harvest, and so forth. The boys who paraded naked through the streets of Rome at the Floralia (April 28) or who, at the Lupercalia, touched women to exorcise their sterility; the liberties permitted throughout India on the occasion of the Holi festival; the licentiousness which was the rule in central and northern Europe at the time of the harvest festival and against which the ecclesiastical authorities struggled so unavailingly —all these manifestations also had a superhuman prototype and tended to institute universal fertility and abundance.

For the purpose of this study, it is of no concern that we should

3. Trans. E. H. Palmer, *Sacred Books of the East*, VI, p. 33.

know to what extent marriage rites and the orgy created the myths which justify them. What is important is that both the orgy and marriage constituted rituals imitating divine gestures or certain episodes of the sacred drama of the cosmos—the legitimization of human acts through an extrahuman model. If the myth sometimes followed the rite—for example, preconjugal ceremonial unions preceded the appearance of the myth of the preconjugal relations between Hera and Zeus, the myth which served to justify them—the fact in no wise lessens the sacred character of the ritual. The myth is "late" only as a formulation; but its content is archaic and refers to sacraments—that is, to acts which presuppose an absolute reality, a reality which is extrahuman.

84. WOMAN, EARTH, AND FECUNDITY

Woman . . . is mystically held to be one with the earth, childbearing is seen as a variant, on the human scale, of the telluric fertility.[1] All religious experiences connected with fecundity and birth *have a cosmic structure*. The sacrality of woman depends on the holiness of the earth. Feminine fecundity has a cosmic model—that of Terra Mater, the universal Genetrix.

In some religions Mother Earth is imagined as capable of conceiving alone, without the assistance of a coadjutor. Traces of such archaic ideas are still found in the myths of the parthenogenesis of Mediterranean goddesses. According to Hesiod, Gaia (= Earth) gave birth to Ouranos "a being equal to herself, able to cover her completely" (*Theogony*, 126 f.). Other Greek goddesses likewise gave birth without the help of gods. This is a mythical expression of the self-sufficiency and fecundity of Mother Earth. Such mythical conceptions have their counterparts in beliefs concerning the spontaneous fecundity of woman and in her occult magico-religious powers, which exert a determining influence on plant life. The social and cultural phenomenon known as matriarchy is connected with the discovery of agriculture by woman. It was woman who first cultivated food plants. Hence it is she who becomes owner of

Source: *SP*/144–46; cf. *PCR*/308–9, on tree marriages.
1. Telluric: pertaining to the earth. Eds.

the soil and crops. The magico-religious prestige and consequent social predominance of woman have a cosmic model—the figure of Mother Earth.

In other religions the cosmic creation, or at least its completion, is the result of a hierogamy between the Sky-God and Mother Earth. This cosmogonic myth is quite widely disseminated. It is found especially in Oceania—from Indonesia to Micronesia—but it also occurs in Asia, Africa, and the two Americas. Now, as we have seen, the cosmogonic myth is pre-eminently the paradigmatic myth; it serves as model for human behavior. This is why human marriage is regarded as an imitation of the cosmic hierogamy. . . . As we should expect, the divine myth is the paradigmatic model for the human union. But there is another aspect which requires emphasis—*the cosmic structure of the conjugal ritual*, and hence of human sexual behavior. For nonreligious man of the modern societies, this simultaneously *cosmic* and *sacred* dimension of conjugal union is difficult to grasp. But as we have had occasion to say more than once, it must not be forgotten that religious man of the archaic societies sees the world as fraught with messages. Sometimes the messages are in cipher, but the myths are there to help man decipher them. . . .

85. COSMIC HIEROGAMIES

The cosmic hierogamy, the marriage between Heaven and Earth, is a cosmogonic myth of the widest distribution. . . . This myth is more or less similar to that of which Hesiod tells us in his *Theogony* (126, etc.). Ouranos, Heaven, unites with Gaia, the Earth, and the divine pair engender the gods, the Cyclops and other monstrous beings. "The holy Heaven is intoxicated (with desire) to penetrate the body of Earth," says Aeschylus in his *Danaids* (Nauck, fragm. 44). All that exists—the Cosmos, the Gods and Life—takes birth from this marriage.

Although so widely distributed, the myth of the cosmic hierogamy is not, however, universal: thus, it is not recorded from among the Australians, the Arctic peoples, the Fuegians or the hunting and

SOURCE: *MDM*/172–74; cf. *MDM*/185–87.

herding peoples of Northern or Central Asia, etc. Some of these peoples—the Australian and the Fuegian, for instance—are reckoned among the most ancient; their culture is, indeed, still at the paleolithic stage. According to their traditional mythology, the Universe was created by a celestial Supreme Being; sometimes, we are even told that this God is a creator *ex nihilo*. When he has a consort and children, it is still he himself who created them. One may presume that, at the paleolithic stage of culture and religion, the myth of the cosmic hierogamy was unknown. This does not necessarily mean that nothing was known about a great Goddess of the Earth and of universal fertility. On the contrary, paleolithic deposits in Asia and Europe have yielded a great many bone statuettes representing a nude Goddess, very probably the prototype of the innumerable goddesses of fecundity, of which some occur everywhere from all times since the neolithic. We know, on the other hand, that Mother-Goddesses are not an appanage[1] of the agricultural societies; they only attained to their privileged position after the invention of agriculture. Great Goddesses were also known to the hunting peoples: there is, for instance, the Great Mother of the Animals, Mother of the Wild Beasts, whom we find in the Far North of Asia and in the Arctic regions.

Nevertheless the absence of the hierogamic myth from the earliest strata of the "primitive" religions is of significance from our point of view. Two hypotheses could be advanced to explain it. The first is as follows: at the archaic stage of culture—which, be it remembered, corresponds with the paleolithic period—hierogamy was inconceivable, because the supreme Being, a god of celestial character, was believed to have created the world, life and men, all by himself. It follows that the figurines of bone found in paleolithic sites are easy to explain—assuming that they do indeed represent goddesses—in the light of the Australian, Fuegian or Arctic religions and mythologies: such Mother-Goddesses had themselves been created by the supreme Being, as is the case, for instance, among the Australians and in the Zuni myth we have described above. In any case, we cannot deduce from the *presence* of the paleolithic female statuettes, the *nonexistence* of the worship of a divine masculine Being. In still more ancient paleolithic sites—

1. Appanage: adjunct aspect. Eds.

namely, the caves of Wildkirchli, Wildemannlisloch and Drachen-loch, in the Swiss Alps, and in that of Petershöhle in Mittelfranken —remains of sacrifices have been found, which it is allowable to identify as offerings to the heavenly Gods. There is, indeed, an astonishing resemblance between these remains—skulls of cave-bears set up on stones built into the form of an altar—and the sacrifice of the heads of animals which the hunting peoples of the Arctic regions, even today, are still offering up to the heavenly Gods.

This hypothesis would appear to have a very good chance of proving correct. The trouble is that it applies only to the paleolithic, and can tell us nothing about the situation before the stone ages. Men had been living for about half a million years before they left us any traces—either of their culture or of their religion. About that pre-lithic humanity we have no exact knowledge.

86. MYSTICAL EROTICISM

. . . Anthropo-cosmic homologies and, especially, the sacramentalization of physiological life that ensues have preserved all their vitality even in highly evolved religions. For but one example, we need only think of the prestige that sexual union as ritual acquired in Indian tantrism. . . .

* * *

Maithuna[1] was known from Vedic times, but it remained for tantrism to transform it into an instrument of salvation. In pre-tantric India, we must distinguish two possible ritual values of sexual union —both of which, we may note, are archaic in structure and of unquestionable antiquity: (1) conjugal union as a hierogamy; (2) orgiastic sexual union, to the end either of procuring universal fecundity (rain, harvests, flocks, women, etc.) or of creating a "magical defense." We shall not dwell upon the marital act transformed into a hierogamy: "I am the heaven; thou, the earth," says the husband to the wife.[2] The union is a ceremony, comprising

SOURCE: *SP*/170; *Y*/254–56; cf. *Y*/241–45.
1. *Maithuna*: "coupling," sexual union; see selection 87. Eds.
2. *Brihadaranyaka Upanishad*, VI, 4, 20; trans. Hume, *Thirteen Principal Upanishads*, p. 171.

many preliminary purifications, symbolical homologizations, and prayers—just as in the performance of the Vedic ritual. The woman is first transfigured; she becomes the consecrated place where the sacrifice is performed: "Her lap is a sacrificial altar; her hairs, the sacrificial grass; her skin, the somapress. The two lips of the vulva are the fire in the middle [of the vulva]. Verily, indeed, as great as is the world of him who sacrifices with the Vajapeya ('Strength-libation') sacrifice, so great is the world of him who practices sexual intercourse, knowing this."[3] Let us note a fact that is of importance. From the *Brihadaranyaka Upanishad* on, the belief becomes prevalent that the fruit of "works"—the result of a Vedic sacrifice —can be obtained by a ritually consummated marital union. The identification of the sacrificial fire with the female sexual organ is confirmed by the magical charm cast on the wife's lover: "You have made a libation in my fire," etc.[4] A ritual detail of the union, when it is wished that the woman shall not conceive, suggests certain obscure ideas concerning the reabsorption of semen: "He should first exhale, then inhale, and say: 'With power, with semen, I reclaim the semen from you!' Thus she comes to be without seed."[5] Hence the Hatha-yogic technique may have existed, at least in the form of a "magical spell," from the period of the Upanishads. In any case, the preceding text connects the aspiration of semen with a respiratory act and a magical formula.

Conception takes place in the name of the gods:

> Let Vishnu make the womb prepared!
> Let Tvashtri shape the various forms!
>
> Prajapati, let him pour in!
> Let Dhatri place the germ for thee!
> O Sinivali, give the germ;
> O give the germ, thou broad-tressed dame!
> Let the Twin Gods implace thy germ—
> The Ashvins, crowned with lotus-wreaths![6]

An adequate comprehension of such behavior will suffice to show us that here sexuality was no longer a psychophysiological situa-

3. *Brihadaranyaka Upanishad*, VI, 4, 3; trans. Hume, p. 168.
4. *Ibid.*, VI, 4, 12; trans. Hume, p. 170.
5. *Ibid.*, VI, 4, 10; trans. Hume, p. 169.
6. *Ibid.*, VI, 4, 21; trans. Hume, p. 172.

tion, that it was valorized as ritual—whereafter the way was open to the tantric innovations. If the sexual plane is sanctified and homologized to the planes of ritual and myth, the same symbolism also operates in the opposite direction—the ritual is explained in sexual terms. . . .

87. MAITHUNA

Every naked woman incarnates *prakriti*.[1] Hence she is to be looked upon with the same adoration and the same detachment that one exercises in pondering the unfathomable secret of nature, its limitless capacity to create. The ritual nudity of the *yogini* has an intrinsic mystical value: if, in the presence of the naked woman, one does not find in one's inmost being the same terrifying emotion that one feels before the revelation of the cosmic mystery, there is no rite, there is only a secular act, with all the familiar consequences (strengthening of the karmic chain, etc.). The second stage consists in the transformation of the woman-*prakriti* into an incarnation of the Shakti; the partner in the rite becomes a goddess, as the yogin must incarnate the god. The tantric iconography of divine couples (in Tibetan: *yab-yam*, "father-mother"), of the innumerable "forms" of Buddha embraced by their Shaktis, constitutes the exemplary model of *maithuna*. We should note the immobility of the god; all the activity is on the side of the Shakti. (In the yogic context, the static *purusha* contemplates the creative activity of *prakriti*.). . . . In the case of Hatha Yoga, in tantrism immobility simultaneously realized on the three planes of "movement"—thought, respiration, seminal emission—constitutes the supreme goal of *sadhana*. Here again, there is imitation of a divine model—the Buddha, or Shiva, pure Spirit, motionless and serene amid the cosmic play.

Maithuna serves, in the first place, to make respiration rhythmical and to aid concentration; it is, then, a substitute for *pranayama* and *dharana*, or rather their "support." The *yogini* is a girl whom the

SOURCE: *Y*/259–60, 262–63.
1. *Prakriti*: eternal power-source; "Nature," yet in the sense of the essential potentiality or cause of all natural objects. Eds.

guru has instructed and whose body has been consecrated (*adhis-thita*) by *nyasas*. Sexual union is transformed into a ritual through which the human couple becomes a divine couple. . . .

* * *

. . . The tantrics are divided into two classes: the *samayins*, who believe in the identity of Shiva and Shakti and attempt to awaken the *kundalini* by spiritual exercises, and the *kaulas*, who venerate the Kaulini (= *kundalini*) and employ concrete rituals. This distinction is no doubt valid, but it is not always easy to be perfectly sure how far a ritual is to be understood literally: we have seen in what sense "drunkenness" carried to the point of "falling to the ground" was to be interpreted. Now, coarse and brutal language is often used as a trap for the noninitiate. A celebrated text, the *Shaktisan-gama-tantra*, devoted almost entirely to the *satcakrabheda* (= "pen-etration of the six *cakras*"), employs an extremely "concrete" vo-cabulary to describe spiritual exercises. The ambiguity of the erotic vocabulary of tantric literature cannot be too strongly em-phasized. The ascent of the Candali through the yogin's body is often compared with the dance of the "washerwoman" (*dombi*). "With the *dombi* in [his] neck" (i.e., in the *sambhogakaya* near the neck), the yogin "passes the night in great bliss."

Nevertheless, *maithuna* is also practiced as a concrete ritual. By the fact that the act is no longer profane but a rite, that the partners are no longer human beings but "detached" like gods, sexual union no longer participates in the cosmic plane. The tantric texts fre-quently repeat the saying, "By the same acts that cause some men to burn in hell for thousands of years, the yogin gains his eternal salvation." . . .[2]

88. THE TANTRIC PATH

Viewed from outside . . . tantrism would seem to be an "easy road," leading to freedom pleasantly and almost without imped-iments. For, as we shall presently see, the *vamacaris* expect to attain

SOURCE: *Y*/205–7.

2. Indrabhuti, *Jnanasiddhi*, 15; ed. Bhattacharyya, *Two Vajrayana Works*, p. 32.

identification with Shiva and Shakti through ritual indulgence in wine, meat, and sexual union. The *Kularnava-tantra* (VIII, 107 ff.) even insists that union with God can be obtained only through sexual union. And the famous *Guhyasamaja-tantra* categorically affirms: "No one succeeds in attaining perfection by employing difficult and vexing operations; but perfection can be gained by satisfying all one's desires."[1] The same text adds that sensuality is permitted (one may, for example, eat any kind of meat, including human flesh),[2] that the tantrist may kill any kind of animal, may lie, steal, commit adultery, etc.[3] Let us not forget that the aim of the *Guhyasamaja-tantra* is rapid arrival at Buddhahood! And when the Buddha reveals this strange truth to the countless assembly of the Bodhisattvas, and they protest, he points out that what he is teaching them is nothing but the *bodhisattvacarya*, the "conduct of a Bodhisattva." For, he adds,[4] "the conduct of the passions and attachments [*ragacarya*] is the same as the conduct of a Bodhisattva [*bodhisattvacarya*], that being the best conduct [*agracarya*]." In other words: all contraries are illusory, extreme evil coincides with extreme good. Buddhahood can—within the limits of this sea of appearances—coincide with supreme immorality; and all for the very good reason that only the universal void *is*, everything else being without ontological reality. Whoever understands this truth (which is more especially the truth of the Madhyamika Buddhists, but to which other schools subscribe, at least in part) is saved—that is, becomes a Buddha.

But the "easiness" of the tantric path is more apparent than real. Certainly, the metaphysical ambiguity of the *shunya* encouraged and, in sum, justified many excesses among the *vamacaris* (for example, the "tantric orgies"). But aberrant interpretations of dogma appear in the history of all mystical cults. The fact is that the tantric road presupposes a long and difficult *sadhana*, which at times suggests the difficulties of the alchemical *opus*. To return to the text just quoted, the "void" (*shunya*) is not simply a "nonbeing"; it is more like the *brahman* of the Vedanta, it is of an adamantine essence, for which reason it is called *vajra* (= diamond). "*Shunyata*,

---

1. Ed. B. Bhattacharyya, p. 27.
2. *Ibid.*, p. 26, etc.
3. *Ibid.*, pp. 20, 98, 120 ff.
4. *Ibid.*, p. 37.

which is firm, substantial, indivisible and impenetrable, proof against fire and imperishable, is called *vajra*."[5] Now, the ideal of the Buddhist tantrika is to transform himself into a "being of diamond"— in which, on the one hand, he is at one with the ideal of the Indian alchemist, and, on the other, renews the famous Upanishadic equation *atman* = *brahman*. For tantric metaphysics, both Hindu and Buddhist, the absolute reality, the *Urgrund*, contains in itself all dualities and polarities, but reunited, reintegrated, in a state of absolute Unity (*advaya*). The creation, and the becoming that arose from it, represent the shattering of the primordial Unity and the separation of the two principles (Shiva-Shakti, etc.); in consequence, man experiences a state of duality (object-subject, etc.)—and this is suffering, illusion, "bondage." The purpose of tantric *sadhana* is the reunion of the two polar principles within the disciple's own body. "Revealed" for the use of the *kali-yuga*, tantrism is above all a practice, an act, a realization (= *sadhana*). But although the revelation is addressed to all, the tantric path includes an initiation that can be performed only by a *guru*; hence the importance of the master, who alone can communicate the secret, esoteric doctrine, transmitting it "from mouth to ear." . . .

89. SANCTIFICATION OF SEXUAL LIFE

The Indian example shows to what a degree of mystical refinement sacramentalization of the organs and of physiological life can be brought—a sacramentalization that is already amply documented on all the archaic levels of culture. We should add that the valorization of sexuality as a means of participating in the sacred (or, in India, of gaining the superhuman state of absolute freedom) is not without its dangers. In India itself, tantrism has provided the occasion for aberrant and infamous ceremonies. In the primitive world too, ritual sexuality has been accompanied by many orgiastic forms. Nevertheless, the example still retains its suggestive value, for it reveals an experience that is no longer accessible in a desacralized society—the experience of a sanctified sexual life.

SOURCE: *SP*/172; cf. *PCR*/356–59 on sacred orgies.
5. *Advayavajra-samgraha*, ed. H. Shāstri, p. 37.

90. COSMIC PATTERNS AND CONSTRUCTION RITES

If sexuality can be sanctified in tantrism, so can almost anything constructed be made sacred. Selections 90, 91, and 92 relate construction (as, construction of buildings) to world-construction; the house itself can be a microcosm, and hence we are led into ritual sacrifices to establish the "creation" of this micorcosm.

The creation of the world is the exemplar for all constructions. Every new town, every new house that is built, imitates afresh, and in a sense repeats, the creation of the world. Indeed, every town, every dwelling stands at the "center of the world," so that its construction was only possible by means of abolishing profane space and time and establishing sacred space and time. Just as the town is always an *imago mundi*, the house also is a microcosm. The threshold divides the two sorts of space; the home is equivalent to the center of the world. The central pillar in the dwellings of the primitive peoples (*Urkulturen* of the Graebner-Schmidt school) of the Arctic and North America (Samoyeds, Ainus, Indians of northern and central California, Algonquins) is likened to the cosmic axis. When the dwelling is of a different shape (as, for instance with the shepherds and cattle-breeders of central Asia), and the house is replaced by the yurt, the mystical and religious function of the central pillar is assured by the opening in the roof through which the smoke escapes. When its inhabitants are offering sacrifice, they bring into the yurt a tree, the top of which goes through that opening. The sacrificial tree with its seven branches symbolizes the seven spheres of heaven. Thus the house on the one hand corresponds to the universe, and on the other is looked upon as situate at the "center" of the world, with the opening for smoke directly facing the polar star. Every dwelling, by the paradox of the consecration of space and by the rite of its construction, is transformed into a "center." Thus, all houses—like all temples, palaces and cities —stand in the selfsame place, the center of the universe. It is, we must remember, a transcendent space, quite different in nature from profane space, and allows of the existence of a multiplicity and even an infinity of "centers."

SOURCE: *PCR/379–80*; cf. *SP/45–58* and *PCR/371–74* on construction of sacred space.

In India, just before a house is built, the astrologer will decide
which foundation stone must be laid upon the head of the serpent
upholding the world. The master mason sticks a stake into the appointed spot, so as to "fasten down" the head of the earth-serpent
firmly, and so avoid earthquakes. Not only does the construction
of the house take place in the center of the world, but in a sense
it also repeats the creation. We know, indeed, that in innumerable
mythologies the world came from the cutting up of a primeval
monster, often serpentine in form. Just as all dwellings are, by
magic, placed at the "center of the world," so too their building
takes place in the *same* moment of the dawn of the creation of the
worlds. Like sacred space, mythical time can be repeated *ad infinitum* with every new thing man makes.

91. CONSTRUCTION SACRIFICES

In the form of attenuated ritual, of legend, or of vague beliefs,
constructional sacrifices are found almost all over the world. A considerable number of facts has been collected in modern India,
where the belief certainly had a ritual reality in ancient times. Similar sacrifices are found in the Central American cultures, but also
in Oceania and Polynesia, in Indochina, in China, and in Japan. Special mention must be made of the sacrifice at the founding of a village among the Mande people of the Sudan—a complex ritual,
fully studied by Frobenius, the symbolism of which is not without
resemblances to the symbolism implicit in the foundation of Rome.[1]
Obviously, in each instance individual studies must determine to
what extent the immolation of victims is documented ritually and
to what extent it survives only as legend or superstition.

A large volume would be required for an adequate exposition
and discussion of the many forms this type of sacrifice has assumed
down the ages and in different cultural contexts. To put it briefly,
we will only say that, in the last analysis, all these forms depend
upon a common ideology, which could be summarized as follows:

Source: Z/181–83.
1. L. Frobenius, *Kulturgeschichte Afrikas* (Leipzig, 1933), pp. 177–80; G.
Cocchiara, "Il Ponte di Arta e i sacrifici di construzione," in *Annali del
Museo Pitrè* 1 (Palermo, 1950): 38–51, 64–65.

to last, a construction (house, technical accomplishment, but also a spiritual undertaking) must be animated, that is, must receive both life and a soul. The "transference" of the soul is possible only by means of a sacrifice; in other words, by a violent death. We may even say that the victim continues its existence after death, no longer in its physical body but in the new body—the construction —which it has "animated" by its immolation; we may even speak of an "architectonic body" substituted for a body of flesh. The ritual transference of life by means of a sacrifice is not confined to constructions (temples, cities, bridges, houses) and utilitarian objects: human victims are also immolated to assure the success of an undertaking, or even the historical longevity of a spiritual enterprise.

92. BLOOD SACRIFICES AND COSMOGONIC MYTHS

The exemplary model for all these forms of sacrifice is very probably a cosmogonic myth, that is, the myth that explains the Creation by the killing of a primordial Giant (of the type of Ymir, Purusa, P'an-ku): his organs produce the various cosmic regions. This motif was disseminated over an immense area; it occurs with the greatest frequency in eastern Asia. In general, the cosmogonic myth has been shown to be the model for all myths and rites related to a "making," a "work," a "creation." The mythical motif of a "birth" brought about by an immolation is found in countless contexts: it is not only the Cosmos that is born as the result of the immolation of a Primordial Being and from his own substance; the same is true of food plants, human races, or different social classes. Best known of all are the Indonesian and Oceanian myths that relate the voluntary immolation of a Woman or Maiden in order that the different species of food plants may spring from her body.

It is in this mythical horizon that we must seek the spiritual source of our construction rites. If we remember, too, that the traditional societies saw the human dwelling as an *imago mundi*, it becomes still clearer that every work of foundation symbolically reproduced the cosmogony. The cosmic meaning of the dwelling

was reinforced by the symbolism of the Center; for, as is beginning
to be better seen today, every house—*a fortiori* every palace, temple, city—was believed to be at the "Center of the World." . . . The
homologation house-Cosmos (in many variants: the tent assimilated
to the celestial vault, the central pole to the *axis mundi*, etc.) is one
of the distinguishing characteristics of the nomadic hunting and pastoral cultures of America, northern and central Asia, and Africa.
But the idea of a Center through which the *axis mundi* passes and
which, in consequence, makes communication between Sky and
Earth possible is also found at a still earlier stage of culture. The
Achilpa of Australia always carry a sacred pole with them on their
wanderings and decide what direction they shall take by the direction toward which it leans. Their myth relates that the divine being
Numbakula, after "cosmicizing" the territory of the future Achilpa,
creating their ancestor, and founding their institutions, disappeared
in the following way: he made the sacred pole from the trunk of a
gum tree, anointed it with blood, and climbed up it into the sky.
The sacred pole represents the cosmic axis, and settling in a territory
is equivalent to a "cosmicization" from a center of radiation. In
other words, despite their being constantly on the move, the Achilpa
never leave the "Center of the World": they are always "centered"
and in communication with the Sky into which Numbakula
vanished.

We can, then, distinguish two conceptions in regard to the religious function of the human dwelling: (1) the earlier, documented
among hunting peoples and nomadic pastoralists, consecrates the
dwelling and, in general, the inhabited territory by assimilating
them to the Cosmos through the symbolism of the "Center of the
World"; (2) the other, and more recent, conception (it first
appears in the societies of the paleocultivators, the *Urpflanzer*)
is characterized, as we have seen, by repetition of the cosmogonic
myth: because the world (or food plants, men, etc.) arose from
the primordial sacrifice of a Divine Being, every construction demands the immolation of a victim. We should note that, in the
spiritual horizon concomitant with this conception, the actual substance of the victim is transformed into the beings or objects that
issue from it after its death by violence. In one myth the mountains are the bones of the Primordial Giant, the clouds his brain,
and so on; in another the coconut is the actual flesh of the Maiden

Hainuwele. On the plane of construction rites the immolated being, as we have seen, acquires a new body: the building that it has made a "living," hence enduring, thing by its violent death. In all these myths death by violence is creative.

From the viewpoint of cultural history, it is in the conception of the paleocultivators that we must situate the blood rites integral to construction. A. E. Jensen came to a similar conclusion, chiefly on the evidence of the rites that accompany the building of the "men's house" (*dárimo*) among the Kiwai.[1] According to Landt-mann, the ceremony is conducted as follows: When it is de-cided to build a *dárimo*, the village chooses an elderly couple and informs their eldest son of the choice; he rarely refuses: he daubs his face with mud and begins to mourn for his old parents, for it is the common belief that they will not outlive the completion of the building. The old man receives the name "father of the *dárimo*," and his old wife that of "burning woman." It is they who play the principal part in the building of the cult house. The work com-prises the erection of a central pillar, anointing it with the blood of an enemy, and, above all, the sacrifice of a prisoner, for a new cult house is not fit for use before such a sacrifice.[2] The myth that pro-vides the basis and the justification for this ritual relates how the divinity who was immolated *in illo tempore* became the first of the dead: the *dárimo*, the cult house, is the terrestrial reproduction of the beyond. According to Jensen, the Kiwai rite represents the archetype of the *Bauopfer*, and all the other forms of construc-tional sacrifice found throughout the world are connected with the same exemplary model. We consider it difficult to follow him so far. Rather, we believe that the Kiwai rite represents an already special-ized variant of the original scenario, which included only the fol-lowing moments: immolation of a divine being, followed by a "cre-ation," that is, his metamorphosis into a substance or a form that did not exist before. The Kiwai sequence—especially the immola-tion of the divinity, his transformation into the realm of the dead, and the reproduction of the latter in the cult house—already pre-sents an amplification of the original schema.

1. A. E. Jensen, *Das religiöse Weltbild einer frühen Kultur*, p. 58; Jensen, *Mythos und Kult bei Naturvölkern* (Wiesbaden, 1951), pp. 210 ff.
2. Gunnar Landtman, *The Kiwai Papuans of British New Guinea* (London, 1927), pp. 10 ff., 17 ff.

93. THE RETURN TO THE PAST

The cosmogonic myths are functional when establishing, or con-structing, as we have just seen; they also have an important purpose in regenerating, recharging. One "returns to the past" for partici-pating in the primal creative power—a power that is especially forceful because in the creative era there were no divisions, no pain or grief.

Return to the past, then, as a sort of archaic therapy—but there is also a return to the past in the "cargo cults" that focus upon a com-ing future time of restoration. Eliade suggests that these cargo-and millenarian-cults are primarily to be understood as seeking restoration of a more ideal past, even though the imagery may point toward the future. (Studies of Ancient Near Eastern mythol-ogy bear out this observation: imagery of the "endtimes" is fre-quently derived from creation-language, imagery of the "first times.")

. . . In some widely dissimilar cultures the cosmogonic myth is re-enacted not only upon such occasions as the New Year, but also at the enthronement of a new chief, at a declaration of war, or in order to save a threatened harvest or, lastly, to cure an illness. This last is of the greatest interest to us. It has been shown that a fairly large number of peoples, ranging from the most primitive to the most civilized (the Mesopotamians, for instance), made use of sol-emn recitation of the cosmogonic myth as a therapeutic method. We can easily see why: by making the patient symbolically "re-turn to the past" he was rendered contemporary with the Creation, he lived again in the initial plenitude of being. One does not *repair* a worn-out organism, it must be *remade*; the patient needs to be born again; he needs, as it were, to recover the whole energy and potency that a being has at the moment of its birth. And such a re-turn to the "beginning" is rendered possible by *the patient's own memory*. The cosmogonic myth is recited before him and for him; it is the sick man who, by recollecting one after another the episodes of the myth, relives them, and therefore becomes contemporary with them. The function of memory is not to *conserve* the memory

SOURCE: *MDM*/48–53; cf. *AR*/96, 58 f. (selection 23 here), *MR*/88–91, and on the shaman as the specialist in "remembering," *RSI*/102, and *MDM*/163 f.

of the primordial myth, but to transport the patient to *where that event is in process of accomplishment*—namely, to the dawn of Time, to the "commencement."

This "return to the past" by the vehicle of memory, as a means of magical cure, naturally invites us to widen our research. How can we but compare this archaic procedure with the techniques of spiritual healing, nay even with the soteriologies and philosophies elaborated in historical civilizations infinitely more complex than those we have just been considering? We are reminded first of all of one of the fundamental techniques of yoga, in use among the Buddhists as well as the Hindus: needless to add, the comparisons we shall draw do not imply the least depreciation on our part of either Greek or Indian thought; nor do we attach any undue value to archaic thinking. But modern sciences and discoveries, whatever their immediate frame of reference, can claim a certain solidarity, and the results obtained in any one field of study may invite us to make new approaches in others related to it. It seems to us that the importance allowed to Time and to History in contemporary thought, as well as the findings of depth-psychology, may shed further light upon certain spiritual dispositions of archaic humanity.

According to the Buddha, as indeed in Indian thought as a whole, man's life is doomed to suffering by the very fact that it is lived in Time. Here we touch upon a vast question which could not be summarized in a few pages, but it may be said, as a simplification, that suffering in this world is based upon, and indefinitely prolonged by, *karma*, therefore by the temporal nature of existence. It is the law of *karma* which imposes the innumerable transmigrations, the eternal return to existence and therefore to suffering. To deliver oneself from the karmic law, to rend the veil of Maya—this is equivalent to spiritual "cure." The Buddha is "the king of physicians" and his message is proclaimed as the "new medicine." The philosophies, the ascetic and contemplative techniques and the mystical system of India are all directed to the same end: to cure man of the pain of existence in Time. It is by "burning up" even the very last germ of a future life that one finally breaks out of the karmic cycle and attains deliverance from Time. Now, one of the methods of "burning up" the karmic residua is a technique for "returning to the past," becoming conscious of one's previous lives. This is a technique that is universal in India. It is attested in the *Yoga-sutra* (III, 18), and was known to all the sages and contemplatives contemporary with the Buddha, who himself practiced and recommended it.

The method is to cast off from a precise instant of time, the nearest to the present moment, and to retrace the time backwards (*pratiloman* or "against the stream") in order to arrive *ad originem*, the point where existence first "burst" into the world and unleashed Time. Then one rejoins that paradoxical instant before which Time was not, because nothing had been manifested. We can grasp the meaning and the aim of this technique: to re-ascend the stream of time would necessarily bring one back ultimately to the point of departure, which coincides with that of the cosmogony. To relive one's past lives would also be to understand them and, to a certain degree, "burn up" one's "sins"; that is, the sum of the deeds done in the state of ignorance and capitalized from one life to the next by the law of *karma*. But there is something of even greater importance: one attains to the beginning of Time and enters the Timeless —the eternal present which preceded the temporal experience inaugurated by the "fall" into human existence. In other words, it is possible, starting from any moment of temporal duration, to exhaust that duration by retracing its course to the source and so come out into the Timeless, into eternity. But that is to transcend the human condition and to regain the nonconditioned state, which preceded the fall into Time and the wheel of existences.

We must abstain from the intricacies into which we should be led by any attempt to do justice to this technique of the yogis. Our purpose here is simply to indicate the therapeutic virtue of memory as the Hindus have understood it, and, indeed, its soteriological function. For India, the knowledge which leads to salvation is founded upon memory. Ananda and other disciples of Buddha could "remember births," they were numbered among "those who remembered births" (*jatissaro*). Vamadeva, the author of a well-known Rigvedic hymn, said of himself: "Finding myself in the womb, I knew all the births of the gods"; Krishna himself "knew all previous existences".[1] Now, he who *knows*, in this sense, is one who *can recollect the beginning*, or, more exactly, one who has become contemporaneous with the birth of the world, when existence

1. *Rig Veda*, IV, 27, 1 and *Bhagavad-Gita*, IV, 5.

and Time first became manifest. The radical "cure" of the suffering of existence is attained by retracing one's footsteps in the sands of memory right back to the initial *illud tempus*—which implies the abolition of profane time.

We can now see the sense in which such a soteriological philosophy is comparable to those archaic therapies which, in their way, are also intended to render the patient contemporaneous with the cosmogony. (As we need hardly protest, there can be no question of confusing the two categories of facts—of an attitude on one side and a philosophy on the other.) The man of the archaic society is trying to transport himself back to the beginning of the world in order to re-absorb the initial plenitude and recover, intact, the reserves of energy in the new-born babe. The Buddha, like most of the yogis, will have nothing to do with "origins"; he regards any search for first causes as futile: he is simply seeking to neutralize the consequences that those first causes have brought upon every individual in particular. His aim is to sever the succession of transmigrations; and one of the methods is this retracing of the course of one's previous lives, through the memory of them, back to the moment when the Cosmos came into existence. In this respect, therefore, there is an equivalence between the two methods: in both cases, the "cure" and, consequently, the solution of the problem of existence, becomes possible by the Remembrance of the primordial deed, of that which came to pass *at the beginning*.

Another parallelism is evident in the *anamnesis*. Without stopping to analyze the famous Platonic doctrine and its probably Pythagorean origin, let us note, incidentally, the way in which an archaic attitude has been developed to philosophic advantage. We know very little about Pythagoras, but the surest thing we do know is that he believed in metempsychosis and remembered his previous lives. Xenophon and Empedocles[2] described him as "a man of an extraordinary knowledge," for "when he put forth all the powers of his mind he could easily see what he had been in ten, or twenty, human lives." Tradition is insistent upon the importance given to memory training in the Pythagorean brotherhoods.[3] The Buddha and the yogis were not alone, then, in being able to remember

2. Xenophon, *frag.* 7 and Empedocles, *frag.* 129.
3. Diodorus, X, 5; and Iamblichus, *Vita Pyth.*, 78 ff.

their previous lives: and the same kind of prestige was accorded to the shamans; which need not surprise us, since the shamans were "those who had memory of the beginnings." In their ecstasies they re-entered the primordial *illud tempus.*

It is now generally agreed that the Platonic doctrine of *anamnesis* was derived from the Pythagorean tradition. But with Plato it is no longer a matter of personal recollection of personal lives, but of a kind of "impersonal memory" buried deep in each individual, made up of memories of the time when the soul was directly contemplating the Ideas. There can be nothing personal in these recollections: if there were, there would be a thousand ways of understanding the triangle, which obviously would be absurd. We remember only the Ideas; and the differences between individuals are due solely to the imperfections of their *anamnesis.*

It is in the Platonic doctrine of the Remembrance of impersonal realities that we find the most astonishing persistence of archaic thought. The distance between Plato and the primitive world is too obvious for words; but that distance does not imply a break in continuity. In this Platonic doctrine of Ideas, Greek philosophy renewed and revalorized the archaic and universal myth of a fabulous, pleromatic *illud tempus,* which man has to remember if he is to know the *truth* and participate in *Being.* The primitive, just like Plato in his theory of *anamnesis,* does not attach importance to *personal* memories: only the myth, the exemplary History is of importance to him. One might even say that Plato comes nearer than Pythagoras to traditional thinking: the latter, with his personal recollections of ten or twenty previous lives, is more nearly in line with the "elect"—with Buddha, the yogis and the shamans. In Plato it is only the pre-existence of the soul in the timeless universe of Ideas that matters; and the *truth (aletheia)* is the remembrance of that impersonal situation.

94. THE EXPECTATION OF THE DEAD AND RITUAL INITIATION

In all Melanesian "cargo-cults," the expectation of the catastrophe which will precede the Golden Age is marked by a series of

SOURCE: *TO*/137–40; cf. *Q*/88–111.

actions expressing an absolute detachment from ordinary values and behaviour. Pigs and cows are massacred; all savings are spent in order to be done with European money, and coins are even thrown into the sea, barns are built to store provisions; the cemeteries are tidied and planted with flowers, new paths are made, men stop work in order to await the dead around the banquet tables. In the John Frum movement a certain licence is allowed on the occasion of these collective feasts; Friday, the day on which the Golden Age will begin, is the holy day, and Saturday is spent in dancing and drinking *kava*. The young men and women live in a communal house; they bathe together by day and dance during the night.

Divorced from their syncretist and Christian elements, all these Melanesian minor religions share the same central myth; the coming of the dead is taken as the sign of cosmic renewal. Now, we know that this is a fundamental religious idea of the Melanesians. The "cargo-cults" have merely resumed, amplified, revalorized, and charged with prophetic and millenary power the traditional religious theme that the Cosmos renews itself periodically, or to be more exact that it is symbolically re-created every year. New Year's day is a replica of the cosmogony: a new World has just been born, a fresh, pure, rich world with all its potentialities intact and unworn by time; in other words the World as it was on the first day of Creation. This idea, which is, by the way, very widespread, reveals the religious man's desire to deliver himself from the weight of his past, to escape the work of Time, and to begin his life again *ab ovo*.

In Melanesia the great agricultural feast of the New Year contains the following elements: the coming of the dead, the prohibition of work, offerings on platforms for the enjoyment of the dead or a banquet offered to spirits, in fact a collective feast of an orgiastic kind. In this lay-out for the great agricultural New Year's feast it is easy to recognize the most characteristic elements of the "cargo cults": expectation of the dead, enormous holocaust of domestic animals, offerings to the spirits, orgiastic rejoicings, and the refusal to work. Europeans were particularly struck by the vast destruction of goods and the absolute stopping of activity. To confine ourselves to one example, this is how an Acting Resident Magistrate described his visit to one of the regions of Papua infected by what was called Vailala Madness. "They all sat motionless and not a word was uttered for the several minutes that I stayed there looking at them. It was enough to make anyone furious, to see them behaving in this idiotic manner: a whole group of strong, well-built natives, wearing new clean clothes and sitting in silence like stones or tree-trunks in the full afternoon, instead of working or attending to some job like reasonable beings. You would have said that they were ripe for a lunatic asylum."[1]

It was difficult for a Westerner to understand this ritual immobility: it was not just laziness but pure madness. And yet, the natives were engaged in celebrating a rite: they were waiting for the dead and were therefore forbidden to work. But now it was not merely the return of the dead on New Year's day, and the annual renewal of the World; they were watching for what might be called the inauguration of a new cosmic era, the beginning of a Great Year. The dead would come back for good, never to leave the living again. The abolition of death, old age and sickness would destroy all differences between the living and the dead. This radical renewal of the world was practically the inauguration of Paradise. And therefore, as we have just seen, it was to be preceded by terrible cataclysms; earthquakes, floods, darkness, fiery rain, etc. This time there would be a total destruction of the old world, to allow of a new cosmogony, the inauguration of a new way of life: a paradisaical existence.

If so many "cargo-cults" assimilated millenarist Christian ideas, it is because the natives rediscovered in Christianity their old, traditional eschatological myth. The resurrection of the dead, proclaimed by Christianity, was a familiar idea to them. If the natives were disappointed by the missionaries, if the majority of "cargo-cults" ended by becoming anti-Christian, it was not because of Christianity itself, but because the missionaries and converts did not seem to behave like true Christians. The natives were frequently and tragically disappointed by their encounters with official Christianity. For what most attracted them to Christianity was precisely the proclamation of a radical renewal of the World, of the imminent coming of Christ and the resurrection of the dead; it was

---

1. *Papua, Annual Report*, 1919–20, appendix v, text reproduced by P. Worsley, *The Trumpet Shall Sound* (London, 1957), p. 84.

the prophetic and eschatological aspects of the Christian religion that woke the deepest echo in them. But these were just the aspects of Christianity that the missionaries and converts seemed to pass over and despise. The millenarist movements became wildly anti-Christian when their chiefs realized that the missionaries, who had indirectly inspired them, did not believe in the reality of the ships of the dead with their cargos of gifts; in fact did not believe in the imminence of the Kingdom, the resurrection of the dead and the inauguration of Paradise.

One of the most significant episodes in the conflict between the millenarist ideology of the "cargo-cults" and official Christianity is the misadventure of the famous Yali, a figure of the first importance in the prophetic movements of the Madang religion. I will end this account of the Melanesian millenary cults by telling his story. Yali had been drawn by the popular fervour into a millenarist movement which contained many features drawn from Christian eschatology. But in 1947 he was summoned to Port Moresby, the capital of Papua in New Guinea, to a meeting with certain high officials who were alarmed by his activities. While he was at Port Moresby, he learnt that the European Christians did not believe in the reality of the marvelous cargo-boat. A native showed him a book on evolution, and informed him that European Christians *really* believed in this theory. The information deeply disturbed Yali; he discovered that the Europeans believed they were descended from animals, in other words, shared the old totemist belief of his own tribe. Yali felt he had been deceived, became rabidly anti-Christian and returned to the religion of his ancestors. He preferred to acknowledge his descent from one of his familiar totemic animals rather than from an obscure monkey who was said to have lived, far away from his island, in a fabulous geological era.

95. MILLENARIAN MOVEMENTS (AUSTRALIA)

. . . Many other . . . wandering cults were noticed at the turn of the century. In almost every one of them the "black magic" elements were strongly emphasized. One could describe their emer-

Source: *AR*/179–83; cf. *AR*/172–79.

gence and growth in the following terms: a dynamic and magically oriented cult originates from a partial disintegration of the traditional pattern, accompanied by a reorganization and re-evaluation of the traditional symbolism and ritual scenario. As far as we can judge, the success of the magically oriented wandering cults was due to a certain dissatisfaction with the traditional tribal religion. Moreover, as is clearly shown by the brilliant career of Kuràngara, even if the cult emerged and developed initially in an aboriginal milieu, utilizing exclusively archaic and pan-Australian elements, its popularity and rapid diffusion in later stages are largely due to the consequences of the various tribes' contacts with white man's tools, powers, and beliefs.

Until a few years ago, the only known case of a prophetic millenarian cult stimulated directly by contact with Western culture was *molonga* or *mulunga*. Having originated in east central Australia and Queensland at the turn of the century, in only a few years *mulunga* reached all the tribes of central and southern Australia. The corroboree lasted five consecutive nights, and many dances portrayed a future war against the whites. At the end appeared Ka'nini, the Spirit of the "Great Mother from the Water," who, in a series of pantomimes, swallowed all the whites.[1] This nativistic and millenarian cult presents a certain analogy with Kuràngara: the mischievous *mulunga* spirit, just like the Djanba, is invisible to all except the medicine men. But the analogy stops here, for the Djanba are desert spirits, whereas *mulunga* is related to the waters.[2]

In 1960, Helmut Petri and Gisela Petri-Odermann noticed a sort of revivalist movement in the Canning Desert of western Australia, but one lacking prophetic, nativistic, and millenaristic ideas. In 1963, however, the situation was radically changed; the natives refused to accept the two anthropologists again in their traditional cere-

---

1. O. Siebert, "Sagen und Sitten der Dieiri und Nachbarr-Stämme in Zentral-Australien," *Globus* 97 (1910): 57–59; cf. summary by Petri, "Der australische Medizinmann," Part II, pp. 166–67.

2. Helmut Petri, "Der australische Medizinmann," Part II, p. 167. In his book *Movimenti religiosi di libertà e di salvezza* (Milano, 1960), V. Lanternari included Kuràngara among the prophetic cults (cf. pp. 220 ff.), but he did not discuss the *mulunga*, whose prophetic-millenaristic structure is obvious.

monies, and the anti-European feelings were high.[3] The Petris found out from a sympathetic native that a new cult was expected to arrive in the region. They learned that Jinimin (= Jesus) had appeared recently amidst the aborigines. He has black and white skin, and he announced that the entire country will belong to the natives, and also that no distinction will exist between whites and blacks. This will happen only when the natives become powerful enough to conquer the whites. The victory, however, is certain provided the "old law" be faithfully respected. Jesus appears thus as a revivalist prophet of the traditional culture. He is said to have descended from heaven one early afternoon, creating a great surprise. Some people photographed him. He ascended back to heaven at twilight, leaving the Worgaia cult as the means to attain the millennium. Worgaia is a Great Mother type of cult, probably originally from Arnhem Land. Its dynamism was first noticed in 1954.[4]

Another myth from this cult tells of a stone boat sent by Jesus from heaven. The same informants stated definitely that the ship was there from the beginnings of time, from the *bugari-gara*. This is equivalent to saying that Jesus is classified among the mythical Heroes of the tribe. Only as such could he have sent the ship in the primordial time. The ship is invested with two functions: (1) it will serve as Noah's ark when the diluvial rains will kill all the whites with "sacred water"; (2) it is described as loaded with gold and crystals; in other words, it expresses the idea of the richness of an Australian society that suffered the influence of the white man's economics.

Thus, concluded the Petris, an originally nonaggressive revivalism evolved into an aggressive nativistic and millenarian cult through a Christian-sectarian reinterpretation. The process took place after the liberalization of official politics with regard to the aborigines and after the aborigines received equal rights with the whites. This indicates that nativistic and millenarian movements are related more to mystical nostalgias than to purely economic and political circumstances; or, to put it otherwise, it proves how

3. Helmut Petri and Gisela Petri-Odermann, "Nativismus und Millenarismus in gegenwärtigen Australien," *Festschrift für Ad. E. Jensen*, II (Munich, 1964), especially, 462.

4. *Ibid.*, p. 464, n. 8.

much a politically oriented nativistic movement is permeated with religious symbolism and mystical values.

Though manifestly syncretistic, this new millenarian cult is grounded essentially in a pan-Australian religious pattern. Jesus is metamorphosed into one of the Culture Heroes of the mythical time, and the strength and ultimate "salvation" of the tribe is declared to be dependent on the respect of tradition. The results of increasing contact with the Western world are therefore not always disruptive of traditional values. Moreover, an anti-Western attitude does not necessarily result in pessimism and despair, nor are the purely magical elements inevitably exalted. In sum, the emergence of this cult proves again that future modifications of a "primitive" religion cannot be anticipated. The Australian mind reacts creatively, and therefore diversely, to the challenges raised by acculturation. Even the "political" aspect of some of the new cults represents a creative innovation, being, in fact, a drastic re-evaluation of the traditional understanding of "power."

In all these wandering cults the role of some gifted and dynamic personalities—either medicine men, "black magicians," or "inspired" men and women—seems to have been decisive. The central issue was always a reaction against tradition or a reinterpretation of some of its aspects. As the examples which we discussed illustrate abundantly, even the most violent rejection of the "old law" was expressed in "new" forms that utilized the archaic pan-Australian pattern. The process underlying these radical disruptions and transformations observed in the last sixty to seventy years may help us to understand the less dramatic changes that took place earlier in Australia, as a result of Oceanian and Asian cultural influences.

96. MILLENIALISMS AS RELIGIOUS MOVEMENTS

The morphology of primitive millennialisms is extremely rich and complex. For our purpose the important aspects are these: (1) the millennialist movements may be considered a development of the mythico-ritual scenario of the periodic renewal of the World; (2) the influence, direct or indirect, of Christian eschatology almost always seems beyond question; (3) though attracted by Western values and wishing to acquire the religion and education of the whites no less than their wealth and weapons, the adherents of the millennialist movements are always anti-Western; (4) these movements are always begun by strong religious personalities of the prophetic type, and are organized or expanded by politicians for political ends; (5) for all of them the millennium is imminent, but it will not come without cosmic cataclysms or historical catastrophes.

There is no need to dwell on the political, social, and economic character of these movements—it is sufficiently obvious. But their strength, their influence, and their creativity do not reside solely in these socio-economic factors. They are religious movements. Their disciples expect and announce the End of the World in order to achieve a better economic and social condition—but above all because they hope for a re-creation of the World and a restoration of human happiness. They hunger and thirst after worldly goods—but also for the immortality, the freedom, and the bliss of Paradise. For them the End of the World is the condition for establishing a form of human life that will be blissful, perfect, and eternal.

We should add that even where there is no question of a catastrophic end, the idea of regeneration, of a re-creation of the World, is the essential element of the movement. The prophet or founder of the cult proclaims the imminent "return to the origins," and hence the recovery of the first, "paradisal," state. To be sure, in many cases this "original" paradisal state represents the idealized image of the cultural and economic situation before the coming of the whites. This is not the only example of the "original state," a people's "ancient history," being mythicized as an Age of Gold. But what is to our purpose is not the "historical" reality that can sometimes be abstracted and isolated from this exuberant flowering of images, but the fact that the End of a World—the world of colonization—and the expectation of a New World imply a return to origins. The messianic figure is identified with the Culture Hero or the mythical Ancestor whose return was awaited. Their coming is equivalent to a reinstallation of the mythical Times of the origin, hence to a recreation of the World. The political independence and the cultural freedom proclaimed by the millennialist movements among the colonial peoples are conceived as the recovery of an original state of bliss. In short, even without a *visible* apocalyptic destruction, this world, the old world, is symbolically abolished and the paradisal World of the origin is established in its place.

◆

REFLECTING AND MAINTAINING THE SACRED

Man attempts to transcend ritually the limitations of this earthly sphere of existence: symbols speak of overcoming the dualities and tensions, or as in an important theme represented in selection 97, by recognizing the coincidence of the opposites. This rather complex text from *Yoga* shows that the conjunction of opposites is a form of transcendence, but the following materials on magical flight, ladder and stairs images, and other symbols of ascension demonstrate clearly that already archaic man had a definite desire "to live more than twenty-four hours a day," as we might put it, to experience the "other" world as a means of sustaining his daily life in "this" world.

97. THE CONJUNCTION OF OPPOSITES

. . . The tantrist is concerned with *sadhana*; he wants to "realize" the paradox expressed in all the images and formulas concerning the union of opposites, he wants concrete, experimental knowledge of the state of nonduality. The Buddhist texts had made two pairs of opposites especially popular—*prajna*, wisdom, and *upaya*, the means to attain it; *shunya*, the void, and *karuna*, compassion. To "unify" or "transcend" them was, in sum, to attain the paradoxical position of a Bodhisattva—in his wisdom, the Bodhisattva no longer sees persons (for, metaphysically, the "person" does not exist; all that exists is an aggregation of the five *skandhas*), and yet, in his compassion, he undertakes to save persons. Tantrism multiplies the pairs of opposites (sun and moon, Shiva and Shakti, *ida* and *pingala*, etc.) and, as we have just seen, attempts to "unify" them through techniques combining subtle physiology with meditation. This fact must be emphasized: on whatever plane it is realized, the con-

SOURCE: *Y*/269–73; cf. *IS*/85–86, *Y*/55–65, *FC*/124–26.

junction of opposites represents a transcending of the phenomenal world, abolishment of all experience of duality.

The images employed suggest return to a primordial state of non-differentiation; unification of sun and moon represents "destruction of the cosmos," and hence return to the original Unity. In Hatha Yoga, the adept works to obtain "immobility" of breath and semen; there is even supposed to be a "return of semen"—that is, a paradoxical act, impossible to execute in a "normal" physiological context dependent upon a "normal" cosmos; in other words, the "return of semen" stands, on the physiological plane, for a transcendence of the phenomenal world, entrance into freedom. This is but one application of what is termed "going against the current" (*ujana sadhana*), or of the "regressive" process (*ulta*) of the Natha Siddhas, implying a complete "inversion" of all psychophysiological processes; it is, basically, the mysterious *paravritti* that is already to be found in Mahayanic texts, which, in tantrism, also designates the "return of semen." For one who realizes them, this "return," this "regression," imply destruction of the cosmos and hence "emergence from time," entrance into "immortality." In the *Goraksha Vijaya*, Durga (= Shakti, Prakriti) asks Shiva: "Why is it, my Lord, that thou art immortal, and mortal am I? Advise me the truth, O Lord, so that I also may be immortal for ages."[1] It is on this occasion that Shiva reveals the doctrine of Hatha Yoga. Now, immortality cannot be gained except by *arresting manifestation*, and hence the process of disintegration; one must proceed "against the current" (*ujana sadhana*) and once again find the primordial, motionless Unity, which existed before the rupture. This is what the Hatha yogins do when they unite the "sun" and "moon." The paradoxical act takes place on several planes at once: through the union of Shakti (= *kundalini*) with Shiva in the *sahasrara*, the yogin brings about inversion of the cosmic process, regression to the undiscriminated state of the original Totality; "physiologically," the conjunction sun-moon is represented by the "union" of the *prana* and *apana*—that is, by a "totalization" of the breaths; in short, by their arrest. . . .

1. For this and other texts, see S. B. Dasgupta, *Obscure Religious Cults as Background of Bengali Literature* (Calcutta, 1946), pp. 256 ff.

As we have seen, the union of "sun" and "moon" is brought about by unification of the breaths and vital energies circulating in the *ida* and *pingala*; it takes place in the *susumna*. Now, the *Hatha-yogapradipika* (IV, 16–17) says that "the *susumna* devours time." The texts dwell upon the "conquest of death" and the immortality that the yogin who "conquers time" obtains. To arrest respiration, suspend thought, immobilize the semen—these are only formulas expressing the same paradox of the abolishment of time. We have noted that every effort to transcend the cosmos is preceded by a long process of "cosmicizing" the body and the psychomental life, for it is from a perfect "cosmos" that the yogin sets out to transcend the cosmic condition. But "cosmicization," first realized through *pranayama*, already modifies the yogin's temporal experience. The *Kalacakra-tantra* relates inhalation and exhalation to day and night, then to the half months, months, years, thus progressively reaching the longest cosmic cycles. This is equivalent to saying that, through his own respiratory rhythm, the yogin repeats and, as it were, relives the cosmic Great Time, the periodical creations and destructions of the universes (the cosmic "days and nights"). By arresting his breathing, by "unifying" it in the *susumna*, he transcends the phenomenal world, he passes into that nonconditioned and timeless state in which "there is neither day nor night," "neither sickness nor death"—naïve and inadequate formulas to signify "emergence from time." To transcend "day and night" means to transcend the opposites. In the language of the Natha Siddhas, it is the reabsorption of the cosmos through inversion of all the processes of manifestation. It is the coincidence of time and eternity, of *bhava* and *nirvana*; on the purely "human" plane, it is the reintegration of the primordial androgyne, the conjunction, in one's own being, of male and female—in a word, the reconquest of the completeness that precedes all creation.

In short, this nostalgia for the primordial completeness and bliss is what animates and informs all the techniques that lead to the *coincidentia oppositorum* in one's own being. We know that the same nostalgia, with an astonishing variety of symbolisms and techniques, is found almost everywhere in the archaic world; we know, too, that many aberrant ceremonies have their basis and theoretical justification in the desire to recover the "paradisal" state of primordial man. Most of the excesses, cruelties, and aberrations referred to as "tantric orgies" spring, in the last analysis, from the same traditional metaphysics, which refused to define ultimate reality otherwise than as the *coincidentia oppositorum*. . . .

But we have still to emphasize an aspect of tantric *sadhana* that is generally overlooked; we refer to the particular meaning of cosmic reabsorption. After describing the process of creation by Shiva (I, 69–77), the *Shiva Samhita* describes the inverse process, in which the yogin takes part: he sees the element earth become "subtle" and dissolve in water, water dissolve in fire, fire in air, air in ether, etc., until everything is reabsorbed into the Great Brahman. Now, the yogin undertakes this spiritual exercise in order to anticipate the process of reabsorption that occurs at death. In other words, through his *sadhana*, the yogin already witnesses the reabsorption of these cosmic elements into their respective matrices, a process set in motion at the instant of death and continuing during the first stages of existence beyond the world. The *Bardo Thödol* gives some invaluable information on the subject. Viewed from this angle, tantric *sadhana* is centered on the experience of initiatory death, as we should expect, since every archaic spiritual discipline implies initiation in one form or another—that is, the experience of ritual death and resurrection. In this respect the tantrist is a "dead man in life," for he has experienced his own death in advance; he is, by the same token, "twice born," in the initiatory sense of the term, for he has not gained this "new birth" on a purely theoretical plane, but by means of a personal experience. It is possible that many references to the yogin's "immortality," references that are especially frequent in Hatha-yogic texts, ultimately stem from the experiences of such "dead men in life."

98. "MAGICAL FLIGHT"

Siberian, Eskimo, and North American shamans fly. All over the world the same magical power is credited to sorcerers and medicine men. In Malekula the sorcerers (*bwili*) are able to change into animals, but they usually choose to change into hens and falcons, for the faculty of flight makes them like spirits. The Marind sorcerer

SOURCE: *S*/477–82; cf. *S*/119–22, 125–27, 131–35, 407–12; *PCR*/102–8; 132–34.

"goes to a sort of lodge that he has built in the forest from palm leaves, and equips his upper arms and forearms with long plumes from a heron. Finally, he sets fire to his hut, without leaving it . . . the smoke and flames are to lift him into the air, and, like a bird, he flies where he will. . . ."[1]

All this makes us think of the ornithomorphic symbolism of the Siberian shamans' costumes. The Dyak shaman, who escorts the souls of the deceased to the other world, also takes the form of a bird. We have seen that the Vedic sacrificer, when he reaches the top of the ladder, spreads his arms as a bird does its wings and cries: "We have come to the heaven," and so forth. The same rite is found in Malekula: at the culminating point of the sacrifice the sacrificer spreads his arms to imitate the falcon and sings a chant in honor of the stars. According to many traditions, the power of flight extended to all men in the mythical age; all could reach heaven, whether on the wings of a fabulous bird or on the clouds. There is no need to repeat all the details of flight symbolism recorded earlier in these pages (feathers, wings, etc.). We will add that a universal belief, amply documented in Europe, gives wizards and witches the ability to fly through the air. . . . The same magical powers are credited to yogins, fakirs, and alchemists. We should make it clear, however, that here such powers often take on a purely spiritual character: "flight" expresses only intelligence, understanding of secret things or metaphysical truths. "Among all things that fly the mind [*manas*] is swiftest," says the *Rig Veda*.[2] And the *Pancavimsha Brahmana* adds: "Those who know have wings."[3]

An adequate analysis of the symbolism of magical flight would lead us too far. We will simply observe that two important mythical motifs have contributed to give it its present structure: the mythical image of the soul in the form of a bird and the idea of birds as psychopomps. Negelein, Frazer, and Frobenius have assembled much material regarding these two myths of the soul. What concerns us in this instance is the fact that sorcerers and shamans are able, *here on earth* and *as often as they wish*, to accomplish "com-

1. P. Wirz, *Die Marind-anim von Holländisch-Süd-Neu-Guinea* (Hamburg, 1922–25), 2: 74, cited in L. Lévy-Bruhl, *La Mythologie primitive. Le Monde mythique des Australiens et de Papous* (Paris, 1935), p. 232.

2. VI, 9, 5 (trans. R. T. H. Griffith).

3. XIV, I, 13 (trans. W. Caland).

ing out of the body," that is, the death that alone has power to transform the rest of mankind into "birds"; shamans and sorcerers can enjoy the condition of "souls," of "disincarnate beings," which is accessible to the profane only when they die. Magical flight is the expression both of the soul's autonomy and of ecstasy. The fact explains how this myth could be incorporated into such different cultural complexes: sorcery, mythology of dream, solar cults and imperial apotheoses, techniques of ecstasy, funerary symbolisms, and many others. It is also related to the symbolism of ascension. This myth of the soul contains in embryo a whole metaphysics of man's spiritual autonomy and freedom; it is here that we must seek the point of departure for the earliest speculations concerning voluntary abandonment of the body, the omnipotence of intelligence, the immortality of the human soul. An analysis of the "imagination of motion" will show how essential the nostalgia for flight is to the human psyche. The point of primary importance here is that the mythology and the rites of magical flight peculiar to shamans and sorcerers confirm and proclaim their transcendence in respect to the human condition; by flying into the air, in bird form or in their normal human shape, shamans as it were proclaim the degeneration of humanity. For as we have seen, a number of myths refer to a primordial time when *all human beings* could ascend to heaven, by climbing a mountain, a tree, or a ladder, or flying by their own power, or being carried by birds. The degeneration of humanity henceforth forbids the mass of mankind to fly to heaven; only death restores men (and not all of them!) to their primordial condition; only then can they ascend to heaven, fly like birds, and so forth.

Once again, without undertaking a thorough analysis of this flight symbolism and the mythology of the bird-soul, we will remind the reader that the concept of the bird-soul and, hence, the identification of the deceased with a bird, are already documented in the religions of the archaic Near East. The Egyptian Book of the Dead describes the deceased as a falcon flying away,[4] and in Mesopotamia the dead were imagined as birds. The myth is probably even older. In the prehistoric monuments of Europe and Asia the Cosmic Tree is depicted with two birds in its branches; in addition to

4. Ch. XXVIII, etc.

their cosmogonic value, these birds seem to have symbolized the Ancestor-Soul. For, it will be remembered, in the mythologies of Central Asia, Siberia, and Indonesia the birds perched on the branches of the World Tree represent men's souls. Because shamans can change themselves into "birds," that is, because they enjoy the "spirit" condition, they are able to fly to the World Tree to bring back "soul-birds." The bird perched on a stick is a frequent symbol in shamanic circles. It is found, for example, on the tombs of Yakut shamans. A Hungarian *táltos* "had a stick or post before his hut and perched on the stick was a bird. He sent the bird wherever he would have to go."[5] The bird perched on a post is already found in the celebrated relief at Lascaux (bird-headed man) in which Horst Kirchner has seen a representation of a shamanic trance. However this may be, it is certain that the motif "bird perched on a post" is extremely archaic.

From these few examples it is clear that the symbolism and mythologies of "magical flight" extend beyond the bounds of shamanism proper and also precede it; they belong to an ideology of universal magic and play an essential part in many magico-religious complexes. Yet we can understand the incorporation of this symbolism and of all these mythologies into shamanism; for did they not evince and emphasize the shaman's superhuman condition, his freedom, in the last analysis, to move safely among the three cosmic zones and to pass indefinitely from "life" to "death" and vice versa, exactly like the "spirits" whose abilities he had appropriated? The "magical flight" of sovereigns manifests the same autonomy and the same victory over death.

In this connection we may remember that the levitation of saints and magicians is also attested in both the Christian and Islamic traditions. Roman Catholic hagiography has gone so far as to record a large number of "levitations" and even of "flights"; Olivier Leroy's compilation of instances is there to prove it. The outstanding example is that of St. Joseph of Cupertino (1603–1663). A witness describes his levitation as follows: ". . . he rose into space, and, from the middle of the church, flew like a bird onto the high altar,

5. G. Róheim, "Hungarian Shamanism," in *Psychoanalysis and the Social Sciences* (New York, 1951), p. 38; cf. id., *Hungarian and Vogul Mythology* (New York, 1954), pp. 49 ff.

where he embraced the tabernacle. . . ."[6] Sometimes, too, he was
seen to fly to the altar of St. Francis and of the Virgin of the Gro-
tello. . . ."[7] Another time he flew into an olive tree, "and he remained kneeling for half an hour on a branch, which was seen to
sway as if a bird had perched on it."[8] In another ecstasy he flew,
about seven feet above the ground, to an almond tree a hundred
feet away.[9] Among the countless other examples of levitation or
flight by saints or pious persons, we will also cite the experience of
Sister Mary of Jesus Crucified, an Arabian Carmelite. She rose
high into the air, to the tops of the trees, in the garden of the Carmelite nunnery in Bethlehem, "but she began by raising herself with
the help of some branches and never floated free in space."[10]

99. LADDERS AND STAIRS

. . . The Tatar or Siberian shaman climbs a tree, and the Vedic
sacrificer mounts a ladder: the two rites are directed to the same
end, the ascension into Heaven. A good many of the myths speak
of a tree, of a creeper, a cord, or a thread of spider-web or a ladder
which connects Earth with Heaven, and by means of which certain privileged beings do, in effect, mount up to heaven. These
myths have, of course, their ritual correlatives—as, for instance,
the shamanic tree or the post in the Vedic sacrifice. The ceremonial
staircase plays an equally important part, of which we will now give
a few examples:

Polyaenus (*Stratagematon*, VII, 22) tells us of Kosingas, the
priest-king of certain peoples of Thrace, who threatened to desert
his subjects by going up a wooden ladder to the goddess Hera;
which proves that such a ritual ladder existed and was believed to
be a means whereby the priest-king could ascend to Heaven. The
ascension to Heaven by ritually climbing up a ladder was probably

Source: *IS*/48–51.
6. *Le Lévitation* (Paris, 1928), p. 125.
7. *Ibid.*, p. 126.
8. *Ibid.*, p. 127.
9. *Ibid.*, p. 128.
10. *Ibid.*, p. 178.

part of an Orphic initiation; in any case, we find it again in the Mithraic initiation. In the mysteries of Mithra the ceremonial ladder (*climax*) had seven rungs, each being made of a different metal. According to Celsus (Origen, *Contra Celsum*, VI, 22), the first rung was made of lead, corresponding to the "heaven" of the planet Saturn; the second of tin (Venus); the third of bronze (Jupiter); the fourth of iron (Mercury); the fifth of "monetary alloy" (Mars); the sixth of silver (the Moon) and the seventh of gold (the Sun). The eighth rung, Celsus tells us, represented the sphere of the fixed stars. By going up this ceremonial ladder, the initiate was supposed to pass through the seven heavens, thus uplifting himself even to the Empyrean—just as one attained to the ultimate heaven by ascending the seven stages of the Babylonian *ziqqurat*, or as one travelled through the different cosmic regions by scaling the terraces of the Temple of Barabudur, which in itself, as we saw, constituted a Cosmic Mountain and an *imago mundi*.

We can easily understand that the stairway in the Mithraic initiation was an Axis of the World and was situated at the Center of the Universe: otherwise the rupture of the planes would not have been possible. "Initiation" means, as we know, the symbolic death and resurrection of the neophyte or, in other contexts, the descent into Hell followed by ascension into Heaven. Death—whether initiatory or not—is the supreme case of a rupture of the planes. That is why it is symbolized by a climbing of steps, and why funerary rites often make use of ladders or stairways. The soul of the deceased ascends the pathways up a mountain, or climbs a tree or a creeper, right up into the heavens. We meet with something of this conception all over the world, from ancient Egypt to Australia. In Assyrian, the common expression for the verb "to die" is "to clutch the mountain." Similarly in Egyptian, *myny*, "to clutch" is a euphemism for "to die." In the Indian mythological tradition, Yama, the first man to die, climbed up the mountain and over "the high passes" in order to show "the path to many" as it is said in the *Rig Veda* (X, 14, 1). The road of the dead, in popular Ural-Altaic beliefs, leads up the mountains: Bolot, the Kara-Kirghiz hero and also Kesar, legendary king of the Mongols, enter into the world of beyond by way of an initiatory ordeal, through a cave at the summit of the mountains: the descent of the shaman into Hell is also effected by way of a cavern. The Egyptians have preserved, in their funerary texts, the expression *asket pet* (*asket* means "a step") to indicate that the ladder at the disposal of Re is a real ladder, linking Earth to Heaven. "The ladder is set up that I may see the gods," says the *Book of the Dead*, and again, "the gods make him a ladder, so that, by making use of it, he may go up to Heaven." In many tombs of the periods of the archaic and the middle dynasties, amulets have been found engraved with a ladder (*maqet*) or a staircase. The custom of the funerary ladder has, moreover, survived until our days: several primitive Asian peoples—as, for instance, the Lolos, the Karens and others—set up ritual ladders upon tombs, to enable the deceased to ascend to heaven.

As we have just seen, the ladder can carry an extremely rich symbolism without ceasing to be perfectly coherent. *It gives plastic expression to the break through the planes necessitated by the passage from one mode of being to another*, by placing us at the cosmological point *where communication between Heaven, Earth and Hell becomes possible*. That is why the stairway and the ladder play so considerable a part in the rites and the myths of initiation, as well as in funerary rituals, not to mention the rites of royal or sacerdotal enthronement or those of marriage. But we also know that the symbolism of climbing-up and of stairs recurs often enough in psychoanalytic literature, an indication that it belongs to the archaic content of the human psyche and is not a "historical" creation, not an innovation dating from a certain historical moment (say, from ancient Egypt or Vedic India, etc.). I will content myself with a single example of a spontaneous rediscovery of this primordial symbolism.

Julien Green notes, in his Journal for the fourth of April 1933, that "in all my books, the idea of fear or of any other fairly strong emotion seems linked in some inexplicable manner to a staircase. I realised this yesterday, whilst I was passing in review all the novels that I have written . . . (here follow the references). I wonder how I can have so often repeated this effect without noticing it. As a child, I used to dream I was being chased on a staircase. My mother had the same fears in her young days; perhaps something of them has remained with me. . . ."

We now know why the idea of fear, for Julien Green, was associated with the image of a staircase, and why all the dramatic events he described in his works—love, death, or crime—happened upon a staircase. The act of climbing or ascending symbolizes *the way towards the absolute reality*; and to the profane consciousness, the approach towards that reality arouses an ambivalent feeling, of fear and of joy, of attraction and repulsion, etc. The ideas of sanctification, of death, love and deliverance are all involved in the symbolism of stairs. Indeed, each of these modes of being represents a cessation of the profane human condition; that is, a breaking of the ontological plane. Through love and death, sanctity and metaphysical knowledge, man passes—as it is said in the *Brihadaranyaka Upanishad*, from the "unreal to the reality."

But it must not be forgotten that the staircase symbolizes these things because it is thought to be set up in a "center," because it makes communication possible between the different levels of being, and, finally, because it is a concrete formula for the mythical ladder, for the creeper or the spider-web, the Cosmic Tree or the Pillar of the Universe, that connects the three cosmic zones.

100. FLIGHT AND ASCENSION

What strikes us first about the mythology and folklore of the "magical flight" are their primitivity and their universal diffusion. It is agreed that the theme of the *Magische Flucht* is one of the most ancient motifs in folklore: it is found everywhere, and in the most archaic of cultural strata. Strictly speaking, what is in question is not a "flight" but a dizzy trajectory, mostly in a horizontal direction, as one would expect if, as the students of folklore think, the fundamental point of the story is the escape of a young hero from the kingdom of death, pursued by a terrifying figure who personifies Death itself. It would be interesting to analyze the structure of the space in which the magical flight takes place at greater length than we can do here: we should find in it all the elements of anxiety, of the supreme effort to escape from an imminent danger, to free oneself from a dreaded presence. The hero flees more quickly than magic coursers, faster than the wind, as quick as thought—and yet it is not until the end that he manages to shake off his pursuer.

SOURCE: *MDM*/103–7; cf. *MDM*/Ch. 5; *PCR*/102–8, 111; *S*/119–22, 125–27, 131–35, 407–12.

Note, moreover, that he does not fly away towards Heaven; he is not escaping upwards, or not vertically only. The spatial universe of the *Magische Flucht* remains that of man and of death, it is never transcended. The speed rises to a fantastic pitch, yet there is no change of dimension. Divinity does not intervene in this nightmare, this rout of man before Death; it is only friendly animals or fairies who help the fugitive, and it is by the magical objects that he throws over his shoulder, and which transform themselves into grandiose natural obstacles (mountains, forests, seas), that he is at last enabled to escape. This has nothing in common with the "flight." But in this universe of anxiety and vertiginous speeds it is important to distinguish one essential element: the desperate effort to *be rid of* a monstrous presence, to *free oneself*.

Space takes on quite a different aspect in the countless myths, tales and legends concerning human or superhuman beings who fly away into Heaven and travel freely between Earth and Heaven, whether they do so with the aid of birds' feathers or by any other means. It is not the speed with which they fly, nor the dramatic intensity of the aerial voyage that characterize this complex of myth and folklore; it is the fact that *weight is abolished*, that an ontological mutation has occurred in the human being himself. It is not possible here to pass in review all the species and varieties of this "flight" and of the communications between Earth and Heaven. Let it suffice to say that the motif is of universal distribution, and is integral to a whole group of myths concerned both with the celestial origin of the first human beings and with the paradisiac situation during the primordial *illud tempus* when Heaven was very near to Earth and the mythical Ancestor could attain to it easily enough by climbing a mountain, a tree or a creeper.

One fact of outstanding importance for our purpose is that the motifs of flight and of ascension to Heaven are attested at every level of the archaic cultures, as much in the rituals and mythologies of the shamans and the ecstatics as in the myths and folklore of other members of the society who make no pretence to be distinguished by the intensity of their religious experience. In short, the ascension and the "flight" belong to an experience common to all primitive humanity. That this experience constitutes a profound dimension of spirituality is shown by the subsequent history of the symbolism of ascension. Let us remember the importance assumed

by the symbols of the soul as a bird, of the "wings of the soul,"
etc., and the images which point to the spiritual life as an "elevation," the mystical experience as an ascension, etc. The amount of
documentation now at the disposal of the historian of religions is
such, that any enumeration of these motifs and these symbols
would be likely to be incomplete. So we must resign ourselves to a
few allusions bearing upon the symbolism of the bird. It is probable
that the mythico-ritual theme "bird—soul—ecstatic flight" was already extant in the paleolithic epoch; one can, indeed, interpret in
this sense some of the designs at Altamira (man with the mask of a
bird), and the famous relief of Lascaux (man with a bird's head),
in which Horst Kirchner sees the representation of a shamanic
trance.[1] As for the mythical conceptions of the soul as a bird and
as a spirit-guide (psychopomp), they have been studied enough
for us to content ourselves here with a mere allusion. A great many
symbols and significations to do with the spiritual life and, above all,
with the power of intelligence, are connected with the images of
"flight" and "wings." The "flight" signifies intelligence, the understanding of secret things and metaphysical truths. "Intelligence
(*manas*) is the swiftest of birds," says the *Rig Veda* (VI, 9, 5);
and the *Pancavimcsha Brahmana* (IV, 1, 13), states that "he who
understands has wings." We can see how the archaic and exemplary
image of "flight" becomes charged with new meanings, discovered
in the course of new awakenings of consciousness. We shall return
presently to consideration of this process of revalorization.

The extreme archaism and the universal diffusion of the symbols,
myths and legends relating to the "flight" present a problem which
extends beyond the sphere of the historian of religions into that of
philosophic anthropology. We cannot however neglect it; and it
was, indeed, part of our intention to show that the documents of
ethnography and of the history of religions, inasmuch as they deal
with the original spiritual situations, are of interest to the phenom-
enologist and the philosopher. Now, if we consider the "flight" and
all the related symbolisms as a whole, their significance is at once
apparent: they all express a break with the universe of everyday

---

1. Horst Kirchner, "Ein archäologischer Beitrag zur Urgeschichte des
Shamanismus" in *Anthropos* 47 (1952): 244–86, esp. 271 ff.; cf. 258 ff. upon
the symbolism of birds.

experience; and a dual purposiveness is evident in this rupture: both *transcendence* and, at the same time, *freedom* are to be obtained through the "flight." Needless to add, terms denoting "transcendence" or "freedom" are not to be found at the archaic levels of culture in question—but the experience is present, a fact that has its importance. On the one hand, it proves that the roots of freedom are to be sought in the depths of the psyche, and not in conditions brought about by certain historical moments; in other words, that the desire for absolute freedom ranks among the essential longings of man, irrespective of the stage his culture has reached and of its forms of social organization. The creation, repeated to infinity, of these countless imaginary universes in which space is transcended and weight is abolished, speaks volumes upon the true nature of the human being. The longing to break the ties that hold him in bondage to the earth is not a result of cosmic pressures or of economic insecurity—it is constitutive of man, in that he is a being who enjoys a mode of existence unique in the world. Such a desire to free himself from his limitations, which he feels to be a kind of degradation, and to regain spontaneity and freedom—the desire expressed, in the example here discussed, by symbols of the "flight"—must be ranked among the specific marks of man.

The breaking of the plane effected by the "flight" signifies, on the other hand, an act of transcendence. It is no small matter to find already, at the most archaic stage of culture, the longing to go beyond and "above" the human condition, to transmute it by an excess of "spiritualization." For one can only interpret all the myths, rites and legends to which we have been referring, by a longing to see the human body behaving like a "spirit," to transmute the corporeal modality of man into a spiritual modality. . . .

101. SACRIFICE OF THE MESSENGER

Human sacrifice is surely the most extreme form of ritual! While it cannot be said to be frequent, it does appear with enough frequency to cause us need to interpret it. And again Eliade relates an important dimension to the cosmogonic myth.

SOURCE: Z/48–50; cf. Z/24, 183–87.

Human sacrifice is documented in the history of religions both among the paleocultivators and among certain peoples whose civilization is more complex (for example, the Mesopotamians, the Indo-Europeans, the Aztecs, etc.). Such sacrifices are offered for a great variety of reasons: to assure the fertility of the soil (cf. the well-known example of the Khonds in India); to strengthen the life of the gods (as among the Aztecs); to re-establish contact with the mythical Ancestors or with recently dead relatives; or to repeat the primordial sacrifice of which the myths tell, and hence to assure the continuity of life and the society (cf. the example of Hainuwele). . . .[1]

It is clear that the sacrifice Herodotus[2] describes does not belong to any of these types. Its essential element is the sending of a messenger designated by lot and charged with communicating "their needs" to Zalmoxis. In essence, the sacrifice makes possible the sending of a message, in other words, *it reactualizes direct relations between the Getae and their god.*

This type of sacrifice is especially prevalent in Southeast Asia and the regions adjoining the Pacific, where slaves are immolated to inform the Ancestor of his descendants' desires. In the form that it assumes in southern Asia and in the Pacific region, the sacrifice of the slave-messenger does not represent one of the most archaic phases. Behind this mythic-ritual scenario we discern an earlier idea and one much more widely disseminated throughout the world, that is, the hope of being able to reactualize the primordial (i.e., mythical) situation when men could communicate, directly and *in concreto*, with their gods. According to the myths, this situation came to an end after a certain event, which obliged the gods to withdraw to Heaven and break off concrete communications with the Earth and men (the Cosmic Mountain was flattened, the Tree or Vine connecting Earth and Heaven was cut, etc.).

It is in this category of rituals that we must put the sacrifice of the Getic messenger. He is not a slave or a prisoner of war, as is the case in Asia and Oceania, but a free man, and, if our interpretation is correct, an "initiate" into the "Mysteries" established by Zalmoxis. Classical antiquity provides other examples of the cus-

---

1. On Hainuwele, see *MR*/103–7. Eds.
2. Cf. the discussion of the material from Herodotus, selections 72–73. Eds.

tom of sending messengers or letters to the gods. A still more striking parallel is the Altaic shaman's ecstatic journey to the seventh or
ninth heaven, to carry the prayers of the tribe to Bai Ülgän and
receive the god's blessings and the assurance that he will take
thought for the well-being of his worshipers. The journey to heaven
is made in "ecstasy," that is, in the spirit: it is only the shaman's
soul that undertakes the celestial ascent. But according to certain
mythological traditions, in the beginning, *in illo tempore*, the
meeting with the god took place in the flesh.

Every five years the Getac sent Zalmoxis the "soul" of a messenger, in order to re-establish contact with the god and to inform
him of their "needs." This ritual renewal of a relationship that was
formerly *concrete* between Zalmoxis and his worshipers is equivalent to the symbolic or sacramental *presence* of certain Mystery
divinities at cult banquets. In both cases the *original situation*—
that is, the time when the cult was established—is recovered. The
worshipers can again communicate as a group, with their god. The
fact that a messenger is sent every five years clearly shows that the
sacrifice is related to the years of Zalmoxis' occultation in his "underground chamber." The reappearance of the god in the myth corresponds to the re-establishment, in the ritual, of concrete communications (personal "needs") between Zalmoxis and his worshipers. The sacrifice and sending of the messenger in some sort
constitute a symbolic (because ritual) repetition of the establishment of the cult; in other words, Zalmoxis' epiphany after three
years of occultation is reactualized with all that it implies, especially the assurance of the soul's immortality and bliss. . . .

102. HUMAN SACRIFICE AMONG THE
AZTECS AND KHONDS

We possess evidence of human sacrifice being offered for the harvest by certain peoples of Central and North America, in some parts
of Africa, a few Pacific islands, and by a number of the Dravidian
tribes of India. In order to get a clear grasp of the nature of these
human sacrifices, we will limit ourselves here to a small number of
examples, but those we will examine in detail.

SOURCE: *PCR*/343–45; cf. *PCR*/349, 354.

Sahagun has left us a detailed description of the maize rites of the Aztecs of Mexico. As soon as the plant began to germinate, they went to the fields "to find the god of the maize"—a shoot which they brought back to the house and offered food, exactly as they would to a god. In the evening, it was brought to the temple of Chicome-coatl, goddess of sustenance, where a group of young girls were gathered, each carrying a bundle of seven ears of maize saved from the last crop, wrapped in red paper and sprinkled with sap. The name given to the bundle, *chicomolotl* (the sevenfold ear), was also the name of the goddess of the maize. The girls were of three different ages, very young, adolescent, and grown up—symbolizing, no doubt, the stages in the life of the maize—and their arms and legs were covered in red feathers, red being the colour of the maize divinities. This ceremony, intended simply to honour the goddess and obtain her magic blessing upon the newly germinated crop, did not involve any sacrifice. But three months later, when the crop was ripe, a girl representing the goddess of the new maize, Xilonen, was beheaded; this sacrifice opened the door to using the new maize profanely, for food, which seems to suggest that it was in the nature of an offering of the first-fruits. Sixty days later, at the conclusion of the harvest, there was another sacrifice. A woman representing the goddess Toci, "our Mother" (the goddess of the maize gathered for using), was beheaded and immediately afterwards skinned. One priest arrayed himself in the skin, while a piece taken from the thigh was carried to the Temple of Cinteotl, god of the maize, where another participant made himself a mask out of it. For several weeks, this person was looked upon as a woman in childbirth—for what this rite probably meant was that Toci, once dead, was reborn in her son, the dried maize, the grain that would provide the winter's food. A whole series of ceremonies followed upon these: the warriors marched by (for, like many eastern gods and goddesses of fertility, Toci was also the goddess of war and of death), dances were performed and, finally, the king, followed by all his people, threw everything that came to hand at the head of the person representing Toci and then withdrew. It seems as though Toci ended up as a scapegoat, and took upon herself, when she was driven out, all the sins of the community, for the person who played the part bore the skin to a fortress at the frontier and left it hanging there with its arms wide.

And the mask of Cinteotl was taken there as well. Other American tribes, like the Pawnees, used to sacrifice a girl, cut her body up and bury each piece in a field. And that same custom of cutting up a body and placing the pieces in furrows occurs in certain African tribes also.

But the best known example of human sacrifice in connection with agriculture is that practiced until about the middle of the nineteenth century by the Khonds, a Dravidian tribe of Bengal. Sacrifices were offered to the earth goddess, Tari Pennu or Bera Pennu, and the victim, who was known as the Meriah, was either bought from his parents, or born of parents who had themselves been victims. The sacrifices took place upon certain stated feast days or when something exceptional happened, but the victims were always voluntary ones. The Meriahs lived happily for years, looked upon as consecrated beings; they married other "victims" and were given a piece of land as a dowry. Ten or twelve days before the sacrifice, the victim's hair was cut off—a ceremony at which everyone assisted, for the Khonds considered this sacrifice as being offered for the good of all mankind. Then followed an indescribable orgy—and this is something we shall meet in a great many festivals relating to agriculture and natural fertility—and the Meriah was brought in procession from the village to the place of sacrifice which was usually a forest as yet untouched by the axe. There the Meriah was consecrated; he was anointed with melted butter and curcuma and decked with flowers, and seems to have been identified with the divinity, for the throng pressed round to touch him, and the homage offered him bordered on adoration. They danced to music around him, and calling upon the earth they cried: "O God, we offer thee this sacrifice; give us good crops, good weather and good health!" They then addressed the victim: "We have purchased thee, not seized thee by force; now, according to our custom, we sacrifice thee and there is no sin to us!" The orgies are suspended for the night, but taken up again in the morning and last till midday when all once more gather round the Meriah to watch the sacrifice. There are different ways of killing the Meriah: drugged with opium, he is bound and his bones are crushed, or he is strangled, or cut in pieces, or slowly burnt over a brazier, and so on. What matters is that all who are present, and thus every village that has sent its representative to the ceremony, should be given a morsel of the sacrificed body. The priest carefully shares out the pieces and they are at once sent to all the villages and there buried with great pomp in the fields. What is left, particularly the head and bones, is burned, and the ashes spread over the ploughlands with the same object—to ensure a good harvest. When the British author-ities forbade human sacrifice, the Khonds used certain animals in place of the Meriahs (a he-goat or a buffalo).

103. SACRIFICE AND REGENERATION

To find the meaning of these human sacrifices we must look into the primitive theory of the seasonal regeneration of the forces of the sacred. Clearly, any rite or drama aiming at the regeneration of a "force" is itself the repetition of a primal, creative act, which took place *ab initio*. A regeneration sacrifice is a ritual "repeti-tion" of the Creation. The myth of creation includes the ritual (that is, violent) death of a primeval giant, from whose body the worlds were made, and plants grew. The origin of plants and of cereals in particular is connected with this sort of sacrifice; . . . herbs, wheat, vines, and so on grew from the blood and the flesh of a mythical creature ritually sacrificed "at the beginning," *in illo tempore*. The object in sacrificing a human victim for the regenera-tion of the force expressed in the harvest is to repeat the act of crea-tion that first made grain to live. *The ritual makes creation over again*; the force at work in plants is reborn by suspending time and returning to the first moment of the fulness of creation. The vic-tim, cut to pieces, is identified with the body of the primeval being of myth, which gave life to the grain by being itself divided ritually. . . .

104. EARTH-MOTHER AS GODDESS OF DEATH

Among the Aztecs, a very young woman, Xilonen, who sym-bolized the young maize, was beheaded; and three months later an-other woman, incarnating the goddess Toci, "Our Mother" (who

Source: *PCR*/345–46; cf. *Z*/14–19.
Source: *MDM*/188–89.

represented the maize already harvested and ready for use), was also beheaded and flayed. This was the ritual repetition of the birth of the plants by the self-sacrifice of the Goddess.

Here we must stop, though we are far from having dealt with all the attributes or all the significant myths of the Earth-Mother. We have had to select, and inevitably some aspects of the subject have been left aside. We have said little of the nocturnal and funerary aspect of the Earth-Mother as the Goddess of Death, and nothing of her aggressive, terrifying and agonizing characteristics. But even in respect of these negative aspects, one thing that must never be lost sight of, is that when the Earth becomes a goddess of Death, it is simply because she is felt to be the universal womb, the inexhaustible source of all creation. Death is not, in itself, a definitive end, not an absolute annihilation, as it is sometimes thought to be in the modern world. Death is likened to the seed which is sown in the bosom of the Earth-Mother to give birth to a new plant. Thus, one might speak of an optimistic view of death, since death is regarded as a return to the Mother, a temporary re-entry into the maternal bosom. That is why bodies buried in neolithic times are found lying in the embryonic position; the dead were laid in the earth in the attitude of the embryo in the womb, as though they were expected to come back to life again and again. The Earth-Mother, as the Japanese myth told us, was the first to die; but this death of Izanami was at the same time a sacrifice made in order to augment and extend the Creation. It followed that men, too, in their dying and being buried, were sacrifices to the Earth. It is thanks to that sacrifice, after all, that life can continue, and that the dead hope to be able to come back to life. The frightening aspect of the Earth-Mother, as the Goddess of Death, is explained by the cosmic necessity of sacrifice, which alone makes possible the passage from one mode of being to another and also ensures the uninterrupted circulation of Life.

105. CREATION AND SACRIFICE

Let us linger a moment over this mythic motif, for the matter is becoming complicated. It would seem that we are now dealing with

Source: *MDM*/183–85; cf. *FC*/27–33, 64 f.

a myth of extremely wide distribution, and one which appears in a considerable number of forms and variants. But this is the essential theme: that Creation cannot take place except from *a living being who is immolated*—a primordial androgynous giant, or a cosmic Male, or a Mother Goddess or a mythic Young Woman. We note, too, that this "Creation" applies on all the levels of existence: it may refer to the Creation of the Cosmos, or of humanity, or of only one particular human race, or of certain vegetable species or certain animals. The mythic pattern remains the same: nothing can be created without immolation, without sacrifice. It is thus that certain myths tell us about the creation of the world out of the actual body of a primordial Giant: Ymir, P'an-Ku, Purusha. Other myths reveal to us how human races or different social classes came to birth, always from a primordial Giant or an Ancestor who is sacrificed and dismembered. Finally, as we have just seen, the edible plants have a similar origin; they sprang from the body of an immolated divine being.

This myth of creation by a violent death transcends, therefore, the mythology of the Earth-Mother. The fundamental idea is that Life can only take birth from another life which is sacrificed. The violent death is creative—in this sense, that the life which is sacrificed manifests itself in a more brilliant form upon another plane of existence. The sacrifice brings about a tremendous transference: the life concentrated in one person overflows that person and manifests itself on the cosmic or collective scale. A single being transforms itself into a Cosmos, or takes multiple rebirth in a whole vegetable species or race of mankind. A living "whole" bursts into fragments and disperses itself in myriads of animated forms. In other terms, here again we find the well-known cosmogonic pattern of the primordial "wholeness" broken into fragments by the act of Creation.

From this we can understand why the myth of the creation of the useful plants and animals out of the body of a sacrificed divine being was incorporated into the mythology of the Earth-Mother. The Earth is the universal Genetrix and Nurse above all others: she creates by hierogamy with Heaven, but also by parthenogenesis[1] or by self-immolation. Traces of the parthenogenesis of the

1. Parthenogenesis: birth that does not presuppose fertilization. Eds.

Earth-Mother survive even in highly evolved mythologies like the Greek: Hera, for instance, conceived by herself to give birth to Typhon, to Haephestos and to Ares. The Earth-Mother embodies the archetype of fecundity, of inexhaustible creativity. That is why she has a tendency to assimilate the attributes and the myths of the divinities of fertility, whether they are human, aquatic or agricultural. But the converse of this is also true: these divinities appropriate the attributes of the Earth-Mother, and sometimes even replace her in the cult. And we can see why: the Waters, like the Mother, are rich with the germs of life, and the Moon, too, symbolizes the universal becoming, the periodical creation and destruction. As for the goddesses of vegetation and agriculture, it is sometimes difficult to distinguish these from telluric goddesses; their myths reveal to us the same mystery of birth, of creation, and of dramatic death followed by resurrection. Reciprocal borrowings and mutual entanglements occur between the mythologies of all these divinities. One might say that the Earth-Mother constitutes a form that is "open" to, or susceptible of, indefinite enrichment, and that is why it takes in all the myths dealing with Life and Death, with Creation and generation, with sexuality and voluntary sacrifice.

106. COSMOGONY AND BUILDING SACRIFICE

[In India], before the masons lay the first stone the astronomer shows them the spot where it is to be placed, and this spot is supposed to lie above the snake that supports the world. The master mason sharpens a stake and drives it into the ground, exactly at the indicated spot, in order to fix the snake's head. A foundation stone is then laid above the stake. *Thus the cornerstone is at the exact center of the world.* But, in addition, the act of foundation repeats the cosmogonic act; for to drive the stake into the snake's head to "fix" it is to imitate the primordial gesture of Soma or Indra, when the latter, as the *Rig Veda* expresses it, "struck the Snake in his lair" (IV, 17, 9), when his lightning bolt "cut off its head" (I, 52, 10). As we said *the snake symbolizes chaos, the formless, the unmanifested. To behead it is equivalent to an act of creation, passage from the virtual and the amorphous to that which has form.* Again,

Source: *SP*/54–56; cf. Z/164–73.

it was from the body of a primordial marine monster, Tiamat, that the god Marduk fashioned the world. This victory was symbolically repeated each year, since each year the cosmos was renewed. But the paradigmatic act of the divine victory was likewise repeated on the occasion of every construction, for every new construction reproduced the creation of the world.

This second type of cosmogony is much more complex, and it will only be outlined here. But it was necessary to cite it, for, in the last analysis, it is with such a cosmogony that the countless forms of the building sacrifice are bound up; the latter, in short, is only an imitation, often a symbolic imitation, of the primordial sacrifice that gave birth to the world. For, beginning with a certain stage of culture, the cosmogonic myth explains the Creation through the slaying of a giant (Ymir in Germanic mythology, Purusha in Indian mythology, P'an-ku in China); his organs give birth to the various cosmic regions. According to other groups of myths, it is not only the cosmos that comes to birth in consequence of the immolation of a primordial being and from his own substance, but also food plants, the races of man, or different social classes. It is on this type of cosmogonic myth that building sacrifices depend. If a "construction" is to endure (be it house, temple, tool, etc.), it must be animated, that is, it must receive life and a soul. The transfer of the soul is possible only through a blood sacrifice. The history of religions, ethnology, folklore record countless forms of building sacrifices—that is, of symbolic or blood sacrifices for the benefit of a structure. In southeastern Europe, these beliefs have inspired admirable popular ballads describing the sacrifice of the wife of the master mason in order that a structure may be completed (cf. the ballads on the Arta Bridge in Greece, on the Monastery of Argesh in Romania, on the city of Scutari in Yugoslavia, etc.). . . .

107. MYTHS AND RITES OF INTEGRATION

. . . To integrate, unify, make whole, in a word to abolish the contraries and reunite the parts, is in India the royal Way of the Spirit. This is already evident in the Brahman conception of sacri-

SOURCE: *TO*/97–98.

fice. Whatever may have been the role of sacrifice in the Indo-Aryan beginnings and the Vedic era, it is certain that from the time of the Brahmanas sacrifice became chiefly a means of restoring the primordial unity. Indeed, by sacrifice the scattered limbs of Prajapati are reunited, that is to say the divine Being, immolated at the beginning of Time in order that the World may be born from his body, is reconstituted. The essential function of sacrifice is to put together again (*samdha*) that which was broken up *in illo tempore*. At the same time as the symbolic reconstitution of Prajapati, a process of reintegration takes place in the officiant himself. By ritually reuniting the fragments of Prajapati, the officiant "recollects" (*samharati*) himself, that is to say endeavours to regain the unity of his true Self. As Ananda Coomaraswamy writes, the unification and the act of becoming oneself represent at the same time a death, a rebirth and a marriage.[1]

This is why the symbolism of the Indian sacrifice is extremely complex; one is concerned with cosmological, sexual and initiatory symbols, all together.

Sacrifice conceived as the pre-eminent method of unification is one of the numerous examples illustrating the irrepressible aspiration of the Indian spirit to transcend the contraries and rise to a complete reality. The later history of Indian spirituality has developed almost entirely in this direction. This is one reason why Indian thought has refused to concede any value to History, and why traditional India has had no historical consciousness. For, compared with absolute reality, what we call Universal History represents only a particular moment in a vast cosmic drama. India, we insist, has refused to grant undue significance to what, according to its ontology, is no more than a passing aspect of a particular situation; to what we call today "man's situation in History."

108. REACTUALIZING MYTHS

It is not without interest to note that religious man assumes a humanity that has a transhuman, transcendent model. He does not

SOURCE: *SP*/99–102.
1. See *Atmayajna: Self-Sacrifice, Harvard Journal of Asiatic Studies*, 6 (1942): 358–98, 388.

consider himself to be *truly man* except in so far as he imitates the gods, the culture heroes, or the mythical ancestors. This is as much as to say that religious man wishes to be *other* than he is on the plane of his profane experience. Religious man is not *given*; he *makes* himself, by approaching the divine models. These models, as we said, are preserved in myths, in the history of the divine *gesta*. Hence religious man too regards himself as *made* by history, just as profane man does; but the only history that concerns him is the *sacred history* revealed by the myths—that is, the history of the gods; whereas profane man insists that he is constituted only by human history, hence by the sum of the very acts that, for religious man, are of no importance because they have no divine models. The point to be emphasized is that, from the beginning, religious man sets the model he is to attain on the transhuman plane, the plane revealed by his myths. *One becomes truly a man only by conforming to the teaching of the myths, that is, by imitating the gods.*

We will add that, for the primitives, such an *imitatio dei* sometimes implies a very grave responsibility. We have seen that certain blood sacrifices find their justification in a primordial divine act; *in illo tempore* the god had slain the marine monster and dismembered its body in order to create the cosmos. Man repeats this blood sacrifice—sometimes even with human victims—when he has to build a village, a temple, or simply a house. What the consequences of this *imitatio dei* can be is clearly shown by the mythologies and rituals of numerous primitive peoples. To give only one example: according to the myths of the earliest cultivators, man became what he is today—mortal, sexualized, and condemned to work—in consequence of a primordial murder; *in illo tempore* a divine being, quite often a woman or a maiden, sometimes a child or a man, allowed himself to be immolated in order that tubers or fruit trees should grow from his body. This first murder basically changed the mode of being of human life. The immolation of the divine being inaugurated not only the need to eat but also the doom of death and, in consequence, sexuality, the only way to ensure the continuity of life. The body of the immolated divinity was changed into food; its soul descended under ground, where it established the Land of the Dead. A. E. Jensen, who has devoted an important book to this type of divinities—which he calls *dema* divinities—

has conclusively shown that in eating and in dying man participates in the life of the *demas*.[1]

For all these paleo-agricultural peoples, what is essential is periodically to evoke the primordial event that established the present condition of humanity. Their whole religious life is a commemoration, a remembering. The memory reactualized by the rites (hence by reiterating the primordial murder) plays a decisive role; what happened *in illo tempore* must never be forgotten. The true sin is forgetting. The girl who at her first menstruation spends three days in a dark hut without speaking to anyone does so because the murdered maiden, having become the moon, remains three days in darkness; if the menstruating girl breaks the taboo of silence and speaks, she is guilty of forgetting a primordial event. Personal memory is not involved; what matters is to remember the mythical event, the only event worth considering because the only creative event. It falls to the primordial myth to preserve *true history*, the history of the human condition; it is in the myth that the principles and paradigms for all conduct must be sought and recovered.

---

1. A. E. Jensen, *Das religiöse Weltbild einer frühen Kultur* (Stuttgart, 1948). Jensen borrowed the word *dema* from the Marind-anim of New Guinea.